BLAIR'S SUCCESSFUL WAR

Military Strategy and Operational Art
Edited by Professor Howard M. Hensel, Air War College, USA

The Ashgate Series on Military Strategy and Operational Art analyzes and assesses the synergistic interrelationship between joint and combined military operations, national military strategy, grand strategy, and national political objectives in peacetime, as well as during periods of armed conflict. In doing so, the series highlights how various patterns of civil–military relations, as well as styles of political and military leadership influence the outcome of armed conflicts. In addition, the series highlights both the advantages and challenges associated with the joint and combined use of military forces involved in humanitarian relief, nation building, and peacekeeping operations, as well as across the spectrum of conflict extending from limited conflicts fought for limited political objectives to total war fought for unlimited objectives. Finally, the series highlights the complexity and challenges associated with insurgency and counter-insurgency operations, as well as conventional operations and operations involving the possible use of weapons of mass destruction.

Also in this series:

Russian Civil-Military Relations
Robert Brannon
ISBN 978 0 7546 7591 4

Managing Civil-Military Cooperation
Edited by Sebastiaan J.H. Rietjens and Myriame T.I.B. Bollen
ISBN 978 0 7546 7281 4

Securing the State
Reforming the National Security Decisionmaking
Process at the Civil-Military Nexus
Christopher P. Gibson
ISBN 978 0 7546 7290 6

Blair's Successful War
British Military Intervention in Sierra Leone

ANDREW M. DORMAN
King's College London, UK

Routledge
Taylor & Francis Group

LONDON AND NEW YORK

First published 2009 by Ashgate Publishing

2 Park Square, Milton Park, Abingdon, Oxfordshire OX14 4RN
711 Third Avenue, New York, NY 10017

Routledge is an imprint of the Taylor & Francis Group, an informa business

First issued in paperback 2018

Copyright © Andrew M. Dorman 2009

Andrew M. Dorman has asserted his right under the Copyright, Designs and Patents Act, 1988, to be identified as the author of this work.

All rights reserved. No part of this book may be reprinted or reproduced or utilised in any form or by any electronic, mechanical, or other means, now known or hereafter invented, including photocopying and recording, or in any information storage or retrieval system, without permission in writing from the publishers.

Notice:
Product or corporate names may be trademarks or registered trademarks, and are used only for identification and explanation without intent to infringe.

British Library Cataloguing in Publication Data
Dorman, Andrew M., 1966-
  Blair's successful war : British military intervention in
  Sierra Leone. -- (Military strategy and operational art)
  1. Great Britain--Foreign relations--Sierra Leone.
  2. Sierra Leone--Foreign relations--Great Britain.
  3. Sierra Leone--History--Civil War, 1991-2002--Peace.
  4. Humanitarian intervention--Sierra Leone. 5. United
  Nations Assistance Mission in Sierra Leone. 6. Great
  Britain--Politics and government--1997-2007. 7. Great
  Britain--History, Military--20th century.
  I. Title II. Series
  327.4'10664-dc22

Library of Congress Cataloging-in-Publication Data
Dorman, Andrew M., 1966-
  Blair's successful war : British military intervention in Sierra Leone / by Andrew M. Dorman.
     p. cm. -- (Military strategy and operational art)
  Includes bibliographical references and index.
     ISBN 978-0-7546-7299-9 (hardback) -- ISBN 978-0-7546-9169-3 (ebook) 1. Great Britain --Foreign relations--Sierra Leone. 2. Sierra Leon--Foreign relations--Great Britain. 3. Blair, Tony, 1953---Military leadership. 4. Sierra Leone--History--Civil War, 1991-2002. 5. Peacekeeping forces--Sierra Leone--History. 6. Great Britain--Military policy. 7. Intervention (International law) I. Title.
  DA47.9.S5D67 2009
  966.404--dc22

2009031070

ISBN 13: 978-0-7546-7299-9 (hbk)
ISBN 13: 978-1-138-37648-9 (pbk)

Printed in the United Kingdom by Henry Ling Limited

Contents

List of Figure and Tables		*vii*
Glossary of Terms		*ix*
Introduction		1
1	Blair and the Use of Military Force	7
2	Background History: From the Creation of Sierra Leone to the End of Civil War	29
3	Lomé Peace Agreement and UNAMSIL – the UN Peacekeeping Mission	45
4	Evacuation, May 2000	61
5	Saving UNAMSIL and Confronting the RUF	87
6	*Operation Barras* – the Hostage Rescue	103
7	The Defeat of the RUF	115
8	Impact of the Operation	127
Select Bibliography		*147*
Index		*157*

List of Figures and Tables

Figure

2.1   Map of Sierra Leone   30

Tables

4.1   Level of funding committed to Sierra Leone by DFID, 12 May 2000   66
7.1   Composition of UNAMSIL, 30 October 2000   119

Glossary of Terms

1 PARA	1st Battalion of the Parachute Regiment
1 RIR	1st Battalion of the Royal Irish Regiment
2 PARA	2nd Battalion of the Parachute Regiment
42 Cdo	42 Commando, Royal Marines
ABTF	Airborne Task Force
AFRC	Armed Forces Revolutionary Council
AMC	Air Movements Centre
APC	All People's Congress
ARG	Amphibious Ready Group
ARRC	Allied Rapid Reaction Corps
BHC	British High Commission
CDS	Chief of the Defence Staff
DCI	Defence Capabilities Initiative
DDR	Disarmament, demobilisation and rehabilitation
DFID	Department for International Development
DSF	Director of Special Forces
ECOWAS	Economic Community of West African States
ECOMOG	Economic Community of West African States Monitoring Group
EO	Executive Outcomes
EP	Entitled Personnel
EU	European Union
FCO	Foreign and Commonwealth Office
FYR	Former Yugoslav Republic
HQ	Headquarters
GOSL	Government of Sierra Leone
IMATT	International Military Advisory and Training Team
IMF	International Monetary Fund
ISAF	International Security Assistance Force
JFC	Joint Force Commander
JTF	Joint Task Force
JTFC	Joint Task Force Commander
JTFHQ	Joint Task Force Headquarters
KFOR	Kosovo Force
MEU	Marine Expeditionary Unit
MOD	Ministry of Defence
NATO	North Atlantic Treaty Organisation
NEO	Non-combatant Evacuation Operation
NPRC	National Provincial Ruling Council
NTM	Notice to move

ORLT	Operational Reconnaissance and Liaison Team
OSCE	Organsation for Security and Cooperation in Europe
PJHQ	Permanent Joint Headquarters
PMC	Private Military Company
RAF	Royal Air Force
RN	Royal Navy
ROE	Rules of Engagement
RUF	Revolutionary United Front
SAS	Special Air Service
SBS	Special Boat Service
SBU	Small Boys Unit
SLA	Sierra Leone Army
SLPP	Sierra Leone People's Party
UN	United Nations
UNAMSIL	United Nations Mission in Sierra Leone
UNIOSIL	United Nations Integrated Office in Sierra Leone
UNMO	United Nations Military Observer
UNOMSIL	United Nations Observer Mission in Sierra Leone
WEU	Western European Union
WHO	World Health Organisation
WSB	West Side Boys

Introduction

Tony Blair remains a source of fascination, especially given the problems that his successor, Gordon Brown, has encountered as Prime Minister.[1] In many respects he has been Labour's most successful Prime Minister having spent ten years in office and winning three successive general elections.[2] However, Blair's time in office remains debated and highly controversial.[3] The image of a young Tony Blair sweeping into office in 1997 as leader of 'New Labour' in a landslide election has been contrasted with the picture of a visibly much older individual, harried out of office by elements of his own party. He has been compared with Margaret Thatcher, the most recent Prime Minister with a similar level of longevity in office, who also won three successive General Elections and one whose policies he has been associated with.[4] This analogy has been taken a stage further as Blair's successor, Gordon Brown, has been unfavourably compared to John Major[5] and has been the subject of a series of attacks from within his own Cabinet and party[6] as well as from a number of retired military officers.[7] Yet, the manner of his departure from

---

1   See Francis Elliott, 'They came to bury him, not praise him: but Brown lives to fight another day', *The Times*, 9 June 2009, pp. 6–7.

2   See Anthony Seldon, *Blair Unbound* (London: Simon and Schuster, 2007); Patrick Stephens, *Tony Blair: the Price of Leadership* (London: Politico's, 2004); Simon Jenkins, *Thatcher and Sons: A Revolution in Three Acts* (London: Penguin, 2006).

3   See, for example, Mark Bennister, 'Tony Blair and John Howard: Comparative Predominance and "Institution Stretch" in the UK and Australia', *British Journal of Politics and International Relations*, vol. 9, no. 3, August 2007, pp. 327–45; Eoin O'Malley's 'Setting Choices, Controlling Outcomes: The Operation of Prime Ministerial Influence and the UK's Decision to Invade Iraq', *British Journal of Politics and International Relations*, vol. 9, no. 1, February 2007, pp. 1–19; See also Craig McLean and Alan Patterson, 'A Precautionary Approach to Foreign Policy? A Preliminary Analysis of Tony Blair's Speeches on Iraq', *British Journal of Politics and International Relations*, vol. 8, no. 3, August 2006, pp. 351–67; Alex Danchev, 'Tony Blair's Vietnam: The Iraq War and the "Special Relationship" in Historical Perspective', *Review of International Studies*, vol. 33, no. 2, April 2007, pp. 189–203.

4   See Simon Jenkins, *Thatcher and Sons: A Revolution in Three Acts* (London: Penguin, 2006).

5   Anatole Kaletsky, 'The disasters of Brown and Major', *Times Online*, 21 February 2008, http://www.timesonline.co.uk/tol/comment/columnists/anatole_kaletsky/article3406 260.ece, accessed 10 March 2008.

6   Philippe Norton and Philip Webster, 'Brown reshuffle – Caroline Flint plunges in the knife', *Times Online*, 5 June 2009, http://www.timesonline.co.uk/tol/news/politics/article6439062.ece, accessed 6 July 2009.

7   'Brown "shows contempt for forces"', *BBC Online*, 22 November 2007, http://news.bbc.co.uk/1/hi/uk_politics/7108354.stm, accessed 6 March 2008; see also House

office was significantly different from hers. Blair was able to leave at a time of his relative choosing and to the applause of the House of Commons, rather than as a result of a leadership contest which she had won but with an insufficiently large majority.[8] David Cameron, the leader of the official opposition, left Tony Blair with the following words:

> On behalf of everyone on these Benches, may I congratulate the right hon. Gentleman on his remarkable achievement of being Prime Minister for 10 years? [Hon. Members: 'Hear, hear'.] For all the heated battles across the Dispatch Box, for 13 years he has led his party, for 10 years he has led our country, and no one can be in any doubt about the huge efforts he has made in public service. He has considerable achievements to his credit, whether it is peace in Northern Ireland or his work in the developing world, which will endure. I am sure that life in the public eye has sometimes been tough on his family, so on behalf of my party may I wish him and his family well, and wish him every success in whatever he does in future?[9]

Both Blair and Thatcher were associated with a particular policy disaster and arguments over arrogance in office. In Thatcher's case the Poll Tax proved to be her bête noir and in Blair's case the war on Iraq.[10] For many who had voted for 'New Labour' and the politics of change in 1997 the Blair years were years of betrayal marred above all by the Iraq War and his relationship with President George W. Bush.[11] This perception of failure has haunted him to the end of his time in office. This was evident in his last Prime Minister's question time which he opened with the following statement:

> First of all, I know that the whole House will want to join me in sending our deep condolences to the family and friends of Major Paul Harding of the 1st Battalion the Rifles, and Corporal John Rigby of the 4th Battalion the Rifles, both of whom died in Iraq; and Drummer Thomas Wright, of the 1st Battalion the Worcestershire and Sherwood Foresters Regiment. All three of them were outstanding soldiers and will be deeply missed.

---

of Lords Debate on the Armed Forces, 22 November 2007, cols937-1001, http://www.publications.parliament.uk/pa/ld200708/ldhansrd/text/71122-0002.htm#07112238000004, accessed 6 March 2008.

    8   'A dozen Downing Street departures', *BBC Online*, 9 May 2007, http://news.bbc.co.uk/1/hi/uk_politics/6524943.stm, accessed 3 March 2008; Margaret Thatcher, *The Downing Street Years* (London: HarperCollins, 2003).

    9   David Cameron, House of Commons Parliamentary Debates, 'Prime Minister's Engagements', 27 June 2007, col.326, http://www.publications.parliament.uk/pa/cm200607/cmhansrd/cm070627/debtext/70627-0002.htm#07062782000011, accessed 6 March 2008.

    10   Michael Heseltine, *Life in the Jungle: My Biography* (London: Hodder and Stoughton, 2000), pp. 345–6.

    11   For example, see Geoffrey Wheatcroft, *Yo, Blair!* (London: Politico's, 2007).

> Mr Speaker, since this is the last time that this, the saddest of duties, falls to me, I hope that the House will permit me to say something about our armed forces, and not just about the three individuals who have fallen in the past week. I have never come across people of such sustained dedication, courage and commitment. I am truly sorry about the dangers that they face today in Iraq and Afghanistan. I know that some may think that they face these dangers in vain. I do not, and I never will. I believe that they are fighting for the security of this country and the wider world against people who would destroy our way of life. But whatever view people take of my decisions, I think that there is only one view to take of them: they are the bravest and the best.[12]

During his time in office Blair became convinced of the morality of appropriate humanitarian intervention using military forces.[13] According to one of his biographers:

> Revulsion at the brutality of the dictators was a regular Blair theme. 'They asked me why we don't get rid of Mugabe', Peter Storland recalls him saying in March 2003, 'Why not the Burmese lot? ... I don't because I can't, but when you can, you should'. 'He saw Saddam as the Pol Pot of the Middle East', said one close aide. Blair would talk to colleagues enthusiastically about the history of twentieth-century moral intervention by the British left. He would say, 'I cannot understand why people on the left oppose it. Hasn't the left always been committed to fighting injustice in the world?'[14]

As Prime Minister he broke all records for the use of the armed forces ranging from operations in the Balkans to Afghanistan. According to Geoffrey Wheatcroft:

> Blair is most certainly a war Prime Minister. His zeal for waging war was quite unforeseen ten years ago but it is by this that he will be remembered.[15]

This is somewhat ironic given that he began his time in office with virtually no experience of foreign affairs and a clear domestic agenda.[16] For the majority of these military adventures were political and economic disasters yet one operation,

---

12 Tony Blair, House of Commons Parliamentary Debates, 'Prime Minister's Engagements', 27 June 2007, col.323, http://www.publications.parliament.uk/pa/cm200607/cmhansrd/cm070627/debtext/70627-0002.htm, accessed 6 March 2008.

13 Patrick Stephens, *Tony Blair: the Price of Leadership* (London: Politico's, 2004), p. 233.

14 Anthony Seldon, *Blair Unbound* (London: Simon and Schuster, 2007), p. 86.

15 Geoffrey Wheatcroft, *Yo, Blair!* (London: Politico's, 2007), p. 55.

16 'New Labour because Britain deserves better' (London: Labour Party, 1997), http://labour-party.org.uk/manifestos/1997/1997-labour-manifesto.shtml accessed 18 November 2008.

Sierra Leone, the only unilateral deployment, has been viewed on as successful.[17] Yet, the 2007 World Health Organisation (WHO) study placed Sierra Leone at the bottom of most development and health statistics and whilst peace remains the shadow of the civil war still hangs over the country and corruption remains endemic.[18]

This volume sets out to examine the British military operation in Sierra Leone that began in May 2000 and which still involves a commitment of British forces via the British-led International Military Advisory and Training Team (IMATT) which supports the government of Sierra Leone.[19] To accomplish this task the book has been divided into nine chapters. The first chapter examines the Blair legacy and the development of an interventionalist policy which led to *Operation Palliser*, the initial deployment to Sierra Leone, and which ultimately would also lead to the British involvement in Afghanistan in 2001, re-engagement in 2006 and the Iraq War in 2003.

Chapter 2 provides a background history of Sierra Leone that covers the period from its creation to the signing of the Lomé Peace Agreement in 1999. It outlines the formation of Sierra Leone, its colonial days through to decolonisation, the birth of the Revolutionary United Front (RUF) and the outbreak of the civil war, it then considers the impact of the civil war and the role that various groups of mercenaries played, their links to the British government, the intervention of the Economic Community of West African States Monitoring Group (ECOMOG) forces and the original United Nations deployment – the United Nations Observer Mission in Sierra Leone (UNOMSIL).

Chapter 3 analyses the period from the signing of the Lomé Peace Agreement and the deployment of the United Nations peacekeeping mission (UNAMSIL) to the crisis that led to the rebellion of the main rebel group – the RUF – and the initial response of the international community. It will highlight the problems of the Lomé Peace Agreement and the weaknesses of the United Nations mission.

Chapter 4 charts the intial deployment of British forces to evacuate its entitled personnel (EPs) in what would ultimately become the largest unilateral British

---

17 Rita Abrahamsen and Paul Williams, 'Ethics and Foreign Policy: the Antinomies of New Labour's 'Third Way' in Sub-Saharan Africa', *Political Studies*, vol. 49, no. 2, 2001, pp. 249–64.

18 *World Health Statistics 2007* (Geneva: World Health Organisation, 2007), http://www.who.int/whosis/whostat2007.pdf, accessed 23 January 2008; Andrew Stewart, 'An Enduring Commitment: The British Military's Role in Sierra Leone', *Defence Studies*, vol. 8, no. 3, September 2008, pp. 351–68, p. 364.

19 See http://www.fco.gov.uk/servlet/Front?pagename=OpenMarket/Xcelerate/ShowPage&c=Page&cid=1063633918151, accessed 23 January 2008.

deployment since the 1982 Falklands Conflict. It examines how over the course of a weekend the British military successfully deployed to Sierra Leone and secured the capital Freetown before the rebels were able to engage in another wave of brutality and evacuated nearly 500 'Entitled Personnel'. It shows how the military forces leapt ahead of the political process and through luck, calculated risk and by the various elements of the British armed forces competing to deploy first they were able to ensure the escape of those of its citizens who wanted to leave.

Chapter 5 explores how this led to mission creep and developed into a policy of stabilisation and surrogate warfighting via the reorganisation of the Sierra Leone Army allied with the use of UNAMSIL forces until this was interrupted by the seizure of 11 Royal Irish Regiment personnel in August 2000 by a group who referred to themselves as the West Side Boys (WSB). It considers the extent to which government policy followed on from a military lead and the degree to which there was a cross-governmental consensus.

Chapter 6 examines the impact of the seizure of the Royal Irish Regiment seized by the WSB. It analyses how the crisis unfolded, the response of the British government, the negotiations that were undertaken and the dramatic assault of the West Side Boys base by British Special Forces and A Company of the 1st Battalion of the Parachute Regiment (1 PARA) that led to the freeing of the captives under the codename *Operation Barras*. It evaluates the risks that were taken and the government's preparedness to incur significant casualties in order to retrieve its captured personnel.

Chapter 7 then charts the ultimate defeat of the RUF. It examines how the British used the rebuilt Sierra Leone Army with British advisors and some support from UNAMSIL to defeat the RUF and force them into the demobilisation process. It shows how this was linked to wider government policy towards the region and, in particular, towards Liberia and its then leader President Charles Taylor.

Chapter 8 considers the impact of the operation in terms of the impact on the Blair Government, the subsequent impact on British defence and security policy and the lessons drawn in terms of British defence policy, the defence transformation of Britain's military and the creation of the EU battlegroup concept.

Finally, the last chapter draws some conclusions that reflect on the wider lessons that can be drawn from this conflict and what it means for the future of military intervention by the United Kingdom.

Chapter 1
Blair and the Use of Military Force

Introduction

This chapter will examine the Blair government and the development of its approach to the use of military force as a means of achieving its evolving international political aims. The chapter has been subdivided into four parts. The first looks at the controversy that is Tony Blair. The second section then considers the history of military intervention during Blair's time as Prime Minister. It highlights how this evolved over time and how the use of force in Sierra Leone neatly dove-tailed into his developing thinking on the use of the military for humanitarian intervention.[1] The third section then considers how this policy of military intervention fitted within the wider Labour Party and the support it had prior to the Iraq debacle. The final section draws some overall conclusions.

The Controversy that is Tony Blair

Even now, more than two years after his departure from office, Tony Blair remains somewhat of an enigma. Like Margaret Thatcher before him, he had lost much of the support amongst those who elected him both within his own party and in the nation as a whole by the time he left office.[2] There are many who now condemn his policies and time in office especially amongst some of his former cabinet colleagues.[3] His time in office continues to be overshadowed by the war on Iraq

---

1 See Lorraine Elliott and Graeme Cheeseman (eds), *Forces for Good? Cosmopolitan Militaries in the 21st Century* (Manchester: Manchester University Press, 2005); Alex J. Bellamy, 'Motives, outcomes, intent and the legitimacy of humanitarian intervention', *Journal of Military Ethics*, vol. 3, no. 3, 2004, pp. 216–32.

2 Interestingly prior to the economic problems that have beset the world various polls put Tony Blair ahead of both his successor as prime minister, Gordon Brown, and the leader of the Conservative opposition, David Cameron, as the preferred Prime Minister. 'The problem is not just Gordon Brown, it's Labour, too', *Daily Telegraph Online*, 1 August 2008, http://www.telegraph.co.uk/opinion/main.jhtml?xml=/opinion/2008/08/01/dl0101.xml, accessed 18 November 2008.

3 See, for example, Clare Short, *An Honourable Deception? New Labour, Iraq, and the Misuse of Power* (London: The Free Press, 2005). Note also that the issue of Britain's war powers emerged after the 2003 invasion of Iraq. See 'The Governance of Britain', *Cm. 7070* (London: TSO, 2007), http://www.official-documents.gov.uk/document/cm71/7170/7170.pdf, accessed 18 November 2008; 'The Governance of Britain analysis of consultations',

and, whilst he still remains convinced it was the right to undertake the operation, the majority of the British electorate ended up opposed to this deployment.[4] His successor, Gordon Brown, was quick to distance himself from the more unpopular Blair policies, partly as an attempt to court early popularity. Brown initially promised a rapid reduction in the level of British forces in Iraq.[5] However, the reality has been that this reduction has been much slower than that envisaged under Blair and the United Kingdom's commitment was only brought to a virtual end during the first half of 2009 with several hundred personnel staying on beyond this period to help train the Iraqi navy.[6] Moreover, Brown has been criticised for removing Blairism without anything to replace it and his decision to bring Peter Mandelson back into the Cabinet was been viewed by some as a return to Blairism and the 'Third Way'.[7]

Yet, Blair remains unique amongst Labour leaders in that he won three general elections in succession and this allowed Labour to remain in office for an unprecedented period of time. He was in office during a period of unprecedented growth and prosperity. His successor has clearly struggled to fill the newly vacated office and had been severely hampered by the economic downturn.[8] In particular, Brown has been subjected to an unprecedented level of criticism for his relations

---

Cm.7342–III (London: TSO, 2008), http://www.justice.gov.uk/docs/governance-analysis-consultations.pdf, accessed 18 November 2008; House of Lords Select Committee on the Constitution, 'Waging war: Parliament's Role and Responsibility', session 2005–2006, *HL.236–1* (London: TSO, 2006), http://www.publications.parliament.uk/pa/ld200506/ldselect/ldconst/236/236i.pdf, accessed 18 November 2008; Alastair Campbell, *The Blair Years: Extracts from the Alastair Campbell Diaries* (London: Hutchinson, 2007).

4 See YOUGOV summary report http://www.yougov.com/archives/pdf/trackerIraq Trends_060403.pdf and Tony Blair, 'Our Nation's Future', speech made Plymouth, 12 January 2007, http://www.number10.gov.uk/output/Page10735.asp, both accessed 5 December 2007; Sam Coates, 'Straw may curb freedom of information', *The Times*, 25 February 2009, p. 17.

5 Gordon Brown, *House of Commons Parliamentary Debates*, 'Statement on Iraq', 8 October 2008, cols 21–5; http://www.publications.parliament.uk/pa/cm200607/cmhansrd/cm071008/debtext/71008-0004.htm#0710081000001, accessed 15 March 2008.

6 See latest report of the House of Commons Defence Committee, 'Eighth Report: Operational Costs in Afghanistan and Iraq: Spring Supplementary Estimate 2007–8', *HC.400*, session 2007–2008 (London: TSO, 2008), http://www.publications.parliament.uk/pa/cm200708/cmselect/cmdfence/400/400.pdf, accessed 10 March 2008; John Hutton, 'Debate on Defence Policy', Hansard, 30 October 2008, col. 1075, http://www.publications.parliament.uk/pa/cm200708/cmhansrd/cm081030/debtext/81030-0011.htm, accessed 18 November 2008.

7 'The Cabinet: Who's Who', *BBC Online*, 6 October 2008, http://news.bbc.co.uk/1/hi/uk_politics/7642459.stm, accessed 18 November 2008.

8 For an analysis of Gordon Brown see Tom Bower, *Gordon Brown: Prime Minister* (London: HarperCollins, 2004); Robin Cook, *The Point of Departure* (London: Simon and Schuster, 2003), p. 1.

with Britain's military which he has unsuccessfully tried to counter.[9] By the party conference of September 2008, a little over a year after becoming Prime Minister, there was a considerable discussion in the media about replacing Brown.[10] In many respects the subsequent financial crisis looked to be Brown's 'Falklands factor' as his poll ratings began to rise sharply.[11] However, this subsequently fell and his lack of authority within his own cabinet has severely weakened his position. The June 2009 reshuffle that followed on from poor local and European elections have proven disastrous for him. It will, therefore, be interesting to see whether those who examine the Blair record and legacy in subsequent years, rather than in the immediate aftermath of his departure from office, are kinder in their analyses.

A History of Intervention

In 2003 John Kampfner published *Blair's Wars* as a response to Tony Blair's willingness, as Prime Minister, to use military force to achieve his foreign policy objectives.[12] As indicated earlier, Geoffrey Wheatcroft has dubbed him a 'War Prime Minister' whilst Blair himself has argued the case for humanitarian intervention.[13] In his first six years in office Tony Blair had used armed force five times (*Operation Desert Fox* against Iraq in 1998, Kosovo 1999, Sierra Leone 2000, Afghanistan 2001 and Iraq 2003) and that excluded the deployment of forces in support of the United Nations mission to East Timor in 1999 or to provide military assistance with

---

9   See Armed Forces debate in the House of Lords, Hansard, 22 November 2007, http://www.publications.parliament.uk/pa/ld200708/ldhansrd/index/071122.html, accessed 5 December 2007; Andrew Porter and James Kirkup, 'Gordon Brown accused of contempt for Forces', *The Daily Telegraph Online*, 24 November 2007, http://www.telegraph.co.uk/news/main.jhtml?view=DETAILS&grid=A1YourView&xml=/news/2007/11/24/nbrown 124.xml, accessed 5 December 2007; Andrew Dorman, 'Britain and its Armed Forces today', *Political Quarterly*, vol. 78, no. 2, April–June 2007, pp. 320–27; Paul Cornish and Andrew Dorman, 'Blair's Wars and Brown's Budgets', *International Affairs*, vol. 85, no. 2, March 2009, pp. 247–61

10   Sam Coates, 'BBC unwittingly led the Gordon Brown coup plotters to break cover', *BBC Online*, 15 September 2008, http://www.timesonline.co.uk/tol/news/politics/article4754026.ece, accessed 18 November 2008.

11   Anthony Hilton, 'A Falklands factor for Brown?', *Thisismoney*, 30 September 2008, http://www.thisismoney.co.uk/news/columnists/article.html?in_article_id=452949&in_page_id=19&in_author_id=4, accessed 18 November 2008.

12   John Kampfner, *Blair's Wars* (London: The Free Press, 2003).

13   See Tony Blair, Doctrine of the International Community', speech given at Chicago, 24 April 1999, http://www.pbs.org/newshour/bb/international/jan-june99/blair_doctrine4-23.html, accessed 18 November 2008; Tony Blair, 'Our Nation's Future', speech made in Plymouth 12 January 2007, http://www.number10.gov.uk/output/Page10735.asp, accessed 5 December 2007.

the response to foot and mouth disease in the United Kingdom.[14] His subsequent four years witnessed no new wars apart from NATO taking full responsibility for the war in Afghanistan in 2006 from the US-led coalition (of which the United Kingdom was a part).[15] This has resulted in Afghanistan becoming the major focus for Britain's armed forces with a deployment of some 8,300 personnel by January 2009 with a further temporary increase to 9,000 planned in support of President Obama's troop surge and the 2009 presidential elections.[16] Nevertheless, Blair was clearly interested in potentially deploying forces to both Darfur and Lebanon.[17] Instead, the operations in Iraq and Afghanistan have continued whilst Britain has continued to support the NATO/EU missions to the Balkans.

Blair's January 2007 speech on defence articulated the continuing case for a proactive foreign and defence policy which would continue to include the use of hard power along with soft power. In that speech he argued that foreign policy:

> has been governed as much by values as interests; indeed has attempted to suggest that it is by furthering our values that we further our interests in the modern era of globalisation and interdependence ...

He then went on to say:

> There are two types of nations similar to ours today. Those who do war fighting and peacekeeping and those who have, effectively, except in the most exceptional circumstances, retreated to the peacekeeping alone.
>
> Britain does both. We should stay that way.[18]

Although his successor, Gordon Brown, sought to distance himself somewhat from the actions of his predecessor he has largely continued the same internationalist policies as evidenced by the new national security strategy and British forces

---

14 'British troops start work in East Timor', *BBC Online*, 20 September 1999, http://news.bbc.co.uk/1/hi/uk/452208.stm, accessed 15 March 2008; Add Connaughton's PJHQ list JFQ no. 90.

15 See James Ferguson, *A Million Bullets: The Real Story of the British Army in Afghanistan* (London: Bantam Press, 2008).

16 Michael Smith, Sarah Baxter and Jerome Starkey, 'Surge and destroy', *The Sunday Times*, 5 July 2009, p. 11. For further details see MOD website at www.mod.uk, accessed 15 January 2009.

17 Robert Fox, 'Britain prepares to send 3,000 troops into Darfur', *Independent on Sunday*, 26 December 2004, http://findarticles.com/p/articles/mi_qn4159/is_20041226/ai_n12765202, accessed 15 March 2008.

18 Tony Blair, 'Our Nation's Future', speech made Plymouth 12 January 2007, http://www.number10.gov.uk/output/Page10735.asp, accessed 5 December 2007.

continue to be deployed in Iraq, Afghanistan and elsewhere.[19] Moreover, Brown himself made enquiries about military options following the outbreak of violence in Kenya following the elections in December 2007. In this case he was informed there were no forces available because of existing commitments.[20] Brown continues to be subjected to significant criticism over defence, most notably from a group of five former Chiefs of the Defence Staff,[21] and the new Chancellor of Exchequer, Alistair Darling, announced a further £2bn provision for fiscal year 2008–2009 to cover ongoing operations as part of his budget statement.[22] In presenting the new 'National Security Strategy'[23] to Parliament in March 2008 Gordon Brown felt compelled to announce some minor defence expenditures as his opening substantive response to the changing security environment rather than make any significant initiatives:

> To raise recruitment and to improve retention we will match our new £2 million pound public information recruitment campaign launched this week with the Government's first ever cross-departmental strategy for supporting our service personnel, their families and veterans, to be published shortly. In the last two years we have raised general pay levels and introduced the first tax-free bonus of nearly £400 a month for those on operations, as well as a council tax refund. And today the Secretary for Defence is announcing new retention incentives for our armed forces. There will be increased commitment bonuses of up to £15,000 for longer serving personnel. And starting with a new £20 million pound home purchase fund we will respond to the demand for more affordable home ownership.[24]

---

19 See http://interactive.cabinetoffice.gov.uk/documents/security/national_security_strategy.pdf, accessed 21 March 2008.

20 Interview with author.

21 See Armed Forces debate in the House of Lords, Hansard, 22 November 2007, http://www.publications.parliament.uk/pa/ld200708/ldhansrd/index/071122.html, accessed 5 December 2007; Andrew Porter and James Kirkup, 'Gordon Brown accused of contempt for Forces', *The Daily Telegraph Online*, 24 November 2007; see also Paul Cornish and Andrew Dorman, 'Blair's Wars and Brown's Budgets: From Strategic Defence Review to Strategic Decay in Less than a Decade', *International Affairs*, vol. 85, no. 2, March 2009, pp. 247–61; http://www.telegraph.co.uk/news/main.jhtml?view=DETAILS&grid=A1Your View&xml=/news/2007/11/24/nbrown124.xml, accessed 5 December 2007.

22 Alistair Darling, *House of Commons Parliamentary Debates*, 'Budget Statement', 12 March 2008, col. 289, http://www.publications.parliament.uk/pa/cm200708/cmhansrd/cm080312/debtext/80312-0004.htm, accessed 15 March 2008.

23 http://interactive.cabinetoffice.gov.uk/documents/security/national_security_strategy.pdf, accessed 21 March 2008.

24 http://www.number10.gov.uk/output/Page15102.asp, accessed 21 March 2008.

However, Britain's ability to sustain such an internationalist strategy is increasingly doubtful given the economic and military position in which the country finds itself.[25]

The controversy of Iraq not only masks the facts about the legitimacy of the other operations but also that all the operations that Blair authorised proved to be controversial. Not a single one led to complete success for the United Kingdom with the apparent exception of Sierra Leone. The air strikes against Iraq in 1998 (*Operation Desert Fox*)[26] proved unsuccessful in persuading Saddam Hussain to let the United Nations weapons inspectors into his palaces and ultimately in 2003 a US-led coalition, with Britain providing a major contribution, invaded Iraq officially to facilitate the elimination of Iraq's weapons of mass destruction.[27] As we now know these were not found and British and American forces have had to fight a considerable insurgency against various groups.[28] Only now is there an end in sight for the British commitment.[29]

The future of Kosovo remains undecided and concern still remains that fighting in the Balkans could flare up again.[30] The United Kingdom still has small forces deployed in support of the Kosovo and the earlier Bosnian operations and has at times had to send reinforcements as tensions have risen with the most recent deployment in June 2008.[31] Moreover, Kosovo's recent declaration of independence has once again highlighted the divisions within that region that remain unresolved.

---

25 Paul Cornish and Andrew Dorman, 'National Defence in the Age of Austerity', *International Affairs*, vol. 85, no. 4, July 2009, pp. 733–53.

26 See http://news.bbc.co.uk/1/shared/spl/hi/middle_east/02/iraq_events/html/desert_fox.stm, accessed 5 December 2007; Thomas E Ricks, *Fiasco: The American Military Adventure in Iraq* (London: Allen Lane, 2006), pp. 20–22; Michael R. Gordon and Bernard E. Trainor, *Cobra II: The Inside Story of the Invasion and Occupation of Iraq* (London: Atlantic Books, 2007).

27 See motion put before House of Commons for approval to take military action, 18 March 2007, http://www.publications.parliament.uk/pa/cm200203/cmhansrd/vo030318/debtext/30318-06.htm#30318-06_spmin2, accessed 5 December 2007; Paul Cornish (ed.), *The Conflict in Iraq 2003* (Basingstoke: Palgrave Macmillan 2004).

28 See Thomas E. Ricks, *Fiasco: The American Military Adventure in Iraq* (London: Allen Lane, 2006); Michael R. Gordon and Bernard E. Trainor, *Cobra II: The Inside Story of the Invasion and Occupation of Iraq* (London: Atlantic Books, 2007); Sir Hilary Synott, *Bad Days in Iraq* (London: I.B. Tauris, 2008).

29 See Warren Chin, 'Why Did it all go Wrong? Reassessing British Counterinsurgency in Iraq', *Security Studies Quarterly*, vol. 12, no. 4, Winter 2008. pp. 119–35.

30 'Final Kosovo talks end in failure', *BBC Online*, 28 November 2007, http://news.bbc.co.uk/1/hi/world/europe/7116606.stm, accessed 5 December 2007.

31 Adam Ingram, Oral Statement to the House of Commons, 1 March 2007, *MOD Online*, http://www.mod.uk/DefenceInternet/AboutDefence/People/Speeches/MinAF/20070301March2007DrawdownOfUkTroopsInBosnia.htm, accessed 5 December 2007.

In Afghanistan NATO's involvement has escalated and the United Kingdom now maintains the second largest contingent of foreign troops deployed in the country in support of the Afghan government.[32] These continue to be engaged in some of the most intense fighting that British troops have found themselves in since the Korean War[33] and a previous Defence Secretary, Des Browne, has spoken of British forces conducting military operations in Afghanistan for decades to come.[34]

Only in Sierra Leone has there been apparent success. Sierra Leone was Tony Blair's second major military adventure – *Operation Desert Fox* and the deployment of forces to East Timor are viewed as minor operations. It followed on from the NATO-led operation in Kosovo[35] which many saw ultimately as a success for Blair, if not the region, and preceded Britain's involvement in operations in Afghanistan and Iraq which ultimately would tarnish the Blair legacy. In a period of almost unprecedented commitment to the use of military force abroad Sierra Leone remains the one example where Britain undertook unilateral action and coincidently the only beacon of apparent success. It appears to embody much of the ethos contained within Blair's 1999 Chicago speech on the 'Doctrine of the International Community' and it is the one operation that his critics, such as Clare Short the former International Development minister, continue to put forward as an example of success and claim credit for themselves.[36]

---

32 See 'Operations in Afghanistan: British Forces', *MOD Online*, http://www.mod.uk/DefenceInternet/FactSheets/OperationsFactsheets/OperationsInAfghanistanBritishForces.htm, accessed 5 December 2007; Ewen Southby-Tailyour, *3 Commando Brigade: Helmand, Afghanistan – Sometimes the Best Form of Defence is Attack* (London: Random House, 2008); Ed Macy, *Apache: The Man, the Machine, the Mission* (London: HarperCollins, 2008); James Fergusson, *A Million Bullets: The Real Story of the British Army in Afghanistan* (London: Bantam Press, 2008); Patrick Bishop, *3 PARA: Afghanistan, Summer 2006. This is War* (London: HarperCollins, 2007).

33 Kim Sengupta, 'British troops "in worst fighting since Korea"', *The Independent Online*, 11 August 2006, http://news.independent.co.uk/uk/politics/article1218449.ece, accessed 5 December 2007; Patrick Bishop, *3 PARA: Afghanistan, Summer 2006. This is war* (London: Harper Press, 2007).

34 Jane Hutcheon, 'Brit troops in Afghanistan "for decades"', *ABC News Online*, 14 January 2008, http://www.abc.net.au/news/stories/2008/01/14/2137527.htm, accessed 15 April 2008.

35 For the official NATO view see http://www.nato.int/kosovo/history.htm#D, accessed 5 December 2007.

36 Tony Blair, 'Doctrine of the International Community', speech made at the Economic Club, Chicago, 24 April 1999, http://www.number10.gov.uk/output/Page1297.asp, accessed 5 December 2007; for commentary on its formulation see John Kampfner, *Blair's Wars* (London: The Free Press, 2003), pp. 52–3; Anthony Seldon, *Blair Unbound* (London: Simon and Schuster, 2007), p. 86.

The Road to Military Adventurism

Blair's Chicago speech and the military adventurism associated with his time in office are quite extraordinary given Blair's relatively little experience or interest in foreign policy prior to his election in May 1997. According to Nick Childs:

> Britain, in May 1997, had experienced a political sea change. After eighteen years of Conservative government, the Labour Party had swept into power. Tony Blair, who had never previously served in any government, was untried and unknown on the international stage. The imprint that he would leave on the country's foreign, defence, and security policy could hardly have been anticipated at the time.[37]

As John Kampfner has argued, his ideas of humanitarian intervention developed 'as he went along'[38] and only appeared to go awry with the 2003 invasion of Iraq. This adventurism ultimately led to Blair's fall from office in the face of public hostility and concern within his own party. It has left his successor, Gordon Brown, with a legacy of wars and ongoing commitments that he seems ill-equipped to deal with.[39] It has also left Gordon Brown to confront the impact of this adventurism on Britain's armed forces and Brown's handling of the armed forces has led to sea of hostility and a rebellion from a number of former Chiefs of the Defence Staff.[40] It is also noticeable that whilst Tony Blair had four different individuals as Secretary of State for Defence over a decade Gordon Brown has had three in less than two years. This may well explain much of the lack of political direction within the MOD and the abrupt announcement of plans to publish a defence Green Paper in the spring of 2010 in preparation for a full-blown defence review in the next parliament.[41]

---

37   Nick Childs, *The Age of Invincible: The Ship that Defined the Modern Royal Navy* (Barnsley: Pen and Sword, 2009), p. 142.

38   John Kampfner, *Blair's Wars* (London: The Free Press, 2003), p. ix; Anthony Seldon, *Blair Unbound* (London: Simon and Schuster, 2007), p. 86; Rita Abrahamsen and Paul Williams, 'Ethics and Foreign Policy: the Antinomies of New Labour's "Third Way" in Sub-Saharan Africa', *Political Studies*, vol. 49, no. 2, 2001, pp. 249–64.

39   Thomas Harding, 'Gordon Brown's Iraq pullout numbers game', *The Daily Telegraph Online*, 3 October 2007, http://www.telegraph.co.uk/news/main.jhtml?xml=/news/2007/10/03/nbrown203.xml, accessed 5 December 2007.

40   See Armed Forces debate in the House of Lords, Hansard, 22 November 2007, http://www.publications.parliament.uk/pa/ld200708/ldhansrd/index/071122.html, accessed 5 December 2007; Andrew Porter and James Kirkup, 'Gordon Brown accused of contempt for Forces', *The Daily Telegraph Online*, 24 November 2007. http://www.telegraph.co.uk/news/main.jhtml?view=DETAILS&grid=A1YourView&xml=/news/2007/11/24/nbrown124.xml, accessed 5 December 2007.

41   'Strategic Defence Review outline', MOD online, 7 July 2009, http://www.mod.uk/DefenceInternet/DefenceNews/DefencePolicyAndBusiness/StrategicDefenceReviewOutlined.htm, accessed 14 September 2009.

Yet, if we look back to Blair's time in opposition and the clear intent spelled out in the 1997 Labour election manifesto, there was no hint of such adventurism.[42] Rather there was a clear impression that Blair wanted to avoid foreign and defence policy offering areas for the Conservatives to exploit.[43] He therefore played safe in his first appointments in these areas. It was not surprisingly that Blair appointed Robin Cook as his first Foreign Secretary. Cook had held the shadow foreign policy portfolio whilst in opposition and had widespread support from within the party. To have appointed someone else would have potentially created a major opponent and raised questions about his judgement at an early stage. It was, therefore, ironic that it would be Cook that would have a series of gaffes that would pose problems for Blair.[44] It was also Cook who openly espoused the traditional 'New Internationalists' line that had been part of the Labour movement almost from its inception. He spoke initially of an ethical foreign policy,[45] although he rapidly had to modify this when the government was confronted with the issue of supplying arms to Indonesia.[46]

In support of this thesis Blair agreed to separate out the old Overseas Development Administration from the Foreign and Commonwealth Office (FCO) in a new government department – the Department for International Development (DFID) – under Clare Short.[47] In some ways this again represented traditional Labour policy. Harold Wilson had undertaken a similar move in the 1960s when he appointed Barbara Castle to the Cabinet with the responsibility of creating a new department responsible for overseas development.[48] This move was not without opposition, especially from within the FCO who wished to retain control over this area of government.[49] Blair nevertheless went through with the creation of DFID and its mission statement was and remains controversial since it failed to refer to Britain's national interests. Rather its Mission Statement is:

---

42   Available via http://www.psr.keele.ac.uk/area/uk/man/lab97.htm, accessed 5 December 2007.
43   John Kampfner, *Blair's Wars* (London: The Free Press, 2003), p. 5.
44   Alastair Campbell, *The Blair Years: Extracts from the Alastair Campbell Diaries* (London: Hutchinson, 2007), p. 225.
45   'Robin Cook's speech on the government's ethical foreign policy', *The Guardian Unlimited*, 12 May 1997, http://www.guardian.co.uk/indonesia/Story/0,2763,190889,00.html, accessed 5 December 2007; see also John Callaghan, *The Labour Party and Foreign Policy: A History* (London: Routledge, 2007).
46   'Ethical foreign policy row', *BBC Online*, 11 February 2000, http://news.bbc.co.uk/1/hi/uk_politics/639451.stm, accessed 5 December 2007.
47   Clare Short, *An Honourable Deception? New Labour, Iraq, and the Misuse of Power* (London: The Free Press, 2005), pp. 77–8.
48   Harold Wilson, *The Labour Government, 1964–70: A Personal Record* (London: Weidenfeld and Nicolson, 1971), p. 10.
49   Clare Short, *An Honourable Deception? New Labour, Iraq, and the Misuse of Power* (London: The Free Press, 2005), p. 78.

> DFID supports long-term programmes to help tackle the underlying causes of poverty.
> DFID also responds to emergencies, both natural and man-made.
> DFID's work forms part of a global promise to:
> – halve the number of people living in extreme poverty and hunger
> – ensure that all children receive primary education
> – promote sexual equality and give women a stronger voice
> – reduce child death rates
> – improve the health of mothers
> – combat HIV and AIDS, malaria and other diseases
> – make sure the environment is protected
> – build a global partnership for those working in development.[50]

This was supported with the publication of a White Paper in 1997 entitled 'Eliminating World Poverty: A Challenge for the 21st Century'.[51] Blair later sought to pour some cold water on this and inserted some traditional realism into his Chicago speech by emphasising that humanitarian intervention also needed to be linked to the national interest:

> We have learned twice before in this century that appeasement does not work. If we let an evil dictator range unchallenged, we will have to spill infinitely more blood and treasure to stop him later.[52]

However, he failed to get its Mission Statement amended and this remains at odds with that of the FCO and MOD. Short's appointment as the first head of DFID also proved popular within the Labour Party and it had the added benefit of placing her within the confines of cabinet collective responsibility. [53]

From the beginning Blair emphasised Britain's role as a 'Bridge between America and Europe' seeking to restore the traditional 'special relationship' with America whilst also restoring Britain's relations with the rest of Europe.[54] In the

---

50   http://www.dfid.gov.uk/aboutdfid/missionstatement.asp, accessed 8 March 2008.
51   'Eliminating World Poverty: A Challenge for the 21st Century', *Cm.3,749* (London: TSO, 1997), http://www.dfid.gov.uk/pubs/files/whitepaper1997.pdf, accessed 6 March 2008.
52   Tony Blair, 'Doctrine of the International Community', speech made at the Economic Club, Chicago, 24 April 1999, http://www.number10.gov.uk/output/Page1297.asp, accessed 5 December 2007; Andrew Dorman, 'Reconciling Britain to Europe in the Next Millennium: The Evolution of British Defense Policy in the Post-Cold War Era', *Defense Analysis*, vol. 17, no. 2, Summer 2001, pp. 187–202.
53   Interview with author.
54   Tony Blair, speech at Lord Mayor's Banquet', 10 November 1997, http://www.number10.gov.uk/output/Page1070.asp, accessed 5 December 2007; Andrew Dorman, 'Reconciling Britain to Europe in the Next Millennium: The Evolution of British Defense Policy in the Post-Cold War Era', *Defense Analysis*, vol. 17, no. 2, Summer 2001, pp. 187–

area of defence the Labour Party had the legacy of its unilateralist anti-NATO days in the 1980s.[55] For Blair the goal of defence policy was therefore to show that a Labour Government could be relied on by the electorate as a safe pair of hands. It was noticeable that when Blair appointed his first Cabinet he gave the defence portfolio to George Robertson rather than David Clark who had been the Labour defence spokesman in opposition.[56] Robertson was viewed within Westminster and the Labour Party as a safe pair of hands who would not rock the boat and carry out the manifesto pledge of bringing defence policy into alignment with foreign policy.[57] He followed a long tradition of appointing Labour Defence Ministers from the right-multilateral wing of the party, such as Denis Healey (Defence Minister 1964–1970), Roy Mason (1974–1976) and Fred Mulley (1976–1979). Robertson, was an astute politician and cleverly managed the subsequent 1998 'Strategic Defence Review' by embarking on a much wider consultation process than had hitherto been the case.[58] The result was a review that had broad support, even from the Conservative opposition, and certainly from within the armed forces and Ministry of Defence.[59]

More significantly, Blair got on well with the then Chief of the Defence Staff, General Sir Charles (now Lord) Guthrie.[60] According to Kampfner:

202; John Dumbrell, *A Special Relationship: Anglo-American Relations from the Cold War to Iraq* (Basingstoke: Palgrave Macmillan, 2006).

55 See Andrew Dorman, *Defence under Thatcher* (Basingstoke: Palgrave Macmillan, 2002); Anthony Seldon, *Blair* (London: The Free Press, 2004), p. 386.

56 Anthony Seldon, *Blair* (London: The Free Press, 2004), p. 386; Tony Blair, speech at Lord Mayor's Banquet', 10 November 1997, http://www.number10.gov.uk/output/Page1070.asp, accessed 5 December 2007.

57 Available via http://www.psr.keele.ac.uk/area/uk/man/lab97.htm, accessed 5 December 2007.

58 See 'The Strategic Defence Review', *Cm. 3,999* (London: HMSO, 1998), http://www.mod.uk/NR/rdonlyres/65F3D7AC-4340-4119-93A2-20825848E50E/0/sdr1998_complete.pdf%20accessed%205%20December%202007, accessed 23 January 2008; Colin McInnes, 'Labour's Strategic Defence Review', *International Affairs*, vol. 74, no. 4, October 1998, pp. 823–45.

59 See Humphry Crum Ewing, 'After the UK Strategic Defence Review: The Need for an Ongoing Reasoned Critique of Positions, Policies and Operations', *Defense and Security Analysis*, vol. 14, no. 3, 1998, pp. 323–30; Colin McInnes, 'Labour's Strategic Defence Review', *International Affairs*, vol. 74, no. 4, October 1998, pp. 823–45; 'The Strategic Defence Review: The View of the Defence Select Committee', *Defence Management Journal*, vol. 1, no. 2, December 1998, pp. 14–17; Ken Aldred et al., *The Strategic Defence Review: How Strategic? How Much a Review?* (London: Brasseys, 1998); Michael Codner, 'The Strategic Defence Review: How Much? How Far? How Joint is Enough?', *RUSI Journal*, vol. 143, no. 4, August 1998, pp. 5–11; its supposed success have led to calls for the next defence review to follow this pattern.

60 Anthony Seldon, *Blair* (London: The Free Press, 2004), p. 386.

Bluff and charismatic, Guthrie felt similarly respectful of his Prime Minister. He also knew how to work him. It was Guthrie who persuaded him to override the Treasury and provide the first real increases in defence spending since 1985. It was Guthrie who persuaded Blair that the Strategic Defence Review should focus on more flexible and responsive armed forces, capable of moving quickly to overseas trouble-spots.[61]

Blair was also an astute politician. With the Labour Party having a reputation for being anti-defence reducing the level of cutbacks to defence proposed by the Chancellor sent a significant signal. Whilst Chancellor Brown fought for greater savings for investment in other areas,[62] the amount was relatively small compared to that which would go into the government's spending priorities of health and education.[63] It demonstrated to the Armed Forces and wider government that Blair was prepared to overrule the Chancellor and thus show who was in charge of policy.[64]

Blair, like Brown and much of his Cabinet, had risen within the Labour Party based on their work on domestic politics. The only exception was Robin Cook who had had been known as a unilateralist in the 1970s and 1980s as well as acting as an opposition spokesman on foreign affairs.[65] *Operation Desert Fox*, the brief air campaign against Saddam Hussain in December 1998, proved to be Blair's first use of Britain's armed forces on the world stage and he intentionally kept a low profile.[66] Thus, it was not until the Kosovo War from March–June 1999, that Blair first held centre stage in the international arena.[67] According to Kampfner:

> Kosovo, Blair's second war, transformed the world's view of him and transformed his view of the world. It played a decisive role in changing his attitude to conflict and his relationship with the United States.[68]

---

61 John Kampfner, *Blair's Wars* (London: The Free Press, 2003), p. 23.
62 Tom Bower, *Gordon Brown: Prime Minister* (London: HarperCollins, 2007), p. 209.
63 Anthony Seldon, *Blair* (London: The Free Press, 2004), p. 386.
64 Tom Brown, *Gordon Brown: Prime Minister* (London: HarperCollins, 2007), p. 277.
65 Lawrence Freedman, 'Defence', in *Blair's Britain, 1997–2007*, edited by Anthony Seldon (Cambridge: Cambridge University Press, 2007), p. 619; Anthony Seldon, *Blair* (London: The Free Press, 2004), p. 386.
66 John Kampfner, *Blair's Wars* (London: The Free Press, 2003), pp. 29–33.
67 See Alastair Campbell, *The Blair Years: Extracts from the Alastair Campbell Diaries* (London: Hutchinson, 2007), pp. 375–82; Andrew Dorman, 'Kosovo', in *War and Diplomacy: From World War 1 to the War on Terrorism*, edited by Andrew Dorman and Greg Kennedy (Washington, DC: Potomac Books, 2008), pp. 148–67.
68 John Kampfner, *Blair's Wars* (London: The Free Press, 2003), p. 36.

NATO's war against the Serbian forces in Kosovo almost proved disastrous for NATO. As diplomacy foundered and the threat of force by NATO failed to deter President Milošević the NATO governments found themselves in the organisation's first war. Despite hopes to the contrary, the initial air campaign proved unsuccessful and a paralysis appeared to take hold within NATO and particularly in Washington.[69] Up until this point Blair had been content to leave the Balkans and, in particular the issue of Kosovo, to Robin Cook, his Foreign Secretary.

Cook, along with his French counterpart Hubert Vedrine, had sought to get the agreement of the various parties at the Rambouillet.[70] In support of these talks Blair had authorised the deployment of a sizeable British force as part of the NATO deployment to the Former Yugoslav Republic of Macedonia.[71] This was intended to place further pressure on President Milosevic. An agreement was eventually reached on 23 February 1999, which granted Kosovo a high degree of autonomy stipulating that Serb and Yugoslav security forces be withdrawn. It was initially to last three years and a follow up meeting in Paris was supposed to sign the agreement on 15 March.

By mid-March 1999 4,500 British personnel had deployed to the Former Yugoslav Republic of Macedonia to put pressure on Milošević and in preparations for implementing an agreed peace accord. The French, Italians and Germans undertook similar action whilst the United States administration announced the deployment of additional air assets to Europe.[72] After much delay the Kosovo Albanian delegation eventually signed the Rambouillet Agreement on 18 March 1999, although some within the delegation were against continuing to be part of Yugoslavia. However, the Serbian delegation, led by Serb President Milan Milutinovic, refused to sign.

On 19 March 1999 the co-chairmen of the Contact Group sponsoring negotiations at Rambouillet, Hubert Védrine and Robin Cook, announced the adjournment of the talks in the absence of an agreement from Belgrade.[73] The failure of the talks led the Organisation for Security and Cooperation in Europe

---

69   See Alastair Campbell, *The Blair Years: Extracts from the Alastair Campbell Diaries* (London: Hutchinson, 2007), pp. 375–82.

70   This was undertaken under the auspices of the six nations Contact Group which had been set up in 1992 by the London Conference on the Former Yugoslavia. It consisted of France, Germany, Italy, Russia, United Kingdom and United States of America.

71   See www.arrc.nato.int, accessed 5 December 2007; 'The Rambouillet Accords: Interim Agreement for Peace and Self-Government in Kosovo', 23 February 1999, www.kosovo.mod.uk/rambouillet_text.htm, accessed 16 Sepember 2006.

72   For history of mission see website at http://www.osce.org/item/22063.html, accessed 15 March 2008.

73   Tim Judah, *Kosovo: War and Revenge* (London: Yale University Press, second edition 2002), p. 224.

(OSCE) to withdraw the Kosovo Verification Mission on 20 March 1999 from Kosovo.[74] This force had been in place since the previous Autumn and had sought to oversee the earlier peace deal negotiated by the American Richard Holbrooke.[75]

As OSCE monitors pulled out they passed Yugoslav forces which launched a major offensive in the Mitrovica region and along the Prizen-Djakovica-Pec axis. Milošević had called the NATO bluff. Both Clinton and Blair had been advised that Milošević would back down after brief 72 hour bombing campaign.[76] On 23 March 1999 immediately prior to the conflict the House of Commons debated Kosovo. In opening the debate Tony Blair outlined the issues:

> As I speak it is still unclear what the outcome of Mr Holbrooke's talks in Belgrade will be, but there is little cause to be optimistic. On the assumptions that they produce no change in President Milošević's position and that the repression in Kosovo by Serb forces continues, Britain stands ready with its NATO allies to take military action.
>
> We do so for very clear reasons. We do so primarily to avert what would otherwise be a humanitarian disaster in Kosovo. Let me give the House an indication of the scale of what is happening. A quarter of a million Kosovars – more than 10 per cent of the population – are now homeless as a result of repression by Serb forces; 65,000 people have been forced from their homes in the past month, and no fewer than 25,000 in the four days since the peace talks broke down; and only yesterday, 5,000 people in the Srebica area were forcibly evicted from their villages ...
>
> We act also because we know from bitter experience throughout this century, most recently in Bosnia, that instability and civil war in one part of the Balkans inevitably spills over into the whole of it, and affects the rest of Europe, too. I remind the House that there are now more than 1 million refugees from the former Yugoslavia in the European Union ...
>
> We made a very plain promise to the Kosovar people. Thousands of them returned to their homes as a result of the ceasefire negotiated last October. We said to them and to Milošević that we would not tolerate the brutal suppression of the civilian population. After the massacre at Racak, those threats and

---

74 Brigadier-General Michel Maisonneuve, 'The OSCE Kosovo Verification Mission', *Canadian Military Journal*, Spring 2000, pp. 49–52, p. 52, http://www.journal.dnd.ca/engraph/Vol1/no1/pdf/49-54_e.pdf, accessed 15 April 2008.

75 Brigadier-General Michel Maisonneuve, 'The OSCE Kosovo Verification Mission', *Canadian Military Journal*, Spring 2000, pp. 49–52, p. 49, http://www.journal.dnd.ca/engraph/Vol1/no1/pdf/49-54_e.pdf, accessed 15 April 2008.

76 John Kampfner, *Blair's Wars* (London: The Free Press, 2003), p. 43.

warnings to Milošević were repeated. To walk away now would not merely destroy NATO's credibility; more importantly, it would be a breach of faith with thousands of innocent civilians whose only desire is to live in peace, and who took us at our word.[77]

This last line would become the central tenet of Blair's Chicago speech of a month later – national interest in the shape of the preservation of NATO mixed with a moral duty – the protection of thousands of civilians.

Although domestic public opinion was not convinced of the need for Britain to become involved Blair felt he had sufficient domestic and international political support.[78] He had ensured that all three major political parties in parliament supported the proposed NATO action and whilst international opinion was divided the members of NATO did agree that they should act. Paddy Ashdown, the leader of the Liberal Democrats, played a particularly important role and spoke with Blair regularly.[79]

However, the hopes of the air campaign quickly failed to materialise, Milošević did not back down and instead embarked on *Operation Horseshoe*, the massed explusion of the Kosovo Albanians from Kosovo.[80] Reflecting on the first week of the air campaign Air Marshal Day, Deputy Chief of the Defence Staff commented:

> NATO's plans had never envisaged beginning the air campaign with a massive application of air bombardment. This was not the start of a war where we were determined as quickly and as harshly as possible to overwhelm his entire military forces. We were aiming to disrupt his military activity and weaken his capability to conduct such repression in the future. We hoped that he would quickly get the message and not continue with his plans. We hoped for a rapid political solution and that it would not be necessary to move from one phase of our operation to the next and so on. And he is now seeing, we are prepared to continue if necessary.[81]

---

77 Tony Blair, *House of Commons Parliamentary Debates*, Statement on Kosovo, 23 March 1999, vol. 328, session 1998–1999, col. 161, http://www.publications.parliament. uk/pa/cm199899/cmhansrd/vo990323/debtext/90323-06.htm#90323-06_head0, accessed 5 December 2007.

78 See Paddy Ashdown, *The Ashdown Diaries*, Vol. 2, *1997–99* (London: Penguin, 2001), pp. 411–13 for insight here.

79 See Paddy Ashdown, *The Ashdown Diaries*, Vol. 2, *1997–99* (London: Penguin, 2001).

80 House of Commons Foreign Affairs Committee, 'Fourth Report – Kosovo', *HC.28*, session 1999–2000 (London: TSO, 2000), http://www.parliament.the-stationery-office.co.uk/pa/cm199900/cmselect/cmfaff/28/2811.htm, accessed 11 December 2007; see also General Wesley K. Clark, *Waging Modern War* (New York: Public Affairs, 2001).

81 Air Marshal Day, 'Briefing by the Foreign Secretary, Mr Robin Cook, and the Deputy Chief of the Defence Staff, Air Marshal Sir John Day', 1 April 1999, www.kosovo. mod.uk/brief010499.htm, accessed 8 December 2007.

The air campaign highlighted the political and capability differences within NATO.[82] Although all NATO members had eventually agreed to NATO action they were not all prepared or even capable of actively participating.[83] What resulted was a two-three week period of semi-paralysis within NATO as the slowly increasing air campaign appeared to produce no results whilst the media was filled with pictures of Kosovar Albanians being expelled from their country.

As a result, the NATO allies looked to the Clinton administration to take the lead, however, it was paralysed by the Monica Lewinsky scandal.[84] With NATO in a state of shock and the world witnessing the mass expulsion of Kosovar Albanians into the neighbouring states Blair stepped in. For Blair the international community had a moral duty to intervene and from mid-April 1999 onwards he quite surprisingly took the lead in getting political agreement amongst the NATO allies to see the war through and potentially engage in a major ground campaign, despite American reservations about such a war.[85] His Chicago speech in the midst of the war marked the first public articulation of this change and it came as a shock to many including some who had helped draft parts of it.[86] In a visit to see some of the refugees in Stankovic in the Former Yugoslav Republic of Macedonia in early May 1999 Blair spoke out – 'This is not a battle for NATO, this is not a battle for territory, this is a battle for humanity. It is a just cause'.[87]

---

82   Douglas P. Yurovich, *Operation Allied Force: Air Power in Kosovo. A Study in Coercive Victory* (Carlisle, PA: US Army War College, 2001); Dan D. Chipman, 'General Short and the Politics of Kosovo's Air War', *Air Power History*, Summer 2002, pp. 30–39; Grant T. Hammond, 'Myths of the Air War over Serbia: Some "Lessons" Not to Learn', *RAF Air Power Review*, vol. 4, no. 2, Summer 2001, pp. 68–81; General Wesley K. Clark, 'The United States in NATO: The Way Ahead', *Parameters*, vol. 29, no. 4, Winter 1999–2000, pp. 2–15.

83   Andrew Dorman, 'The Irrelevance of Air Power: The Potential Impact of Capability Divergence in NATO post-Kosovo', *Airman Scholar*, Spring 2000, pp. 53–8, www.usafa.af.mil/wing/34edg/airman/A-Spring00.pdf, accessed 5 December 2007.

84   Damian Whitworth, 'Oral History: The Monica Lewinsky Scandal Ten Years On' *The Times Online*, 15 January 2008, http://women.timesonline.co.uk/tol/life_and_style/women/relationships/article3185449.ece, accessed 15 March 2008.

85   See Alastair Campbell, *The Blair Years: Extracts from the Alastair Campbell Diaries* (London: Hutchinson, 2007), pp. 375–82.

86   Tony Blair, 'Doctrine of the International Community', speech made at the Economic Club, Chicago, 24 April 1999, http://www.number10.gov.uk/output/Page1297.asp, accessed 5 December 2007; Tim Dunne, 'Fighting for Values: Atlanticism, Internationalism and the Blair Doctrine', paper presented to the ISA Conference, Hawaii, 1–5 March 2005; Paul Reynolds, 'Blair's "International Community" doctrine', *BBC Online*, 6 March 2004, http://news.bbc.co.uk/1/hi/uk_politics/3539125.stm, accessed 10 March 2008.

87   Anthony Seldon, *Blair* (London: The Free Press, 2004), p. 401.

Blair was made acutely aware of the constraints of time and the need to resolve the situation so that the mass of refugees could return to some form of shelter before the winter set in. Charles Guthrie, then Chief of the Defence Staff, informed Blair that any ground deployment would have to begin by the middle of June if a ground campaign were to be started by mid-September and allowing time for the vast number of refugees to return before the first snow arrived. The US Defense Secretary is alleged to have argued that 'You're just pushing for it because it's American guys who are going to get killed'.[88] In response, George Robertson, the British Defence Secretary, with Blair's approval, pledged 50,000 British troops with the acceptance that casualties would run into thousands.[89] The implications were significant, the deployment would actually involve closer to 80,000 personnel and would have required the call out of a major element of the reserve forces amounting to some 10,000–12,000.[90] Committing over half of the regular British Army would also have led to major reductions in the commitments elsewhere, particularly Cyprus and Northern Ireland, which the government was prepared to accept. The pledge was therefore more than a symbolic gesture, it represented a step change in the readiness of the new government to use military force and was in stark contrast to the previous Major government's policy of incrementalism.[91] Fortunately a NATO ground war was not required. Milošević backed down and NATO forces acting on behalf of the United Nations were able to enter Kosovo peacefully in June 1999 to oversee the peace process.

For the United Kingdom, and indeed for the whole of NATO, the Kosovo operation highlighted a series of weaknesses within Britain and NATO's military forces.[92] In particular, the technological dominance of the United States and the consequential dependence of the other allies was manifest. It brought home to many the overall weakness of Europe's military capabilities. As a direct result, the United Kingdom, in conjunction with France, sought to enhance European defence capabilities. They agreed a series of measures at an Ango-French Summit

---

88 John Kampfner, *Blair's Wars* (London: The Free Press, 2003), p. 48.
89 Anthony Seldon, *Blair* (London: The Free Press, 2004), p. 406; John Kampfner, *Blair's Wars* (London: The Free Press, 2003), pp. 48–9; Tim Judah, *Kosovo: War and Revenge* (London: Yale University Press, second edition 2002), p. 270.
90 Interview with author.
91 Rod Thornton, 'Case Study 5 – Bosnia 1992–6', *The British Approach to Low Intensity Operations Part 2*, Report for the Office of Defense Transformation and United Kingdom's Ministry of Defence, 2007, p. 149, http://www.oft.osd.mil/initiatives/ncw/docs/LIO%20Part%20II%20Final%20with%20UK%20MOD%20Release.pdf, accessed 11 March 2008.
92 See *Kosovo: Lessons from the Crisis* (London: TSO, 2000), http://www.mod.uk/NR/rdonlyres/31AA374E-C3CB-40CC-BFC6-C8D6A73330F5/0/kosovo_lessons.pdf, accessed 5 December 2007.

held in London in November 1999.[93] These then formed the basis on an agreement set out at the December 1999 Helsinki European Council of the European Union which:

> agreed that member state should, by 2003, be able to deploy and sustain for at least one year military forces of up to 50,000 to 60,000 troops, capable of a range of tasks essentially defined as humanitarian and rescue missions, peacekeeping and peace enforcement.[94]

This built on the earlier Defence Capability Initiatives (DCI) commissioned by NATO and the similar process undertaken by the Western European Union (WEU).[95] The former aimed at improving the European members of NATO's overall capabilities as part of re-balancing burden-sharing within the alliance whilst the latter had as its goal the construction of a European capability to deal with military challenges in the Balkans without necessarily requiring the United States to become involved.

The Sierra Leone operation would take this transformation in Europe's defence capabilities a step further and provide, along with the French deployment to Ivory Coast, the role model for the European Union's new Battlegroup concept as well as a change in geographical emphasis from the Balkans to Africa.[96]

---

93 'Summit backs Euro force', *BBC Online*, 26 November 1999, http://news.bbc.co.uk/1/hi/uk_politics/536638.stm, accessed 5 December 2007; Mark Oakes, 'European Defence: From Pörtschach to Helsinki', House of Commons Library Research Papers 00/20 21 February 2000, http://www.parliament.uk/commons/lib/research/rp2000/rp00-020.pdf, accessed 5 December 2007

94 Tony Blair, *House of Commons Parliamentary Debates,* Statement on Helsinki European Council 13 December 1999, session 2000–2001, col. 22; 'Presidency Conclusions, Helsinki European Council, 10–11 December 1999', www.ue.eu.int/ueDocs/cms_Data/docs/pressData/en/ec/ACFA4C.htm, accessed 5 December 2007.

95 'Defence Capabilities Initiative', *NATO Press Release NAC-S (99)69*, 25 April 1999, http://www.nato.int/docu/pr/1999/p99s069e.htm, accessed 11 March 2008; 'Audit of Assets and Capabilities for European Crisis Management Operations', presented to the WEU Council of Ministers, Luxembourg, 22–23 November 1999, available from http://www.weu.int/, accessed 1 March 2009.

96 'Letter from Rt Hon Geoffrey Hoon MP, Secretary of State, Ministry of Defence to the Chairman', House of Lords Select Committee on the European Union, 19 February 2005, http://www.publications.parliament.uk/pa/ld200506/ldselect/ldeucom/16/16100.htm, accessed 7 December 2007; Gerrard Quille, '"Battle Groups" to Strengthen EU Military Crisis Management?', *European Security Review*, no. 22, 2003, http://www.forum-europe.com/publication/ESR22BattleGroup.pdf, accessed 5 December 2007; EU Council Secretariat Factsheet, 'EU Battlegroups', *EU BG 02*, November 2006, http://www.consilium.europa.eu/ueDocs/cms_Data/docs/pressData/en/esdp/91624.pdf, accessed 5 December 2007; General Henri Bentégeat, '1998–2008: 10 years of ESDP', *Impetus: Bulletin of the EU Military Staff*, Autumn/Winter 2008, pp. 6–7.

For the United Kingdom there were also a significant number of national lessons from the Kosovo conflict and it reinforced a number of previous conclusions highlighting aspects in which the Strategic Defence Review needed to be adjusted. Firstly, strategic lift was identified as of critical importance. On 10 June 1999 when the NATO-led KFOR force[97] entered Kosovo the United Kingdom had by far the greatest force immediately available but the number of troops deploying into Kosovo was less than the number of Serbian security forces leaving.[98] This, in part, explains the reluctance of the Allied Rapid Reaction Corps (ARRC) Commander, Lieutenant-General Sir Mike Jackson, to seize Pristina airport ahead of a Russian column moving from Bosnia.[99] The friction also indicated a growing British preparedness to take a more independent line.

Secondly, the Kosovo operation also highlighted a number of weaknesses in the Royal Air Force (RAF).[100] For example, whilst most commentators have highlighted the inability of the British to launch precision attacks in all weathers, few noticed the United Kingdom's inability to create its own air tasking order – a daily programme that sets out all the various air missions that are going to take place. The operation in Sierra Leone would come at just the point in time when such a capability was being exercised.

Thirdly, it emphasised the importance of seizing the initiative and coordinating the diplomatic and military lines of operation. This was nothing new but an area that had not been part of NATO's Cold War remit whilst nationally it had largely been forgotten as the United Kingdom had tended to avoid the use of force externally from the early 1970s onwards.[101]

'New Internationalism'

The 'new internationalism' had wide support within Cabinet and fitted into Cook's 'ethical foreign policy'. Ironically, Clare Short, as the International Development minister, proved to be as robust as anyone over the use of military action to

---

97 See http://www.nato.int/KFOR/, accessed 23 January 2008.
98 Lieutenant-General Sir Mike Jackson, 'KFOR: the inside story', *The RUSI Journal*, vol. 145, no. 1, February 2000, pp. 13–9, p. 15.
99 General Sir Mike Jackson, *Soldier: The Autobiography* (London: Bantam Press, 2007), pp. 274–5.
100 See MOD, *Kosovo: Lessons from the Crisis* (London: MOD, 1999), ch. 7, http://www.mod.uk/NR/rdonlyres/31AA374E-C3CB-40CC-BFC6-C8D6A73330F5/0/kosovo_lessons.pdf, accessed 6 July 2009.
101 See Andrew Dorman and Greg Kennedy (eds), *War and Diplomacy* (Washington, DC: Potomac Books, 2008).

resolve the Kosovo situation.[102] Later on she would be equally supportive of the use of military action to restore the situation in Sierra Leone and in the initial operations by the US-led coalition in Afghanistan. Only when it subsequently went wrong in Iraq would she begin to redefine her position.[103] The only major change in personalities between Kosovo and the deployment to Sierra Leone was Robertson's replacement as Secretary of State for Defence by Geoff Hoon who had been Minister of State at the FCO. Robertson's move to the post of NATO Secretary-General meant that Sierra Leone would be Hoon's first major operation in what would become a very busy time in office.[104]

Sierra Leone represented the next stage in the evolution of the 'New Internationalist' policy from one based on involvement in such operations as part of an alliance to unilateral action. The irony of Sierra Leone is that it began in the midst of policy disaster.[105] The British government, particularly in the form of the FCO and DFID, had put a considerable amount of time and resources into supporting the fledgling Lomé Peace Agreement as a mechanism for ending the vicious civil war in Sierra Leone.[106] This agreement had involved bringing the various warring factions into the Government of Sierra Leone with the United Nations overseeing the disarmament, demobilisation and reintegration process (DDR). The involvement of the British MOD had limited comprising the provision of a few officers to act as United Nations Military Observers (UNMO).[107]

It began in the midst of a United Nations peacekeeping mission that was in meltdown as elements of the RUF seized various elements of the UN peacekeeping force and started to march on Freetown, the capital, much to the consternation of the international community. The British response in Sierra Leone appeared to show how a relatively small force of highly trained soldiers can transform a situation bringing hope where there was despair.[108] As the deployment began *The Economist* painted a bleak picture of the situation:

---

102   John Kampfner, *Blair's Wars* (London: The Free Press, 2003), p. 47.

103   See Clare Short, *An Honourable Deception? New Labour, Iraq, and the Misuse of Power* (London: The Free Press, 2004).

104   Hoon would eventually become Britain's second longest serving Defence Minister, missing Denis Healey's record by less than 40 days. Other operations undertaken during Hoon's time in office include Afghanistan, Iraq and the fire-fighter's strike.

105   Richard Beeston, 'Cook needs an exit strategy from West African foray', *The Times*, 28 August 2000.

106   Clare Short, *An Honourable Deception? New Labour, Iraq, and the Misuse of Power* (London: The Free Press, 2004), p. 99.

107   See Phil Ashby, *Unscathed: Escape from Sierra Leone* (London: Macmillan, 2002).

108   Richard Connaughton, 'The Mechanics and Nature of British Interventions into Sierra Leone (2000) and Afghanistan (2001–2)', *Civil Wars*, vol. 5, no. 2, Summer 2002, pp. 77–95.

> At the start of the 19th century, Freetown was remote and malarial, but also a place of hope ... At the start of the 21st century, Freetown symbolises failure and despair ... The United Nations' peacekeeping mission had degenerated into a shambles, calling into question the outside world's readiness to help end the fighting not just in Sierra Leone but in any of Africa's many dreadful wars. Indeed, since the difficulties of helping Sierra Leone seemed intractable, and since Sierra Leone seemed to epitomise so much of the rest of Africa, it began to look as though the world might just give up.[109]

What had happened to change this? In early May 2000 the United Kingdom successfully deployed a force of around 4,500 personnel including an aircraft carrier, an Amphibious Ready Group – an amphibious force based around a Royal Marine Commando – similar in size to an infantry battalion but trained for amphibious operations – with supporting assets such as artillery and engineers capable of a rapid response, a Parachute battalion, Special Forces and a balanced air force, containing all the various elements of air power such as air defence, strike, reconnaissance, transport aircraft and helicopters and command and control assets – over a distance of 3,500 miles in seven days.[110] In the course of that week they evacuated approximately 500 civilians, stemmed the advance of the rebel RUF, breathed new life into the United Nations peacekeeping mission and ensured that the democratically elected government of Sierra Leone remained in power.

As a result, just two years later, the Prime Minister Tony Blair was able to indicate that the future might not be so bleak, that using the military as a 'force for good' had worked.[111] By 2007 Sierra Leone was able to successfully hold democratic elections in which power was transferred from the government to the opposition, something that a number of other African countries had found challenging.[112] The situation in Sierra Leone has now been transformed and the prospect for peace and even prosperity much improved, however, this success has been lost in the noise of Iraq and Afghanistan.

---

109 'Hopeless Africa', *The Economist*, 13 May 2000, p. 17.
110 See Brigadier David Richards, 'Operation Palliser', *Journal of the Royal Artillery*, vol. CXXVII, no. 2, Autumn 2000, pp. 10–15.
111 Mark Doyle, 'Britain's Future in Sierra Leone', *BBC Online*, 9 February 2002, http://news.bbc.co.uk/1/hi/world/africa/1811731.stm, accessed 11 March 2008; Steve Bloomfield, 'Sierra Leone is like a tinderbox. It will only take one spark', *The Independent Online*, 28 November 2006, http://www.independent.co.uk/news/world/africa/sierra-leone-is-like-a-tinderbox-it-will-only-take-one-spark-426104.html, accessed 11 March 2008.
112 Andrew Stewart, 'An Enduring Commitment: The British Military's Role in Sierra Leone', *Defence Studies*, vol. 8, no. 3, September 2008, pp. 351–68, p. 351.

Conclusions

What is already readily apparent is that Britain's military involvement in Sierra Leone in 2000 could not have been predicted when New Labour entered office in May 1997 under the leadership of Tony Blair. Defence. The use of the armed forces was not part of the New Labour agenda which was almost entirely focused on domestic issues. Instead, what was seen was a policy that evolved overtime as successive crises are confronted and dealt with apparent success and its clearest articulation remains Tony Blair's 'Doctrine of the International Community' speech in Chicago 1999. It was, however, a policy that drew upon Labour's internationalist roots and in general had the support of the wider party until the invasion of Iraq in 2003.

Given this background it is highly likely that the current flow of the tide away from such operations will most likely change in the future subject to any major calamity that might befall British forces currently deployed in Afghanistan. Moreover, the Sierra Leone example shows how individuals can have a significant impact within the British system of government which means that whilst an individual such as Blair, may not have articulated a particular policy before coming to power they are quite at liberty to pursue it once in power with limited checks and balances. This individuality also means that there is an in-built fragility as individuals rise and fall within the system.

Chapter 2
Background History: From the Creation of Sierra Leone to the End of Civil War

Introduction

This chapter briefly outlines the background history of Sierra Leone from its creation to the end of the civil war. In doing so it highlights a number of the long term tensions within Sierra Leonean society and provides an understanding of the context that led to the deployment of the United Nations mission to oversee the rebuilding of the country. To undertake this task the chapter has been divided into six parts. The first provides a background to Sierra Leone in terms of its geography and social construction. This is followed by a series of sections that analyse the pre-colonial, colonial and post-civil war periods. The fifth section them looks at the birth of the RUF and the ensuing civil war up to the Lomé Peace Agreement of 1999 before a final section draws some conclusions.

Background to Sierra Leone

Sierra Leone is a former British colony on the west coast of Africa. To the north and east of Sierra Leone is Guinea and to the south Liberia. To the west is the Atlantic Ocean. Sierra Leone covers an area of 71,740 square kilometres,[1] which is roughly equivalent to the size of Scotland and slightly smaller than the state of South Carolina. The capital city is Freetown which is located on the Atlantic coast and is separated from the main airport by the harbour and the Sierra Leone River which flows into the sea. Whilst estimates vary, the World Health Organisation (WHO) has estimated the population of the country at around 5.5 million people.[2] This is similar to Norway and Croatia. The indigenous population is made up of some 20 ethnic groups, with the largest being the Temne in the north (30 per cent) and the Mende in the south (30 per cent). The Creole or Krio make up a further 10 per cent and are the descendents of Jamaican slaves freed in the eighteenth century and concentrated in and around the capital Freetown. The religious make of this population is also divided with Muslims comprising approximately 60 per cent of

---

[1] CIA World Factbook, https://www.cia.gov/library/publications/the-world-factbook/geos/sl.html, accessed 10 December 2007.
[2] See http://www.who.int/countries/sle/en/, accessed 10 December 2007.

Figure 2.1 Map of Sierra Leone

the population, Christians 10 per cent and the various indigenous beliefs some 30 per cent.[3]

It has a largely agricultural based economy and is relatively rich in raw materials, including diamonds, bauxite and rutile,[4] which are much in demand. Yet, despite its richness in raw materials, the country has been decimated by civil war. This meant that in 1999, shortly before the British deployment, the United Nations assessed Sierra Leone as the least developed country in the world, largely due to the political instability that has continued since the late 1960s. This legacy remains with the country. Its gross national income per capita was estimated to be US$900 in 2006 placing it 220th out of 229 countries and this represented a relatively significant rise compared to a few years earlier.[5] In other words the Sierra Leone economy remains significantly behind the average for Africa which is itself the lowest in the world.[6] For comparison the figures for gross national income per capital for the United Kingdom and the United States are $31,800 and $43,800 respectively.[7] The roots of this situation preceded the civil war, according to Michael Chege, and can be directly traced to the slow-motion, self-destructive policies pursued by the government of President Siaka 'Pa' Stevens (1968–1985). These trends rapidly accelerated under the incompetence of his chosen successor, Joseph Momoh, who led the country from 1985 to 1992.[8]

Overall literacy levels in Sierra Leone stand at 35 per cent with a decided imbalance between the sexes. The male level has been estimated at roughly twice the female level – 47 per cent compared to 24 per cent.[9] The relative poverty of the country is also reflected in the life expectancy figures. In 2004 the average life expectancy for men was 37 years and women 40.[10] By way of contrast the United Kingdom and United States figures are 76 and 81 and 75 and 81 respectively. This means that the average age of the population is dramatically lower 17.5 for Sierra Leone compared to the United Kingdom (40) or the United States (37).

---

3   CIA World Factbook, https://www.cia.gov/library/publications/the-world-factbook/geos/sl.html, accessed 10 December 2007.

4   A natural form of titanium dioxide – it is a major ore of titanium, a metal used for high technology alloys. It is also an important element within the gemstone market. www.minerals.galleries.com/minerals/oxides/rutile/rutile.htm, accessed 10 December 2007.

5   See https://www.cia.gov/library/publications/the-world-factbook/rankorder/2004rank.html, accessed 10 December 2007.

6   See http://www.who.int/countries/sle/en/, accessed 10 December 2007.

7   See https://www.cia.gov/library/publications/the-world-factbook/rankorder/2004rank.html, accessed 10 December 2007.

8   Michael Chege, 'Sierra Leone: The State that Came Back from the Dead', *Washington Quarterly*, vol. 25, no. 3, Summer 1992, pp. 147–60, p. 151.

9   CIA World Factbook, https://www.cia.gov/library/publications/the-world-factbook/geos/sl.html, accessed 10 December 2007.

10   See http://www.who.int/countries/sle/en/, accessed 10 December 2007.

In other words, the average life expectancy for a Sierra Leone male is the same as the average age of an American citizen and the average life expectancy for a Sierra Leone woman is the same as the average age of a British citizen. With such a young population the pressures on the institutions of the state are greater and their inability to support the population has been part of the reason for the poor literacy rates.

Nevertheless, the potential for change remains if there is a period of stability, resources are put into building the economy and supporting the needs of the population and the endemic corruption is brought to an end. One ray of hope was the success of the most recent presidential elections was relatively democratic and power was transferred from one president to another from a different political party.[11]

Pre-Colonial Times

For the European explorers the area that became Sierra Leone was amongst the first to be explored in West Africa. In 1462 the Portuguese explorer Pedro de Cintra mapped the area around what is today Freetown Harbour. Reflecting upon the shape of the hills that surrounded the harbour he named them *Serra Lyoa*, which is the Portuguese for Lion Mountains. The Spanish translation is *Sierra Leone* which later became the country's name.

In 1652 the first slaves destined for North America were brought from the area that is now Sierra Leone. By the mid-eighteenth century the area had become a major trading base for slaves based on Bance Island (now Bunce) on the Sierra Leone River which was about 20 miles from Freetown and the furthest point inland the ocean going ships could reach. It was therefore the natural meeting place for European slave traders arriving in large sailing ships and African slave traders coming along the rivers of the interior to meet. The majority of the slaves were sent to Georgia and South Carolina in the United States where the farmers valued their rice planting skills.

By the late eighteenth century opposition to slavery had begun to grow in Britain[12] and in 1787 a plan was implemented by the St George's Bay Company, whose directors included William Wilberforce and Thomas Clarkson, to settle

---

11 'Landmark elections in Sierra Leone', *Times Online*, 11 August 2007, http://news.bbc.co.uk/1/hi/world/africa/6941558.stm, accessed 6 July 2009.

12 See William Hague, *William Pitt the Younger* (London: HarperCollins, 2004), pp. 291–304; Simon Schama, *Rough Crossings: Britain, the Slaves and the American Revolution* (London: BBC Books, 2005).

some of the black poor from London.[13] Many of these had been loyalists to the crown during the American War of Independence and had been promised their freedom on joining the British Army.[14] They landed in what they referred to as the 'Province of Freedom', later renamed Freetown. The majority of them quickly perished as a result of disease and the hostility of the indigenous people. A second group of nearly 2,000 followed on from Nova Scotia in Canada where they had settled after the British defeat in the American War of Independence. Each male was offered 20 acres of land plus 10 acres for his wife and five acres for every child.[15] Freetown was established in 1792 and the settlement was destroyed two years later by French warships. It was again rebuilt and by 1799 it was a self-supporting settlement of some 1,200 inhabitants.

Not surprisingly there were problems including an unsuccessful revolt in 1799 against the Sierra Leone Company which dominated the area. Nevertheless, over time thousands of former slaves continued to move to Sierra Leone joining the existing settlers. They became known as the Creole people because they had been cut off from their homes and traditions, shared similar experiences of slavery and had assimilated some aspects of British life. They built a flourishing trade on the West African coast and the Creole language rooted in eighteenth century African-American English, quickly spread across the region as a common language of trade and Christian evangelism in the region.

Colonial History

Sierra Leone formerly became one of the United Kingdom's first colonies in West Africa in 1808 as the nineteenth century witnessed the dramatic expansion of Britain's empire in Africa.[16] Freetown became the centre of operations, as well as a key refuelling port for Royal Navy ships. It provided an important staging post during the Second World War for convoys to and from the United Kingdom and it was again used during the Falklands Conflict when the *SS Canberra* visited the port. As a result, by the beginning of the twentieth century Freetown had become the residence of the British governor responsible for overseeing British rule of its various territories in West Africa which included modern day Ghana and Gambia. It therefore served as the education centre for West Africa and for more than a

---

    13   William Hague, *Wilberforce* (London: HarperCollins, 2007), p. 223.
    14   See Simon Schama, *Rough Crossings: Britain, the Slaves and the American Revolution* (London: BBC Books, 2005); William Hague, *Wilberforce* (London: HarperCollins, 2007), pp. 222–6.
    15   William Hague, *Wilberforce* (London: HarperCollins, 2007), p. 223.
    16   Andrew Stewart, 'An Enduring Commitment: The British Military's Role in Sierra Leone', *Defence Studies*, vol. 8, no. 3, September 2008, pp. 351–68; Christopher Fyfe, *A History of Sierra Leone* (Oxford: Oxford University Press, 1962).

century, it had the only European-style university in western Sub-Saharan Africa.[17] This made the demise of the country into civil war and anarchy all the more stark.

This does not mean that colonial rule was correct or untroubled. Moreover, the use of the Creole community by the British as the principal vehicle of their rule added to the tensions between the various groups that comprised Sierra Leone. The indigenous people mounted several unsuccessful revolts against British rule. All were put down and colonial rule maintained but the tensions created between the Creole community and the indigenous groups became a running sore that would lead to a rapid breakdown in the democratic institutions and subsequently fuel the civil war.

Nevertheless, the majority of the period of colonial rule was peaceful. One notable event was the granting of a monopoly on mineral mining to the De Beers to run the Sierra Leone Selection Trust in 1935. This was scheduled to last for 99 years and gave the company a monopoly on the mining of Sierra Leone diamonds. It led to the establishment of a small Lebanese community in Sierra Leone linked directly to the trade in diamonds.

As mentioned above, during the Second World War Freetown served as a major staging and assembly point for convoys travelling to and from the United Kingdom. Members of the Sierra Leone community also served in the British Armed Forces during the Second World War and the Sierra Leone Regiment formed part of the 81st (West African) Division which served in India and Burma with distinction. The Sierra Leone Regiment drew its origins from the Royal West African Frontier Force and ultimately became the basis on the Sierra Leone Army that was formed as part of the process of decolonisation.[18]

From Independence until the Outbreak of the Civil War

The process of decolonisation began soon after the end of the Second World War. In 1951 a constitution was created to provide the basis for independence. In 1953 local ministerial responsibility was introduced with Sir Milton Margai becoming the Chief Minister. Milton Margai had worked in the colonial administration from 1928 after attending medical school at Newcastle University. In partnership with Siaka Stevens he founded the nationalist Sierra Leone People's Party (SLPP) in 1949. In 1951 he was elected to the new Legislative Council and was given

---

17 Michael Chege, 'Sierra Leone: The State that Came Back from the Dead', *Washington Quarterly*, vol. 25, no. 3, Summer 1992, pp. 147–60, p. 148.

18 See Edward Turay and Arthur Abraham, *The Sierra Leone Army: A Century of History* (Basingstoke: Macmillan, 1987); R.P.M Davis, *History of the Sierra Leone Battalion of the Royal West Africa Frontier Force* (Freetown: Government Printer, 1932).

responsibility for Health, Agriculture, and Forestry before later becoming the Chief Minister. In this latter role he oversaw the creation of a new constitution for the colony and its adoption in 1958 which provided for a parliamentary form of democracy as a prelude to decolonisation.

Margai's leadership was soon challenged from within his own party when in that same year his younger brother, Albert Margai, narrowly won the internal party leadership election ahead of him. However, Albert declined the leadership of the party and instead left to form the opposition People's National Party, rejoining his brother in a coalition government in 1960. As a result, it was Milton Margai who became Sierra Leone's Prime Minister and he oversaw the colony's independence on 27 April 1961.

An election followed in 1962 under the mandate of universal adult franchise. Milton Margai's SLPP won a majority of seats in the new parliament. He soon stepped down and he was replaced by his brother Albert in the same year. Albert was heavily criticised by the opposition during his three year reign as Prime Minister. He was accused of corruption and of a policy of favouritism towards his own Mende tribe. Moreover, Albert began what subsequently became a common pattern of activity in Sierra Leone when he unsuccessfully attempted to establish a one-party state but he was confronted by the opposition of the All People's Congress (APC) led by Siaka Stevens.

In March 1967 in a closely contested general election the Governor-General declared Siaka Stevens the winner. Within a few hours of taking office, Stevens was ousted in a bloodless coup led by Brigadier David Lansana, a Mende and the commander of the Sierra Leone Army. Martial law was soon declared and a group of junior non-Mende officers organised a counter-coup. This led to the reinstatement of Siaka Stevens as Prime Minister and a return to civilian rule. The by-elections that followed were hailed an APC victory and Stevens appointed an all-APC cabinet. This marked the beginnings of his determination to move towards a one-party state and begin undermining the institution's of the state which would ultimately lead to the civil war two decades later.

The continuing disorder led Stevens to declare a state of emergency in November 1968 and the embers of Sierra Leonean democracy quickly faded away. Criticism from within the Commonwealth led the Sierra Leone Parliament to vote on 19 April 1971 for Sierra Leone to be a republic with Siaka Stevens becoming its first president. To help solidify his position and counter any possible coups by the army Stevens invited troops from Guinea to enter the country to support his regime and they remained present from 1971 to 1973. A number of coups were alleged to have been attempted over the subsequent years with the alleged plotters being tried and executed. In reality, it meant that Stevens was able to partially purge the army of potential opponents. In 1976 he was re-elected without opposition for a second term. In the national parliamentary election that followed in May 1977, the APC won 74 seats and the opposition SLPP won 15. In 1978, a new constitution was adopted, formally making the country a one-party state and the APC was made the only legal political party in Sierra Leone.[19] Stevens retired from office in 1985 and named the commander of the Republic of Sierra Leone military forces, Major-General Joseph Saidu Momoh, as his successor. According to Chege:

> Sierra Leone's misfortune was Steven's misunderstanding of the essential factors underlying the economic and governance structures he had inherited and yet his insistence on continuing in power for 17 years ...
>
> By the time Stevens handed the reins in 1985 to Momoh, a former military officer even less skilled in statecraft than Stevens, public institutions were already a hollow ineffective sham compared to what they had been in the 1960s. In the public's eye, the state lacked legitimacy. Corruption and illegality became the source of livelihood, as educational and health services vanished.[20]

Further parliamentary elections were held in May 1986 and in the next year, following an alleged attempt to overthrow the new president, Momoh purged the ranks of the APC including his deputy Francis Minah. Momoh's rule was marked, however, by increasing abuses of power and corruption and it was this that planted the seeds of the civil war. By 1994 Robert Kaplan, in his usual controversial fashion, summed up the situation when he wrote:

> Sierra Leone is a microcosm of what is occurring through most of West Africa: the withering away of central government, the rise of tribal and regional domains, the unchecked spread of disease and the growing pervasiveness of war.[21]

Birth of the Revolutionary United Front (RUF)

Without an effective army, police, judiciary or administrative system Sierra Leone was inevitably vulnerable to local and external actors especially given the lucrative raw materials it had. The RUF was created by Foday Sankoh, of Temne and Lokko background, and two others – Abu Kanu and Rashid Mansaray. Foday Sankoh, a former corporal in the Sierra Leone Army (SLA), had been trained in Libya and enjoyed a close relationship with Charles Taylor the one time rebel and subsequent

---

19 See William Reno, *Corruption and State Politics in Sierra Leone* (New York: Cambridge University Press), 1995.

20 Michael Chege, 'Sierra Leone: The State that Came Back from the Dead', *Washington Quarterly*, vol. 25, no. 3, Summer 1992, pp. 147–60, p. 151 and pp. 152–3.

21 Robert Kaplin, 'The Coming Anarchy', *Atlantic Monthly*, February 1994, p. 48.

ruler of Liberia.[22] When the RUF started it ran with the slogan 'No More Slaves, No More Masters. Power and Wealth to the People'. Although its principal goal appeared to be the overthrow of the existing corrupt government of Sierra Leone, the RUF gave little indication of what sort of government would replace it. The group did not advocate any particular ideology, ethnicity, religion or nationalism.[23] It did subsequently publish a pamphlet entitled 'Footpaths to Democracy: Toward a New Sierra Leone', which contained some rhetoric references to social justice and pan-Africanism during the negotiations of 1995 but little more.[24]

Ironically in light of its subsequent actions, the RUF was initially popular with Sierra Leoneans who were confronted with terrible social and economic conditions and lacked any means of changing the situation politically. Moreover, many of whom resented a Freetown elite dominated by the Creoles. They hoped that the RUF would overturn the corruption that was rife and many looked forward to the promise of free education, health care and re-distribution of the money from the diamond mines. This meant that there was no shortage of potential recruits initially and the organisation's ranks were soon swelled by idle and violent youths from Freetown's slums.

However, 'the RUF lacked a strong political agenda and was largely motivated by the ambitions of its opportunistic commanders'.[25] As an organisation it lacked political coherence. Instead, the RUF developed a reputation both domestically and internationally, for enormous cruelty during its decade-long struggle. According to Chege:

> Rather than utilize guerrilla training, Sanko and his associates chose to exploit criminality, torture, drugs, plunder, and rape in battle. The RUF distinguished itself in war with forced conscription of adolescent boys; sexual enslavement of girls; shocking human mutilations; and wholesale destruction of settlements, schools, and government buildings. After years of neglect and short of funding, equipment, training, and discipline, the Sierra Leone armed forces soon capitulated to the invading force.[26]

---

22 William Fowler, *Operation Barras: The SAS Rescue Mission: Sierra Leone 2000* (London: Weidenfeld and Nicolson, 2004), p. 37.
23 See http://www.fas.org/irp/world/para/docs/footpaths.htm, accessed 11 March 2008.
24 Available at www.fas.org/irp/world/para/docs/footpaths.htm, accessed 15 January 2008.
25 William Fowler, *Operation Barras: The SAS Rescue Mission: Sierra Leone 2000* (London: Weidenfeld and Nicolson, 2004), p. 36.
26 Michael Chege, 'Sierra Leone: The State that Came Back from the Dead', *Washington Quarterly*, vol. 25, no. 3, Summer 1992, pp. 147–60, p. 149.

Its leader, Foday Sankoh, maintained control:

> through fear, rewards of drugs and alcohol and a strange paternalistic relationship with his younger fighters. Many of these fighters were illiterate children, some as young as seven, who had been kidnapped and press-ganged into loose formations that were dignified with the title 'Small Boys Unit' (SBU). A mixture of coercion, drugs, the exhilaration of war and a kind of anarchic freedom made them formidable and terrifying fighters ...[27]

Despite their brutality the RUF retained coherence as a military force and their links to neighbouring Liberia ensured that they could maintain themselves with equipment and provisions.[28]

Sankoh began to attack villages in eastern Sierra Leone along the border with Liberia in March 1991 with a small band of men. The initial fighting continued for several months and the RUF quickly gained control of the diamond mines in the Kono district pushing the Sierra Leone Army back towards Freetown. As a consequence, arms and diamonds began to flow across the Sierra Leone-Liberian border where Liberia's President Charles Taylor acted as the lynchpin for the supply of arms in return for diamonds.[29]

In response there was another coup in April 1992 which sent Momoh into exile and established the National Provisional Ruling Council (NPRC) under the leadership of Valentine Strasser. The NPRC proved equally ineffective in dealing with the RUF and by January 1995 the RUF had overrun the three most important diamond sites in the country. This stopped the government's principal income stream thereby further undermining their ability to counter the RUF. By April 1995 the RUF were reported to be within 35km of the capital Freetown and thousands of rural Sierra Leoneans had fled their homes. It was estimated that the number of refugees totalled 900,000 (over one-sixth of the estimated population) of which 150,000 had fled to Guinea, 90,000 Liberia and over 600,000 were internally displaced.[30]

In response, Executive Outcomes (EO), a Private Military Company with origins in South Africa, came to Sierra Leone with the blessing of Valentine

---

[27] William Fowler, *Operation Barras: The SAS Rescue Mission: Sierra Leone 2000* (London: Weidenfeld and Nicolson, 2004), p. 36.

[28] Michael Chege, 'Sierra Leone: The State that Came Back from the Dead', *Washington Quarterly*, vol. 25, no. 3, Summer 1992, pp. 147–60, p. 153.

[29] Michael Chege, 'Sierra Leone: The State that Came Back from the Dead', *Washington Quarterly*, vol. 25, no. 3, Summer 1992, pp. 147–60, p. 153.

[30] William Fowler, *Operation Barras: The SAS Rescue Mission: Sierra Leone 2000* (London: Weidenfeld and Nicolson, 2004), p. 39.

Strasser.[31] To entice EO it was guaranteed £840,000 in profits from the Kono diamond mines in return for clearing the RUF.[32] Once in Sierra Leone, EO used the local Kamajor militia, which had been established the previous year, as its' main foil. The Kamajor mainly comprised traditional hunters drawn from the Mende community. To compliment these indigenous forces EO also brought with it some advance weaponry to give it a technological advantage. This included Mi-24 Hind helicopter gunships and Mi-17 assault helicopters as well as conventional land weaponry such as mortars, heavy machine guns and armoured personnel carriers.

With this mixture of technological superiority, greater acumen and the support of indigenous forces Executive Outcomes was able to clear the coastal areas within a fortnight and a few weeks later the EO contingent recaptured the Kono diamond mines located over 300 km into in the interior of Sierra Leone with the support of elements of the Sierra Leone Army. In addition, Executive Outcomes began training the Sierra Leone Army in company size units to enable them to engage the RUF on their own and thus provide a longer-term solution to the threat posed by the RUF coming across the Sierra Leone-Liberian border.

Initially the prospects for peace looked promising. The defeats suffered by the RUF drove them to the negotiating table. At the same time international pressure on the NPRC government elicited their agreement to hand over power to a civilian government. After presidential and parliamentary elections were held Ahmad Kabbah, a relatively little known Sierra Leone diplomat in the United Nations, was elected President in April 1996, and his party, Milton Margai's Sierra Leone People's Party (SLPP), won 27 out of the 64 seats.[33] Kabbah subsequently signed the Abijan Peace Agreement with the RUF in November 1996.[34] This sought to end the civil war and included a general amnesty. However, one of the terms of the agreement was that Executive Outcomes would leave the country within five weeks whilst the International Monetary Fund (IMF) insisted that the Sierra Leone government reduced its level of defence spending.[35]

---

31 See P.W. Singer, *Corporate Warriors: The Rise of the Privatized Military Industry* (New York: Cornell University Press, 2003); FCO, 'Private Military Companies: Options for Regulation', *HC.577*, session 2001–02 (London: The Stationery Office, 2002), http://www.fco.gov.uk/Files/kfile/mercenaries,0.pdf, accessed 10 September 2007.
32 William Fowler, *Operation Barras: The SAS Rescue Mission: Sierra Leone 2000* (London: Weidenfeld and Nicolson, 2004), p. 40.
33 Kabbah had previously worked for the United Nations for over 20 years.
34 Abiodun Alao and Comfort Ero, 'Cut Short for Taking Short Cuts: The Lome Peace Agreement on Sierra Leone', *Civil Wars*, vol. 4, no. 3, Autumn 2001, pp. 119–20.
35 See http://www.sierra-leone.org/abidjanaccord.html for the terms of the agreement, accessed 11 March 2008; Michael Chege, 'Sierra Leone: The State that Came Back from the Dead', *Washington Quarterly*, vol. 25, no. 3, Summer 1992, pp. 147–60, p. 155.

With Executive Outcomes out of the way a group of junior officers led by Major Johnny Paul Koroma decided to conduct another coup in May 1997. The coup plotters were angered by Kabbah's support for the Kamajors and Kabbah fled to Guinea. The brief 16 month period of democracy therefore came to an end. Koroma formed the Armed Forces Revolutionary Council (AFRC) and then negotiated with the RUF to form a combined regime with Koroma as deputy leader.

As a consequence the Nigerian government sent a force of approximately 700 soldiers, with two naval vessels in support, to Sierra Leone from its ECOMOG forces in Liberia. Initially the Nigerian's actions had the support of the wider international community in the form of the United Nations and African Union.[36] However they were opposed by the existing Sierra Leone government. A combined force of Sierra Leone Army and RUF fighters quickly besieged the Aberdeen Peninsula where the Nigerians were deployed. Fighting continued until a temporary ceasefire was negotiated by the British High Commissioner, Peter Penfold and the ECOMOG forces withdrew. Amidst the chaos the US deployed a Marine Expeditionary Unit (MEU) off the coast. After some negotiation the US evacuated some 1200 foreign nationals on 3 June 1997. As the last of the US troops left the RUF and its supporters in the Sierra Leone Army began the widescale looting, rape and murder of the population, particularly in Freetown area against the Creole community. The brutality of this assault was particularly shocking. No country recognised the Koroma regime and the United Nations Security Council passed Resolution 1132 which imposed an oil and arms blockade.[37] The Nigerian Navy continued to be active and Sierra Leone was again temporarily suspended from the Commonwealth in January 1998.

Whilst in exile in Guinea Kabbah reflected on the role of Executive Outcomes in bringing about a peace. He therefore began negotiations that led to Tim Spicer, then head of the Private Military Company (PMC) Sandline International, being employed to organise a counter-coup and restore Kabbah in power.[38] What resulted was a package of arms and capabilities:

> ... that Spicer called Project Python would include a command and control group to work with the Kamajors and liaise with ECOMOG, the provision

---

36 William Fowler, *Operation Barras: The SAS Rescue Mission: Sierra Leone 2000* (London: Weidenfeld and Nicolson, 2004), p. 43.

37 'United Nations Security Council Resolution 1132', 8 October 1997, http://daccessdds.un.org/doc/UNDOC/GEN/N97/267/13/PDF/N9726713.pdf?OpenElement, accessed 15 March 2008.

38 Richard Beeston, 'Cook needs an exit from West African Foray', *The Times*, 28 August 2000; Tim Spicer, *An Unorthodox Soldier: Peace and war and the Sandline Affair* (Edinburgh: Mainstream, 1999), pp. 189–202.

of helicopter support as a 'force enhancer', a shipment of weapons to enable ECOMOG to arm 8,000 loyal Kamajors and perhaps a special force unit.[39]

In other words, he proposed a package of support very similar to that used by EO so successfully. However, as news of the deal started to become public the British government declared that the Sandline operation was in breach of the United Nations arms embargo. In response Spicer argued that Sandline had received an export approval from the FCO and that he had the tacit support of the British government.[40] According to Peter Penfold, then British High Commissioner to Sierra Leone, the Foreign and Commonwealth Office were fully aware of the deal:

> They also had a copy of my reports that I sent, dated 2nd February, clearly showing that arms and equipment were part of this agreement. I also attached a number of documents which had issued from the Foreign and Commonwealth Office, which clearly showed that, from reading these documents, the understanding of the Foreign and Commonwealth Office was that the sanctions did not apply to President Kabbah.[41]

The affair proved to be embarrassing for the Blair government, especially given Cook's emphasis on an ethical dimension to foreign policy,[42] and the resulting House of Commons Foreign Affairs Committee report made a number of damning conclusions. These included 'that the government policy on individual arms embargoes must never again be stated in a way which could mislead Parliament, the public and even the FCO's own staff' (point 2) and that that any 'change in arms embargo policy is announced to Parliament immediately' (point 5). They were astounded to discover that the High Commissioner was at times required to operate without secure communications (point 10). Whilst it expressed concerns about some of the actions of Peter Penfold (points 12 and 14) they did believe that 'Mr Penfold acted as he thought was in the best interests of the United Kingdom and of Sierra Leone, and that he did not consider that his actions went beyond government policy' (point 15). The report also recommended '(a) in the case of mercenary activities, the publication, within 18 months, of a Green Paper outlining legislative options for the control of private military companies which operate out of the United Kingdom, its dependencies and the British Islands, and (b) in the case

---

39 William Fowler, *Operation Barras: The SAS Rescue Mission: Sierra Leone 2000* (London: Weidenfeld and Nicolson, 2004), p. 49.

40 Tim Spicer, *An Unorthodox Soldier: Peace and War and the Sandline Affair* (Edinburgh: Mainstream Publishing Company (Edinburgh) LTd, 1999, pp. 189–202.

41 'Newsnight Transcript', *BBC Online*, 8 February 2002, http://news.bbc.co.uk/1/hi/events/newsnight/1816794.stm, accessed 17 December 2007.

42 'Robin Cook's speech on the government's ethical foreign policy', *The Guardian Online*, 12 May 1997, http://www.guardian.co.uk/world/1997/may/12/indonesia.ethicalforeignpolicy, accessed 29 April 2008.

of arms trafficking and brokering, that the legislation to control these activities be introduced no later than in the next parliamentary session' (point 31).[43]

With the British engagement temporarily suspended the Economic Community of West African States (ECOWAS), led by Nigeria, again deployed forces (ECOMOG) to oust the AFRC and Kabbah was reinstated in March 1998. In support the United Nations Security Council established the UN Observer Mission in Sierra Leone (UNOMSIL) on 13 July 1998.[44] The remit the UN Security Council gave it included the decisions:

> to establish UNOMSIL for an initial period of six months until 13 January 1999, and further decides that it shall include up to 70 military observers as well as a small medical unit, with the necessary equipment and civilian support staff, with the following mandate:
>
> (a) To monitor the military and security situation in the country as a whole, as security conditions permit, and to provide the Special Representative of the Secretary-General with regular information thereon in particular with a view to determining when conditions are sufficiently secure to allow subsequent deployments of military observers beyond the first phase described in paragraph 7 below;
>
> (b) To monitor the disarmament and demobilization of former combatants concentrated in secure areas of the country, including monitoring of the role of ECOMOG in the provision of security and in the collection and destruction of arms in those secure areas;
>
> (c) To assist in monitoring respect for international humanitarian law, including at disarmament and demobilization sites, where security conditions permit;
>
> (d) To monitor the voluntary disarmament and demobilization of members of the Civil Defence Forces (CDF), as security conditions permit ...

The UNOMSIL force had an impossible mission. It was far too small, the various warring factions were not interested in demobilisation and disarmament and it was largely dependent on the ECOMOG forces for its self-protection. Its total dependence on the willingness of the warring factions to cooperate to achieve

---

43 House of Commons Foreign Affairs Committee, 'Second Report: Sierra Leone', *HC.116*, session 1998–1999 (London: TSO, 1999), http://www.publications.parliament.uk/pa/cm199899/cmselect/cmfaff/116/11601.htm, accessed 15 March 2008.

44 *United Nations Security Council Resolution 1181 (1998)*, 13 July 1998, http://daccessdds.un.org/doc/UNDOC/GEN/N98/203/28/PDF/N9820328.pdf?OpenElement, accessed 11 March 2008.

any of its objectives meant that it was doomed to failure from the beginning. Moreover, international attention was largely focused on the Balkans and on events in Kosovo. This meant that the situation in Sierra Leone was generally not at the forefront of people's agendas.

It was not surprisingly, therefore, that soon afterwards the RUF again attempted to seize power and on 24–25 December 1998 over 80 British and other entitled personnel were evacuated from Freetown by RAF Hercules along with non-essential staff and dependents from the British High Commission as part of *Operation SPARTIC*. At the same time the UNOMSIL force was also withdrawn to Guinea. The ensuing fighting reached Freetown by January 1999, where thousands were killed, maimed and wounded before Nigerian led forces were again able to drive the RUF into retreat. The brutality on both sides was horrific and was captured in the documentary *Cry Freetown*. This award winning documentary was subsequently screened in Britain, France and South Africa but was rejected by the various television channels in the United States because of its' graphic nature. Having let the Nigerian force reinstate Kabbah back in power the international community then forced Kabbah into signing the Lomé Peace Agreement with the RUF in July 1999 before once again returning to issues in the Balkans.[45] Peter Hain, then Minister of State at the FCO, summed up the situation for the Foreign Affairs Committee:

> Together with the international community, we felt it necessary to support a very imperfect Lomé Agreement in which that was provided for, or at least the followup was provided for, because there was literally no alternative. At the risk of repetition, remember where we were. We were in a situation where the RUF had again attacked the elected government, attacked Freetown. The elected government had no army. President Kabbah had no alternative but to negotiate with Foday Sankoh in particular and the other rebels in general. He was backed in that task by ECOWAS, the organisation of African states in West Africa. The Nigerian troops which had been supported and had previously repelled the rebel forces were about to pull out, so he felt the only option he had, and he was supported by ECOWAS, the Organisation for African Unity, the Commonwealth and others, including Britain and the international community, was to strike the best deal that he could.[46]

---

45 William Fowler, *Operation Barras: The SAS Rescue Mission: Sierra Leone 2000* (London: Weidenfeld and Nicolson, 2004), p. 62.
46 Peter Hain, *Foreign Affairs Committee*, Minutes of Evidence, 22 May 2000, Question 16, http://www.publications.parliament.uk/pa/cm199900/cmselect/cmfaff/519/0052203.htm, accessed 20 January 2009.

Conclusions

By 1999 the people of Sierra Leone had suffered a great deal. Independence brought increasing corruption amongst the governing elite and led to a redistribution of the relative power balance within the country. A succession of increasingly failing one-party governments had led to the emergence of the Revolutionary United Front in the early 1990s and the onset of a barbaric civil war in which many were killed and maimed. The cessation of hostilities brought about by the Lomé Peace Agreement offered a glimmer of hope. However the track records of the various warring factions was not strong, nor was the United Nations fully committed to bringing about peace and security for the people of Sierra Leone.

It was perhaps inevitable that the Lomé Peace Agreement would subsequently fail, the question was what would trigger the failure and whether the United Nations force would make any effort to prevent further bloodshed. What was not at all apparent was that the United Kingdom, the former colonial power, would respond militarily when the situation threatened to spiral into anarchy. The involvement of the British government during the 1990s had not been very successful and all indicated that the British would never consider responding militarily. None of the major players, not even within the British government, foresaw the chain of events that would unfurl and lead to the deployment of Britain's armed forces on any capacity other than a few personnel to support the efforts of the United Nations.

Chapter 3
Lomé Peace Agreement and UNAMSIL – the UN Peacekeeping Mission

Introduction

This chapter outlines the implementation of the Lomé Peace Agreement between the deployment of the United Nations force in 1999 and the sudden collapse of the mission in the early days of May 2000. It has been divided into four parts. The first part examines the peace agreement that was signed on 7 July 1999, what it meant to the various belligerents and its initial implementation in 1999 and early 2000. The second section then analyses the enlargement of the United Nations mission from February 2000 onwards into the areas controlled by the Revolutionary United Front and the tensions this created. The third part then considers the spark that caused the immediate crisis and the intial response of the international community through the auspices of the United Nations both in Sierra Leone and at its headquarters in New York. The final section then draws some conclusions.

Lomé Peace Agreement[1]

The Lomé Peace Agreement declared an immediate ceasefire between the Government of Sierra Leone and the RUF which was meant to bring with it a 'total and permanent cessation of hostilities is observed forthwith' (Article I). This was supposed to be monitored by a Cease-fire Monitoring Committee (CMC) chaired by the United Nations Observer Mission in Sierra Leone and include representatives of the Government of Sierra Leone, RUF/SL, the Civil Defence Forces (CDF) and ECOMOG (Article II). As far as governance was concerned the parties:

> ... recognized the right of the people of Sierra Leone to live in peace, and desirous of finding a transitional mechanism to incorporate the RUF/SL into governance within the spirit and letter of the Constitution, agree to the following formulas for structuring the government for the duration of the period before the next elections, as prescribed by the Constitution, managing scarce public

---

1 See http://www.sierra-leone.org/lomeaccord.html, accessed 16 January 2009.

resources for the benefit of the development of the people of Sierra Leone and sharing the responsibility of implementing the peace (intro to Part 2).[2]

The accord transformed the RUF into a legitimate political party (Article III) which enabled its members to hold public office (Article IV) and join a 'Broad-Based Government of National Unity' (Article V). Foday Sankoh, the RUF leader, was offered the 'Chairmanship of the Board of the Commission for the Management of Strategic Resources, National Reconstruction and Development (CMRRD)' with the status of Vice President answerable only to the President of Sierra Leone. He therefore had responsibility for the gold and diamond mines which were largely in RUF controlled territory. In many respects this was, according to Tim Spicer 'like giving the fox the keys to the chicken coop'.[3] Sankoh legitimately had control of much of the countries potential wealth which provided him with the power base to maintain and extend his position.[4] This he exploited and it was noticeable during this time that the level of diamond exports from Sierra Leone dropped significantly. At the same time, exports from neighbouring Liberia, a country with comparatively few diamond mining fields, increased exponentially.[5] In total the RUF gained four posts out an expanded cabinet of 22. In addition a general pardon and amnesty was granted to all the various warring factions.

Furthermore, the accord agreed 'to develop a timetable for the phased withdrawal of ECOMOG, including measures for securing all of the territory of Sierra Leone by the restructured armed forces. The phased withdrawal of ECOMOG will be linked to the phased creation and deployment of the restructured armed forces' (Article XIII). Both the Government of Sierra Leone and the RUF agreed 'to guarantee the safety, security and freedom of movement of UNOMSIL Military Observers throughout Sierra Leone' (Article XV). This was supposed to include the 'complete and unhindered access for UNOMSIL Military Observers in the conduct of their duties throughout Sierra Leone. Before and during the process of Disarmament, Demobilization and Reintegration, officers and escorts to be provided by both Parties shall be required to facilitate this access' (Article XV).

It was also agreed that a neutral peacekeeping force comprising UNOMSIL and ECOMOG should disarm all combatants of the RUF, CDF, Sierra Leone Army and paramilitary groups and that 'the encampment, disarmament and demobilization

---

2 See http://www.sierra-leone.org/lomeaccord.html, accessed 16 January 2009.

3 Tim Spicer, 'Sandline boss blames Blair for carnage in Sierra Leone', *Sunday Telegraph*, 14 May 2000; Douglas Frah, 'Hoodwinked by a Rebel leader', *International Herald Tribune*, 15 May 2000.

4 Alasdair Palmer, 'We helped this monster kill and maim his people', *Sunday Telegraph*, 14 May 2000.

5 William Fowler, *Operation Barras: The SAS Rescue Mission: Sierra Leone 2000* (London: Weidenfeld and Nicolson, 2004), p. 63.

process shall commence within six weeks of the signing of the present Agreement in line with the deployment of the neutral peace keeping force' (Article XV) and that the ex-combatants would retain the right to join a new Sierra Leone Army.

Why was this agreement acceptable to the Government of Sierra Leone and the international community? The hope seems to have been that by including the RUF within the Sierra Leone government it might agree to a form of power sharing and engage in the demobilisation, disarmament and reconciliation process. This agenda certainly appealed to those within the RUF leadership who spoke of a political agenda and wanted to legitimise themselves in some way. They represented an important part of the RUF leadership, however, they were not dominant and there was a sizeable element who wanted to maintain their positions as powerful warlords over the areas they controlled.[6] Moreover, whilst a general pardon for the various crimes was approved this did not remove such atrocities from individual memories and thus for many disarmament was a threat to their personnel security.

To be fair to those who advocated this approach there were few alternatives for the international community unless it was prepared to take the RUF on directly and defeat them militarily. Clearly the Sierra Leone Army and the various militias associated with the government were incapable of undertaking such a task and they were, at times, little better than the RUF.[7] It was unlikely that any government, particularly the United Kingdom, would be prepared to fund the use of a private military company to supplement the Sierra Leone Army after the Sandline Affair. A United Nations or African Union force was equally unlikely and the forces that comprised the ECOMOG contingent were generally keen to reduce their commitment rather than deepen it.

Britain, as the former colonial power, was not interested in participating in any conflict. In fact studies conducted within the MOD indicated that any deployment would have had to occur without a supporting evacuation plan for the force and such a risk was politically unacceptable for the new Labour government.[8] Moreover, the attention of the British government was focused on the worsening situation in the Balkans where the British government had played a major role in NATO's conflict with the Milošević regime over Kosovo.[9] The United Kingdom's 1998 'Strategic Defence Review' had referred to an 'arc of concern' stretching

---

6 C. Ero, 'Sierra Leone Security Complex', *The Conflict, Security and Development Group Working Paper no. 3* (London: Centre for Defence Studies, 2002), p. 29.

7 David Keen, *Conflict and Collusion in Sierra Leone* (New York: Palgrave, 2005), p. 5.

8 Interview with author.

9 See General Sir Mike Jackson, *Soldier: The Autobiography* (London: Bantam Press, 2007).

from North Africa to the Middle East.[10] It did not envisage sending forces south of the Sahara with the exception of potentially having to conduct an operation to evacuate British citizens from Zimbabwe.[11] The deployment of the UK-led NATO Allied Rapid Reaction Corps (ARRC) headquarters to Kosovo, together with a sizeable ground element, was placing significant pressure on the British Army which had no desire to take on any further missions until the scale of the Kosovo deployment could be significantly decreased.[12] The Lomé Peace Agreement, therefore, represented the least worse option for the international community and the best that could be achieved given the level of international disengagement.

The Lomé Peace Agreement called for the United Nations to oversee a new Disarmament, Demobilisation and Rehabilitation (DDR) process and its was envisaged that all the warring parties would begin to surrender their weapons and let their troops enter the rehabilitation process. To support this, the United Nations agreed to establish the United Nations Mission in Sierra Leone (UNAMSIL) to replace the failed UNOMSIL mission. This was approved through United Nations Security Council Resolution 1270.[13] The mandate for this force called upon all the warring factions to 'begin immediately to disband and give up their arms in accordance with the provisions of the Peace Agreement, and to participate fully in the disarmament, demobilization and reintegration programme'.[14] It emphasised that their respective leaderships should promptly engage in the DDR process and announced the the establishment of the United Nations Mission in Sierra Leone (UNAMSIL) in succession to UNOMSIL with immediate effect for an initial period of six months. It was given the following mandate:

a. To cooperate with the Government of Sierra Leone and the other parties to the Peace Agreement in the implementation of the Agreement;
b. To assist the Government of Sierra Leone in the implementation of the disarmament, demobilisation and reintegration plan;
c. To that end, to establish a presence at key locations throughout the territory of Sierra Leone, including at disarmament/reception centres and demobilisation centres;

---

10 'The Strategic Defence Review', *Cm. 3,999* (London: TSO, 1998).

11 Private interview with author.

12 John Spellar, *House of Commons Parliamentary Debates*, Oral Answers, 24 January 2000, col. 18, session 1999–2000, accessed 10 September 2007.

13 United Nations Security Council Resolution 1270 (1999) 22 October 1999, http://daccessdds.un.org/doc/UNDOC/GEN/N99/315/02/PDF/N9931502.pdf?OpenElement, accessed 11 March 2008.

14 United Nations Security Council Resolution 1270 (1999) 22 October 1999, http://daccessdds.un.org/doc/UNDOC/GEN/N99/315/02/PDF/N9931502.pdf?OpenElement, accessed 11 March 2008.

d. To ensure the security and freedom of movement of United Nations personnel;
e. To monitor adherence to the ceasefire in accordance with the ceasefire agreement of 18 May 1999 (S/1999/585, annex) through the structures provided for therein;
f. To encourage the parties to create confidence-building mechanisms and support their functioning;
g. To facilitate the delivery of humanitarian assistance;
h. To support the operations of United Nations civilian officials, including the Special Representative of the Secretary-General and his staff, human rights officers and civil affairs officers;
i. To provide support, as requested, to the elections, which are to be held in accordance with the present constitution of Sierra Leone.[15]

The resolution outlined that UNAMSIL's military component should comprise a maximum of 6,000 military personnel which would include unarmed 260 military observers. The provision of 6,000 UN Peacekeepers to protect the 260 unarmed UN Military Observers represented an improvement on the conditions under which UNOMSIL had tried to operate. However, the force was not large given the size of Sierra Leone and the quality of the various contingents proved to be extremely variable. Most significantly the resolution provided UNAMSIL with a Chapter VII mandate in which 'UNAMSIL may take the necessary action to ensure the security and freedom of movement of its personnel and, within its capabilities and areas of deployment, to afford protection to civilians under imminent threat of physical violence, taking into account the responsibilities of the Government of Sierra Leone and ECOMOG'.[16] These entitled it to potentially use force against the various militia groupings although the overall size of the force encouraged its commanders to adopt a less confrontational approach. That said, the actual peace agreement had few mechanisms within it that could be used to make the participants adhere to their commitments.[17] Moreover, in reality, the majority of the contributing countries effectively operated under a Chapter VI mandate whereby their forces would only operate where all parties gave their consent. The success, therefore, of UNAMSIL's mission was entirely dependent on the willingness of the various groups to abide by the Lomé Peace Agreement and begin to disarm.

---

15 United Nations Security Council Resolution 1270 (1999) 22 October 1999, http://daccessdds.un.org/doc/UNDOC/GEN/N99/315/02/PDF/N9931502.pdf?OpenElement, accessed 11 March 2008.

16 United Nations Security Council Resolution 1270 (1999) 22 October 1999, http://daccessdds.un.org/doc/UNDOC/GEN/N99/315/02/PDF/N9931502.pdf?OpenElement, accessed 11 March 2008.

17 Interview with author.

The resolution also specifically thanked the ECOMOG countries for their forces providing 'security for the areas where it is currently located, in particular around Freetown and Lungi, to provide protection for the Government of Sierra Leone, to conduct other operations in accordance with their mandate to ensure the implementation of the Peace Agreement, and to initiate and proceed with disarmament and demobilization in conjunction and full coordination with UNAMSIL'.[18] This therefore separated the ECOMOG forces from the various militias etc in the eyes of the international community and bestowed them the appropriate recognition.

The first UNAMSIL troops to arrive included Kenyan and Indian battalions which began to relieve the ECOMOG force. Troops from Bangladesh, Ghana, Guinea and Nigeria followed on. Air cover was provided by a force four Ukrainian crewed Mi-24D Hind helicopter gunships plus a mixture of Mi-8 and Mi-26 transport helicopters. In part the significant proportion of African forces reflected a desire for Africa to solve its own problems but it also reflected a lack of willingness from other parts of the world to commit forces. The weakness of the UNAMSIL force and this lack of a wider international involvement helped to undermine any confidence that the various groups within Sierra Leone might have about the future security situation.

UNAMSIL got off to a poor start with a number of hostage crises and a delayed deployment following the granting of its mandate in October 1999 some three months after the peace agreement had been signed.[19] It proceeded according to the old peacekeeping formula that called for non-forceful cooperation with consenting parties, despite the mandate it had been given.[20] It also suffered problems in coordinating the different United Nations elements in Sierra Leone with its headquarters in New York.

Nevertheless, some progress was made in the government controlled western part of Sierra Leone where UNAMSIL initially deployed forces. However, far less progress was made in the areas under the control of the RUF and the disarmament, demobilisation and rehabilitation process was slow to get off the ground.[21] The

---

18 United Nations Security Council Resolution 1270 (1999) 22 October 1999, http://daccessdds.un.org/doc/UNDOC/GEN/N99/315/02/PDF/N9931502.pdf?OpenElement, accessed 11 March 2008.

19 'Crisis in Sierra Leone: The Failure of UN Peacekeeping', *Strategic Comments* (Oxford: Oxford University Press for the IISS), vol. 6, no. 9, November 2000.

20 Brian Urquhart, 'Some Thoughts on Sierra Leone', *New York Book Reviews*, 15 June 2000.

21 'Third Report of the Secretary-General on the United Nations Mission in Sierra Leone', *S/2000/186*, 7 March 2000, p. 2, http://daccess-ods.un.org/TMP/4843224.html, accessed 15 March 2008.

various factions were equally loathed to surrender their weapons until the others had done so. The United Nations Secretary-General's Third Report to the Security Council noted:

> There were several serious incidents involving UNAMSIL and former rebel elements or combatants. On 10 January, RUF elements seized a large number of weapons, ammunition and vehicles from a convoy of Guinean troops moving to join UNAMSIL. In two other incidents, members of the UNAMSIL Kenyan battalion were ambushed and had to surrender their weapons to ex-Sierra Leone Army combatants in the Occra Hills area on 14 January, and to RUF elements near Mekeni on 31 January ... In response to these incidents, the Secretariat and the Force Commander of UNAMSIL, Major General Vijay Kumar Jetley, have urged troop-contributing countries and their contingents to ensure that the troops on the ground fully comply with the mandate and rules of engagement of UNAMSIL and are equipped in accordance with United Nations standards.[22]

The question that remained outstanding was, what would happen if UNAMSIL sought to implement its remit throughout the country and begin to insist that the various warring factions began to disarm?

Expansion of the UN Mission

In February 2000 a further resolution – 1289 – gave UNAMSIL a more robust mandate and expanded its authorised strength to 11,100 including 260 military observers (UNMOs).[23] This was supposed to lead to the deployment of an additional six infantry battalions between May and June to offset the withdrawal of the remaining experienced ECOMOG forces in April and allow UNAMSIL to deploy throughout the entire country. The resolution noted the following:

> 4. Notes with concern that, despite the progress that has been made, the peace process thus far has been marred by the limited and sporadic participation in the disarmament, demobilization and reintegration programme, by the lack of progress on the release of abductees and child soldiers, and by continued hostage-taking and attacks on humanitarian personnel, and expresses its conviction that the expansion of UNAMSIL as provided for in paragraphs 9 to 12 below will

---

22 'Third Report of the Secretary-General on the United Nations Mission in Sierra Leone', *S/2000/186*, 7 March 2000, p. 3, http://daccess-ods.un.org/TMP/4843224.html, accessed 15 March 2008.

23 United Nations Security Council Resolution 1289 (2000), 7 February 2000, http://daccessdds.un.org/doc/UNDOC/GEN/N00/283/50/PDF/N0028350.pdf?OpenElement.

create conditions under which all parties can work to ensure that the provisions of the Peace Agreement are implemented in full; ...[24]

The resolution then went on to call on all the parties plus others involved in the peace agreement to ensure that the DDR process was implemented across the entire country, i.e. it called upon the RUF to follow the example of the other militias and Sierra Leone Army and begin the DDR process.[25] It also noted the intention of the ECOMOG governments to withdraw their contingents and by way of compensation announced the intention to expand the UNAMSIL force to some 11,100 with no change in the number of UNMOs.[26] At the same time the tasks given to UNAMSIL were expanded to include the following:

(a) To provide security at key locations and Government buildings, in particular in Freetown, important intersections and major airports, including Lungi airport;

(b) To facilitate the free flow of people, goods and humanitarian assistance along specified thoroughfares;

(c) To provide security in and at all sites of the disarmament, demobilization and reintegration programme;

(d) To coordinate with and assist, in common areas of deployment, the Sierra Leone law enforcement authorities in the discharge of their responsibilities;

(e) To guard weapons, ammunition and other military equipment collected from ex-combatants and to assist in their subsequent disposal or destruction, authorizes UNAMSIL to take the necessary action to fulfil the additional tasks set out above, and affirms that, in the discharge of its mandate, UNAMSIL may take the necessary action to ensure the security and freedom of movement of its personnel and, within its capabilities and areas of deployment, to afford protection to civilians under imminent threat of physical violence, taking into account the responsibilities of the Government of Sierra Leone; ...[27]

---

24 United Nations Security Council Resolution 1289 (2000), 7 February 2000, http://daccessdds.un.org/doc/UNDOC/GEN/N00/283/50/PDF/N0028350.pdf?OpenElement, accessed 10 September 2007.
25 United Nations Security Council Resolution 1289 (2000), 7 February 2000, http://daccessdds.un.org/doc/UNDOC/GEN/N00/283/50/PDF/N0028350.pdf?OpenElement, accessed 10 September 2007.
26 United Nations Security Council Resolution 1289 (2000), 7 February 2000, http://daccessdds.un.org/doc/UNDOC/GEN/N00/283/50/PDF/N0028350.pdf?OpenElement, accessed 10 September 2007.
27 United Nations Security Council Resolution 1289 (2000), 7 February 2000, http://daccessdds.un.org/doc/UNDOC/GEN/N00/283/50/PDF/N0028350.pdf?OpenElement, accessed 10 September 2007.

The resolution then called on all parties to allow the free and safe movement of all United Nations and associated personnel. This was directed at the RUF as was a subsequent point in the resolution which:

> 18. Emphasizes the importance of the exercise by the Government of Sierra Leone of full control over the exploitation of gold, diamonds and other resources for the benefit of the people of the country and in accordance with Article VII, paragraph 6, of the Peace Agreement, and to that end calls for the early and effective operation of the Commission of the Management of Strategic Resources, National Reconstruction and Development ...[28]

This was a challenge to the RUF's economic basis and indirectly questioned the role that its leader was playing as the cabinet minister responsible for Sierra Leone's strategic resources.[29]

The first challenge for the United Nations commander in Sierra Leone, Major-General Jetley, was to manage this expanded role whilst he lost his experienced ECOMOG forces and only slowly received replacements that would ultimately give him a force almost twice the size of his initial force. In other words, he was required to expand his area of responsibility, confront the lack of adherence to the Lomé Peace Agreement whilst engaging in a force rotation that would initially leave him with a weaker military capability. His solution was to declare in April 2000 that his forces would begin to disarm the RUF forces in Kono district from June onwards, i.e. at a point immediately after the gap between the departure of the experienced ECOMOG forces and arrival of his additional UNAMSIL forces.[30]

However, with the new mandate UNAMSIL was encouraged to begin to establish bases further eastwards in RUF controlled territory and the UNMOs were directed to push forward with the DDR process before UNAMSIL received its reinforcements.[31] Thus the RUF began to be challenged at the same time the relative power balance on the ground altered as the experienced ECOMOG forces began to withdraw and before the UNAMSIL reinforcements began to arrive. The ECOMOG forces, dominated by the Nigerians, had a reputation for dealing with

---

28 United Nations Security Council Resolution 1289 (2000), 7 February 2000, http://daccessdds.un.org/doc/UNDOC/GEN/N00/283/50/PDF/N0028350.pdf?OpenElement, accessed 10 September 2007.
29 United Nations Security Council Resolution 1289 (2000), 7 February 2000, http://daccessdds.un.org/doc/UNDOC/GEN/N00/283/50/PDF/N0028350.pdf?OpenElement, accessed 10 September 2007.
30 David Keen, *Conflict and Collusion in Sierra Leone* (New York: Palgrave, 2005), p. 262.
31 Major Phil Ashby, *Unscathed: Escape from Sierra Leone* (London: Pan Books, 2002), pp. 175–6.

the RUF robustly. The incoming UN forces lacked their experience and, from the beginning, UNAMSIL ran into problems.

On 20 April 2000 two disarmament, demobilisation and reintegration camps in RUF controlled areas became operational. This was nine rather than the planned two months after the Lomé Peace Agreement was signed reflecting the slow pace of implementation but before any of the UNAMSIL reinforcements had arrived. Other camps in government controlled territory had already accepted some 25,000 personnel from the Civil Defence Force (CDF), Kamajors, SLA and other government controlled militias.[32] However, they had not progressed far apart from collecting the weaponry of these groups because they lacked the necessary facilities to commence the rehabilitation process. Each of the camps was supported by a small team of unarmed UNMOs with a small UNAMSIL contingent nearby to support the UNMOs and provide for the protection of the UNMOs and those who had entered the DDR process.

Spark to the Crisis and the Initial Response of the International Community

Although the two camps for the RUF were operational from 20 April little happened initially until 10 former RUF fighters voluntarily came forward and spoke to the UNMO team on 29 April 2000 at Makeni. From these discussions it was clear that whilst the individuals wanted to enter the disarmament process but that their commanders were unaware of their actions and the local UNMO teams at both RUF sites were concerned about the response of the local RUF leadership. They suggested that the disarmament process should only begin once the local RUF leaders had been consulted and agreed. However, they were overruled by the UN headquarters in Freetown who thought that it was worth taking the risk of allowing the 10 RUF fighters enter the disarmament camp.[33] They therefore were asked to return the following day and the DDR process was begun. The 10 RUF fighters subsequently surrendered their weapons and their protection became the formal responsibility of the local UN Kenyan force. The response of the RUF was rapid, as news spread to the local RUF commander of what he referred to as the dissertion of his 10 men he went to the DDR centre at Makeni along with approximately 100 armed guerrillas and demanded their return.[34] When this was refused the UNMOs

---

32 Major Phil Ashby, *Unscathed: Escape from Sierra Leone* (London: Pan Books, 2002), p. 174.
33 Major Phil Ashby, *Unscathed: Escape from Sierra Leone* (London: Pan Books, 2002), p. 189.
34 David Keen, *Conflict and Collusion in Sierra Leone* (New York: Palgrave, 2005), p. 262.

present at the time were seized and abused.[35] The violence quickly escalated and the UN compounds at Makeni and Magburaka were attacked. Troops from the UN Kenyan company fought off the RUF attacks but sustained casualties and were besieged along with their remaining UNMOs and a British DFID team.[36]

Reflecting on what subsequently happened the United Nation Secretary-General's Fourth report to the Security Council outlined the issue as follows:

> During the reporting period, the peace process suffered a very serious setback as the result of the recent unprovoked armed attacks on United Nations personnel, the detention of several hundred United Nations personnel, and the destruction of disarmament and demobilisation camps by fighters of the Revolutionary United Front (RUF).[37]

The problem was that the RUF was made up of several factions with an agenda that changed over time and there was a clear divide between those commanders from its political and military wings. At the top Foday Sankoh seems to have wanted to make the RUF a political party, whilst his deputy, Sam Bockarie, believed that such a move was a 'hasty embrace of peace'.[38] For the RUF's military commanders the DDR process offered them little gain according former UNMO Phil Ashby:

> As rebel fighters, they lived as warlords, with the power of life and death in the areas they controlled and the prettiest girls as bush wives. As uneducated ex-combatants, they would be nobodies, but with many enemies. Worse, they would be with many enemies and no guns.[39]

The RUF's relationship with President Taylor's regime in Liberia was also close, with a thriving cross-border trade in illicit diamonds and arms.[40] Instability in Sierra Leone clearly suited Taylor and he had sponsored similar destabilising action in Guinea. It allowed him to continue his illicit trade in arms and diamonds whilst diverting international attention away from his despotic rule in Liberia.

---

35   Major Phil Ashby, *Unscathed: Escape from Sierra Leone* (London: Pan Books, 2002), p. 193.

36   'UN condemns Sierra Leone rebels', *BBC Online*, 3 May 2000, http://news.bbc.co.uk/1/hi/world/africa/733828.stm, accessed 25 November 2007.

37   'Fourth Report of the Secretary-General on the United Nations Mission in Sierra Leone', *S/2000/455*, 19 May 2000, p. 1, http://daccessdds.un.org/doc/UNDOC/GEN/N00/407/22/IMG/N0040722.pdf?OpenElement, accessed 15 March 2008.

38   C. Ero, 'Sierra Leone Security Complex', *The Conflict, Security and Development Group Working Paper no. 3* (London: Centre for Defence Studies, 2002), p. 29.

39   Major Phil Ashby, *Unscathed: Escape from Sierra Leone* (London: Pan Macmillan Books Ltd, 2002), p. 181.

40   Michael Chege, 'Sierra Leone: The State that Came Back from the Dead', *Washington Quarterly*, vol. 25, no. 3, Summer 1992, pp. 147–60, p. 149.

All that was needed was an incident to spark a revolt. The admission of 10 RUF soldiers into the disarmament process in late April 2000 provided that trigger. Added to this was the knowledge that the United Nations force was at its weakest and it was also about to deploy to the Koidu area which was at the centre of the RUF's diamond mining operations.

In response to the attacks the United Nations Commander, Major-General Jetley spoke with Sankoh to little effect.[41] The UN Special Representative, Oluyemi Odeniji, was also in regular contact with Sankoh prior to Sankoh's disappearance on 8 May and believed that a peaceful resolution was possible.[42] This confidence remained in place despite the fact that United Nations mediators sent to try and resolve the situation were also taken hostage. According to Phil Ashby, one of the three British UNMOs under siege at Makeni:

> No one in the UN HQ in Freetown seemed to be taking our deteriorating security situation seriously. At this stage they were still unwilling to believe anything was amiss. It was exasperating, to put it mildly, to be told by the UN HQ over the radio that 'everything was calm' and we should stop making a fuss.[43]

Further seizures and outbreaks of violence occurred across the area controlled by the RUF and the number of UN personnel seized and taken hostage by the RUF began to grow steadily.

By 3 May 2000 the United Nations Secretariat in New York called for an emergency meeting of the UN Security Council for the 4 May to brief its members on the seizures. The United Nations mission had clearly suffered casualties and a number of its personnel were being held captive. Sankoh remained at large in Freetown and suggested that the situation could be resolved politically. However, he cleverly failed to act and, when he met with both the US Ambassador and Deputy British High Commissioner at his home on 4 May he appeared confident and very much in control of the situation. His reliability was therefore doubted both within the British government and elsewhere.[44] The situation appeared entirely favourable to him and later that day it became apparent that the Zambian battalion sent to the Northern town of Makeni to relieve other UN forces had also been taken hostage

---

41 See 'Interview with Major-General Vijay Kumar Jetley', *Jane's Defence Weekly*, 17 July 2000.

42 Douglas Farah, 'Hoodwinked by a Rebel Leader', *International Herald Tribune*, 15 May 2000.

43 Major Phil Ashby, *Unscathed: Escape from Sierra Leone* (London: Pan Macmillan Books Ltd, 2002), p. 195.

44 Interview with author.

whilst news reached Freetown that the town of Kambia had fallen to the RUF.[45] The conclusion of the US Ambassador was that without external intervention the RUF rebels would be in Freetown within a week.[46] All that appeared to stand between the RUF and Freetown was a weak Sierra Leone Army (SLA) that had been confined to barracks and had surrendered much of its armoury as part of the Lomé Peace Agreement and what remained of the UNAMSIL peacekeeping force.

At the United Nations in New York the Security Council met on the evening of 4 May 2000 to review the situation. After discussion they agreed that the President of the Security Council should issue the following statement:

> The Security Council expresses its grave concern at the outbreak of violence in Sierra Leone in recent days. It condemns in the strongest terms the armed attacks perpetrated by the Revolutionary United Front (RUF) against the forces of the United Nations Mission in Sierra Leone (UNAMSIL), and their continued detention of a large number of United Nations and other international personnel. The Council expresses its outrage at the killing of a number of United Nations peacekeepers of the Kenyan battalion and its deep concern for the UNAMSIL troops who have been wounded or remain unaccounted for.
>
> The Security Council demands that the RUF end its hostile actions, release immediately and unharmed all detained United Nations and other international personnel, cooperate in establishing the whereabouts of those unaccounted for, and comply fully with the terms of the Lomé Peace Agreement (S/1999/777).[47]

The resolution went further, it also decided to hold Foday Sankoh, the leader of the RUF, responsible for the actions of the RUF and complaining that he had failed to 'fulfil his responsibility to cooperate with UNAMSIL in bringing these incidents to an end'.[48] In an attempt to shore up UNAMSIL and its leadership the UN Security Council also praised the efforts of UNAMSIL and its commander to-date and then, no doubt to the discomfort of the British ambassador to the United

---

45 'Sierra Leone hostage crisis deepens', *BBC Online*, 5 May 2000, http://news.bbc.co.uk/1/hi/world/africa/737961.stm, accessed 25 November 2007.

46 Interview with author.

47 Statement by the President of the Security Council at the 4134th meeting of the Security Council, held on 4 May 2000 in connection with the Council's consideration of the item entitled "The situation in Sierra Leone", United Nations Security Council, S/PRST/2000/14, 4 May 2000, http://daccessdds.un.org/doc/UNDOC/GEN/N00/417/77/PDF/N0041777.pdf?OpenElement, accessed 10 September 2007.

48 Statement by the President of the Security Council at the 4134th meeting of the Security Council, held on 4 May 2000 in connection with the Council's consideration of the item entitled "The situation in Sierra Leone", United Nations Security Council, S/PRST/2000/14, 4 May 2000, http://daccessdds.un.org/doc/UNDOC/GEN/N00/417/77/PDF/N0041777.pdf?OpenElement, accessed 10 September 2007.

Nations, 'calls upon all States in a position to do so to assist the Mission in this regard'.[49]

This last point was quickly followed up. As soon as the meeting was over the feelings on the wider international community were made known to the British ambassador. The UN Secretary-General, Kofi Annan, together with the French and United States Ambassadors, made it clear that the situation was rapidly deteriorating and they all felt that Britain, as the former colonial power, had the ultimate responsibility to intervene and rescue the situation and indicated that Britain's reliance solely on the international community to respond via the United Nations was no longer an option.[50] They expected the British government to act to resolve the growing crisis quickly and this message was urgently conveyed back to London. In other words Sierra Leone had now become a British problem in the eyes of the United Nations and international community and the British government was expected to quickly resolve the situation on behalf of the United Nations.[51]

Conclusions

The international community did put a good deal of diplomatic effort into supporting the Lomé Peace Agreement and there were high hopes that this might bring to an end the barbaric civil war that had dominated Sierra Leone for the previous decade. It is difficult to definitively establish whether the RUF ever truly envisaged abiding by the terms of the agreement but it seems highly unlikely. Moreover, the agreement lacked any enforcement mechanisms because the parties involved could not agree any. It is most likely that some elements of the RUF were content with the agreement whilst others were clearly not when it began to be pushed through via the creation of the disarmament, demobilisation and rehabilitation camps in RUF controlled territory.

In retrospect this was probably far too optimistic to expect the process to have worked and the pace of United Nations engagement was altogether far too slow. The DDR camps were supposed to have been in place and ready to operate

---

49 Statement by the President of the Security Council at the 4134th meeting of the Security Council, held on 4 May 2000 in connection with the Council's consideration of the item entitled 'The situation in Sierra Leone', United Nations Security Council, S/PRST/2000/14, 4 May 2000, http://daccessdds.un.org/doc/UNDOC/GEN/N00/417/77/PDF/N0041777.pdf?OpenElement, accessed 10 September 2007.

50 Interview with author; see also David H Dunn, 'Innovation and Precedent in the Kosovo War: The Impact of Operation Allied Force', *International Affairs*, vol. 85, no. 3, May 2009, p. 535.

51 Interview with author.

within 60 days of the signing of the Lomé Peace Agreement when in fact the United Nations Security Council was still to have approved a resolution setting up UNAMSIL. Part of the problem lay in the weaknesses of UNAMSIL and also the United Nations civil administration that accompanied it. A power struggle at the top of UNAMSIL between the commander and head of UNAMSIL Major-General Vijay Jetley and the Nigerian contingent did not help.[52] Jetley was to later make a number of allegations about the collaboration of the Nigerian troops with the RUF in the diamond mining areas as well to name his subordinate, the UN Under-Secretary General Oluyemi Adenji and the former head of ECOMOG.[53] Conversely, Britain's own commander, Brigadier Richards, made a veiled criticism of Jetley – 'While he is socially charming, in some quarters he is viewed as not having done enough to overcome the shortcomings of the UN peacekeeping mission'.[54] Yet, there were few other viable options, and as the next chapters will highlight, the scale of the eventual British response would simply not have been viable in July 1999. At that point Kosovo was dominating the political stage and the armed forces were fully committed to supporting that delicate operation.

---

52 Abiodun Alao and Comfort Ero, 'Cut Short for Taking Short Cuts: The Lomé Peace Agreement on Sierra Leone', *Civil Wars*, vol. 4, no. 3, Autumn 2001, pp. 117–34, p. 129.
53 Abiodun Alao and Comfort Ero, 'Cut Short for Taking Short Cuts: The Lomé Peace Agreement on Sierra Leone', *Civil Wars*, vol. 4, no. 3, Autumn 2001, pp. 117–34, p. 129.
54 Brigadier D.J. Richards, 'Operation Palliser', *Journal of the Royal Artillery*, vol. CXXVII, no. 2, Autumn 2000, pp. 10–15, p. 11.

Chapter 4
Evacuation, May 2000

Introduction

This chapter examines the initial British deployment to facilitate the evacuation of 'Entitled Personnel' which they defined as:

1. British nationals including dual nationals.

2. The UK may also have responsibility for unrepresented EU nationals, unrepresented Commonwealth nationals and/or American nationals.

3. All other nationalities are included on a 'space available' basis and subject to guarantees from their respective governments to repay any evacuation costs.[1]

The chapter has been subdivided into six parts: the first part analyses the reasoning behind the British response. It therefore links to the first chapter and the thinking of the Blair government. The second part will then evaluate the challenges that confronted the British government and its armed forces and their level of preparedness. It will show that the response was complicated by the lack of information, the presence of the United Nations force in Sierra Leone and the need to ensure all entitled personnel were evacuated before the RUF conducted another wave of butchery. The third part will then consider the initial planning, preparation and the dispatch of the Operational Reconnaissance and Liaison Team (ORLT) to Sierra Leone. It will show that, together with the fourth section, the means behind the British response would also help shape the response and subsequent actions. The fourth part will analyse the initial deployment of forces including the the evacuation of entitled personnel. The fifth part will examine the initial response of the British UNMOs in Sierra Leone and will be followed by a section which draws some conclusions.

---

1 'Non-combatant Evacuation Operations', *Joint Warfare Publication 3–51*, Joint Doctrine and Concepts Centre, August 2000, pp. 5–1.

Why Did the British Government Respond?

It is clear that the unfolding situation came as a complete surprise to the British government despite the government's involvement and close links to the Sierra Leone government and involvement in the United Nations mission. As all seemed relatively stable in Sierra Leone and the FCO had organised the transition of its leading diplomat in the country, the British High Commissioner, from the highly experienced but 'troublesome' Peter Penfold to Alan Jones a new individual who was settling down into his first week in post.[2] At the same time the senior British member of the UNAMSIL force also took the opportunity to take some leave.[3]

Likewise the armed forces were seemingly unprepared for an operation as the then Secretary of State for Defence, Geoff Hoon, intimated in the House of Commons defence debate that occurred a few hours before the United Nations Security Council met on 4 May 2000. In opening the debate Geoff Hoon commented:

> Until very recently the operation in Sierra Leone had been remarkably successful and was achieving results. Certainly, there have been difficulties recently which the international community is seeking to address ...
>
> Our previous debate was about how personnel are deployed and managed. This debate is about why they are so deployed, why our armed forces are spread across the globe and why they are so actively engaged in the modern world. In each and every case, there are strong and specific reasons for the deployment of British forces. Indeed, it is a measure of the quality of our forces that they are able to operate as successfully as they do in circumstances where the political environment is often fluid and complicated.
>
> However, the underlying reasons for the deployment of our forces are usually straightforward. As a member of the United Nations Security Council, as a leading member of NATO, the European Union and the Commonwealth and as a comparatively wealthy nation that depends on free trade, Britain has clear responsibilities for, and interests in, peace and stability. The practical imperative is clear: our prosperity depends on trade and on peace and stability, so preserving a peaceful, stable world is clearly in our immediate interests. The United Kingdom is fortunate that it does not at present face a military threat ...

---

2 Andrew Stewart, 'An Enduring Commitment: The British Military's Role in Sierra Leone', *Defence Studies*, vol. 8, no. 3, September 2008, pp. 351–68, p. 367.

3 Major Phil Ashby, *Unscathed: Escape from Sierra Leone* (London: Pan Macmillan Books Ltd, 2002), p. 184.

> For the moment, Britain is fortunate to occupy a peaceful corner of an otherwise troubled world.[4]

Later in that same debate he also acknowledged the pressures on Britain's Armed Forces:

> We have faced problems with overstretch. Last July, some 47 per cent of the trained Army was preparing for, on, or recovering from operations. Such a level of commitment takes its toll on the personal lives of the armed forces and of their families. We are now determined to do something about overstretch, and as a result the figure is now about 27 per cent ...[5]

Although Hoon was aware at the time that a British United Nation's Military Observer had been taken hostage he and the wider MOD were not looking at potential military options other than to hasten the deployment of other national contributions to the UNAMSIL mission.[6] In fact three other British UNMOs had effectively been taken hostage at the Makeni camp in Sierra Leone where they were under siege with their protecting Kenyan force.[7]

Instead, the principal focus for the British armed forces was Kosovo, and the Balkans in general, with brigade level deployments in both Kosovo and Bosnia-Herzegovina on top of the ongoing commitment of forces to Cyprus, Northern Ireland and the Falkland Islands.[8] These existing commitments were already stretching the British forces beyond their perceived current capacity and the government had already agreed to accept operational risk in the high readiness forces. This had involved the Spearhead Battalion and the Airborne Task Force roles being temporarily amalgamated into one based on the 1st Battalion of the Parachute Regiment (1 PARA) to help alleviate the pressure on the army.[9] Although 1 PARA were earmarked for rapid deployment anywhere around the world their principal training focus was either as a back-up to forces already deployed, with Northern Ireland or the Balkans being the obvious places that might require reinforcement, or as a part of a potential deployment to Zimbabwe to

---

4 Geoff Hoon, House of Commons Parliament Debates, 'Defence in the World', 4 May 2000, vol. 504, col. 303.

5 Geoff Hoon, House of Commons Parliament Debates, 'Defence in the World', 4 May 2000, vol. 504, col. 308, accessed 11 November 2008.

6 Geoff Hoon, House of Commons Parliament Debates, 'Defence in the World', 4 May 2000, vol. 504, col. 302, accessed 11 November 2008.

7 For a full account of the three British UNMOs at Makeni see Major Phil Ashby, *Unscathed: Escape from Sierra Leone* (Basingstoke: Macmillan, 2002).

8 Interview with author.

9 Interviews with author; http://www.army.mod.uk/para/history/sierra_leone.htm, accessed 25 November 2007.

evacuate British citizens if the situation their worsened any further. The previous year studies had been undertaken into the possible deployment of forces to Sierra Leone by the Permanent Joint Headquarters (PJHQ)[10] and the conclusion had been drawn that the United Kingdom lacked the capacity to intervene and confront the RUF directly.[11]

Not surprisingly the British government initially looked to the United Nations to co-ordinate international action. The first responses were at the diplomatic level in a variety of forum.[12] At the United Nations headquarters in New York the British mission sought to bring UNAMSIL up to its full complement as soon as possible by bringing forward the deployment of the six additional battalions. This involved widening the diplomatic engagement to a number of states, such as Jordan, which had pledged forces to the expanded UNAMSIL mission but had yet to deploy them to Sierra Leone.[13] This led to the dispatch to New York of some logistics personnel to help facilitate the UN organise the airlift of the additional personnel to UNAMSIL authorised by the February 2000 UN Security Council resolution.[14]

To support these activities the FCO asked what further assistance the MOD might provide. In particular, the FCO wanted to known whether the Royal Air Force (RAF) could start to airlift other nation's forces into Sierra Leone. The response they received was lukewarm. The RAF was already sustaining a number of other operations and was short of transport aircraft.[15] Instead it helped provide advice on contracting aircraft from the civilian market which helped but the bulk of the lift would subsequently be provided by the US Air Force and charged to the United Nations in full.

Once the United Nations Security Council had met on the Thursday evening (New York time, 4 May 2000) and the subsequent messages conveyed by the UN Secretary-General and the French and US Ambassadors to their British counterpart were fed back to London the first moves towards a British response were begun. It meant that at one level the decision of the British government to respond unilaterally to the situation was completely ad hoc and therefore somewhat of a surprise. Clearly, neither the FCO nor the MOD were envisaging

---

10   See http://www.mod.uk/DefenceInternet/AboutDefence/WhatWeDo/DoctrineOperationsandDiplomacy/PJHQ/NorthwoodHeadquarters.htm, accessed 16 January 2008.
11   Interview with author.
12   Interview with author.
13   300 well trained and well equipped troops from Jordan arrived on 12 May. 'Fourth Report of the Secretary-General on the United Nations Mission in Sierra Leone', *S/2000/455*, 19 May 2000, p. 10, http://daccessdds.un.org/doc/UNDOC/GEN/N00/407/22/IMG/N0040722.pdf?OpenElement, accessed 15 March 2008.
14   Michael Evans, 'Cook sends Marines to Sierra Leone', *The Times*, 8 May 2000.
15   Interview with author.

a major military deployment during the evening of 4 May. Yet, at another level it merely represented the next step in the evolution of policy and there were four main elements that drove the response. Firstly, the Blair government was heavily committed to the resolution of the civil war in Sierra Leone and the operation tied into Tony Blair's speech on the 'Doctrine of the International Community'.[16] Moreover, both the FCO and the new DFID had invested a considerable amount of resources in supporting the United Nations mission whilst their respective lead ministers had also invested significant personnel capital which they were not keen to see simply thrown away. In other words there had been a significant amount of government, department and personnel investment and nobody wanted to see that wasted. Writing in *The Times* as the initial deployment of British troops began in secret Michael Binyon commented:

> In the past five years, Britain has spent more money, given more aid per head of population and been more politically engaged in Sierra Leone than in any other African country.
>
> For the Labour Government, Sierra Leone has been an albatross around the neck of the Foreign Office. Every attempt to help the former West African colony get back on its feet after years of civil war has been followed only with greater chaos and instability.[17]

In a written answer George Foulkes, Clare Short's deputy at the Department for International Development, confirmed the level of funding that DFID had already committed to Sierra Leone (see Table 4.1).[18] A failure to respond would have meant that this political and economic capital would have effectively been lost and left the British government open to criticism domestically, especially in the aftermath of the Sandline affair.[19]

Secondly, there were a significant number of British lives potentially at stake. The government had its officials at the British High Commission in Freetown, the various MOD and DFID personnel dispersed around the country and an estimated 1,000 entitled personnel in the country with the majority based in the capital

---

16 Tony Blair, 'Doctrine of the International Community', speech made 23 April 1999, Chicago, www.number-10.gov.uk/output/page917.asp, accessed 18 November 2007.

17 Michael Binyon, 'Labour's expensive African albatross', *The Times*, 8 May 2000.

18 George Foulkes, House of Commons Parliamentary Debates, Written Answers 12 May 2000, col. 489W, session 1999–2000, http://www.publications.parliament.uk/pa/cm199900/cmhansrd/vo000512/text/00512w03.htm#00512w03.html_sbhd2, accessed 16 January 2009.

19 Tim Spicer, *An Unorthodox Soldier: Peace and War and the Sandline Affair* (Edinburgh: Mainstream, 1999).

Table 4.1   Level of funding committed to Sierra Leone by DFID, 12 May 2000

	£ million
Support to the Government of Sierra Leone's National Programme for Disarmament, Demobilisation and Reintegration	12.4
Emergency support to Lungi Demobilisation Camp	1.6
Security Sector Project (SILSEP)	1.7
Support to the Commonwealth Police Development Taskforce (includes Police Humanitarian Fund and Public Order support)	2.45
Provision of an Inspector General of Police	0.25
Military Reintegration Plan (MRP)	3.4
Commonwealth Community Safety and Security Project	12.9
Support to Campaign for Good Governance (Civil Society)	0.2
Support for the return of Paramount Chiefs	2.0
Law Development Project (incl. Legal Draftsman)	2.2
Media Development Project	1.1
Governance assistance programme: British Council project management	1.1
Support to the President's office	0.2
Humanitarian relief and reconstruction	5.0
Budgetary support for essential services/repayment of debts	20.5
Ferry	1.5

Freetown. There was no indication that the RUF would recognise diplomatic niceties and spare any of these individuals.

Thirdly, there was the question of Britain's role in the world. It was clear from the British Ambassador's encounter at the United Nations Security Council that there was an expectation than the United Kingdom should do something. Moreover, the government had emphasised that one of the reasons why Britain should retain its position as a permanent member of the United Nations Security Council with veto rights was because of its representation of the Commonwealth and its good citizenship and not because it had a nuclear deterrent. The crisis in Sierra Leone therefore tapped into both these arguments and placed the government in somewhat of a quandary.

The final driver for a response was the military who said they could conduct an evacuation even with their commitments elsewhere. Two factors helped, firstly, in this case the armed forces found themselves in the fortuitous position of having a number of key assets in relative close proximity to Sierra Leone which meant they would be able to mitigate the risks that such an operation entailed and respond far quicker than expected. Secondly, at this stage the military had not been engaged in the sustained level of operations that they would be required to conduct in the latter years of the Blair administration and therefore they were keen to conduct an operation. This was especially true for the Parachute and Marine units who felt they might be vulnerable to any defence cuts.[20]

Set against these reasons for responding were a number of practical factors. There appeared to be little domestic support for any British response. In fact few in the United Kingdom could probably have located Sierra Leone on a map and given the need to respond quickly and, at least initially, in secret there was no chance of mobilising support. Thus, if things went wrong the government was likely to rapidly lose domestic support whilst the views of the opposition parties were unknown.

Secondly, there was the question of what could be achieved? The Prime Minister's Chicago speech emphasised the practical.[21] A simple evacuation operation would have undermined both the United Nations and the government of Sierra Leone. Anything more substantial ran the risk of leaving British forces deployed in Sierra Leone for the longer term with the risk of being involved in a conflict which had no obvious end in sight.[22] Whilst there was military support for a short evacuation any more substantial and longer lasting operation was likely to be less popular because of the level of other commitments.

On the same day as the United Nations Security Council meeting the Foreign Secretary, Robin Cook, set out his department's view of what was needed to the Secretary of State for Defence, Geoff Hoon. He argued that the evacuation of entitled personnel would be insufficient and that a broader response that would include the strengthening of UNAMSIL was needed urgently.[23] This the MOD did not initially sign up to and it would remain the cause of division.

The differences of view and government indecision would become a consistent feature of the deployment so much so that Briagdier Richards, the commander in Sierra Leone, would not actually receive an official directive from the Chief of the Defence Staff (CDS) until the second day of the evacuation (9 May) and this was

---

20   Interview with author.
21   Tony Blair, 'Doctrine of the International Community', speech made at the Economic Club, Chicago, 24 April 1999, http://www.number10.gov.uk/output/Page1297.asp, accessed 5 December 2007
22   For military planners the identification of 'a clear and unambiguous objective' is the master principle of war and ignoring it often results in failure. 'British Defence Doctrine', *Joint Warfare Publication 0–01*, Joint Doctrine and Concepts Centre, second edition, October 2001, pp. 7–2.
23   Richard Connaughton, 'The Mechanics and Nature of British Interventions into Sierra Leone (2000) and Afghanistan', *Civil Wars*, Summer 2002, pp. 72–95.

then amended later the same day to include securing Lungi Airport to facilitate UNAMSIL reinforcement.[24] To compensate Guthrie gave his own clear verbal instructions whilst the remainder of government coordinated an official response. This would also lead to delays in issuing the troops official Rules of Engagement (ROE) – the government's guidance to its armed forces about when and how force may or may not be used. In this case it did not matter as they defaulted to the guidance they used in Northern Ireland which seemed appropriate in this case.

The Challenge of a Military Intervention

The first question that confronted the officials, both civilian and military, who began the process of exploring the options open to them was what to do? What exactly could or should be expected of the United Kingdom and her armed forces? Ironically this would not be fully decided until September. As mentioned above, the formal directive from the Chief of the Defence Staff to the Joint Task Force Commander was not agreed until the following Tuesday and a second version was dispatched the same day by which time the majority of EPs who wished to leave had already been evacuated. The reality would be that the British government system was incapable of fully identifying what it wanted its armed forces to do and it was effectively left to the commander on the ground in conjunction with the new British High Commissioner to decide policy. Such circumstances were not new to the armed forces, which have frequently been deployed without a clear political objective. For example, the remit of the first British forces sent to support the United Nations mission (UNPROFOR) in Bosnia in 1992[25] was to do something whilst the deployment to Northern Ireland in 1969 which ultimately lasted some 38 years was merely for a weekend to keep the peace.[26]

The biggest challenge was establishing a picture of what was actually going on. Within Sierra Leone the officials of the British High Commission in Freetown sought to engage with the various players involved. Meetings were held with as many of the key power players as possible including Foday Sankoh, the leader of the RUF in Freetown, as well as President Kabbah, some of the other militia leaders, the United Nations Special Representative and UNAMSIL's Indian

---

24   Interview with author.

25   See Rod Thornton, 'Case Study 5 – Bosnia 1992–96', *The British Approach to Low-intensity Operations*, study for the MOD and US Office of Force Transformation, http://www.oft.osd.mil/initiatives/ncw/docs/LIO%20Part%20II%20Final%20with%20 UK%20MOD%20Release.pdf, accessed 18 November 2007.

26   See Rod Thornton, 'Case Study 2 – Northern Ireland August 1969 – March 1972', *The British Approach to Low-intensity Operations*, study for the MOD and US Office of Force Transformation, http://www.oft.osd.mil/initiatives/ncw/docs/LIO%20Part%20II%20 Final%20with%20UK%20MOD%20Release.pdf, accessed 18 November 2007.

commander, Major-General Jetley. These indicated that the UN mission was in crisis and memories of its UNOMSIL predecessor's evacuation were clearly to the fore. Kabbah was nervous and was making preparations to flee the country to Guinea again. He was trying to mobilise forces to support the government but the loyalty of the various militia leaders was never entirely clear and it was likely they would go along with whoever was in power. In other words, the situation in Freetown was extremely tense and the steadily rising prisoner rate of UNAMSIL forces was having a negative effect on the rest of the UNAMSIL contingent, the political elite in Freetown and the civilian population. What was known to the British government was that the Revolutionary United Front had a long history of indiscriminate brutality, including the press ganging of children as soldiers into its service, the repeated abuse of women and involved the systematic use of rape and mutilation as a psychological weapon of war.

The Foreign Secretary's letter to the Defence Secretary emphasised that diplomacy was now not enough; the question was what practical help could be given? The subsequent report to London of the British Ambassador to the United Nations would tip the level of commitment to one of active engagement.[27] The FCO representatives at the United Nations headquarters in New York continued to press for the promised troop contributions to be brought forward and for additional donors to be sought. In response the United Nations Secretariat requested help in the provision of troop lift, and equipment such as body armour, armoured personnel carriers, helmets and an amphibious capability to help protect the approaches to Freetown.

Overnight the Deputy British High Commissioner in Sierra Leone reported on a meeting he and the American ambassador had with Foday Sankoh, leader of the RUF, in Freetown. Sankoh appeared relaxed and completely in control. The announcement by the Sierra Leone Government that he was to be detained played into his hands and incited his followers and allowed him to refuse to move and not cooperate. The conclusion of the British High Commission was that Sankoh felt that he was completely in control of the situation.[28] This view was reinforced when news arrived that the Zambian battalion which the UN had sent to relieve some of its trapped forces had been lost and that Kambia had fallen to the RUF. It seemed that the RUF were now marching on Freetown and there was no credible force in their way. It was hardly surprising that memories of the indiscriminate massacre of civilians in Freetown by the RUF were causing panic and fear to spread amongst the civilian population which was leading some civilians to move westwards ahead of the RUF advance. In the view of the American Ambassador

---

27 Interview with author.
28 Interview with author.

in Sierra Leone the RUF would be in Freetown within a week without external intervention.[29]

Initial Planning, Preparation and the Dispatch of the ORLT

In the United Kingdom the crisis management system began to assess the situation so that options could be presented to the British government. The British government faced several challenges. Firstly, there was the immediate concern for the Briton detained as part of the UNAMSIL force as well as a number of DFID personnel engaged in development work. Strictly speaking the former were all a United Nations responsibility, but the British government's confidence in the ability of UNAMSIL's leadership to resolve the situation was not high and fell further once the reality on the ground became clear. Moreover, the government was not convinced that the RUF would recognise the legal protection provided to the British personnel acting as UNMOs. Secondly, British civilians and the High Commission staff could get caught up in any RUF advance on Freetown and the government owed them a duty of care. Initial estimates put the figure of British citizens at around 1,000. Thirdly, there were also a number of European Union and other nationals for which the British government accepted responsibility as part of a quid pro quo arrangement that covered the globe.

As the diplomatic feedback from the United Nations Security Council meeting was conveyed to London overnight the initial moves towards a military response were begun. The Permanent Joint Headquarters (PJHQ) began to make a series of telephone calls asking various commands about the level of availability of various high readiness units.[30] This led the respective, land, sea and air headquarters to contact their relevant units and ascertain their status. In parallel the Director of Special Forces undertook a similar process for the United Kingdom's Special Forces.

On the Friday morning a COBR[31] meeting was held in the Cabinet Office comprising officials of the FCO, MOD, DFID, the Home Office, Treasury and the intelligence community. They were confronted with a series of disconnected UN requests that reflected the disjointedness of the UN command and it was clear that this was a major setback for UNAMSIL. They were presented with the preliminary military options for an evacuation that had been put together by PJHQ overnight in

---

29 Interview with author.
30 http://www.army.mod.uk/para/history/sierra_leone.htm, accessed 25 November 2007.
31 COBR meetings have at times reached mythical proportions within the press. The name merely refers to the Cabinet Office Briefing Room in which they are held.

discussion with the relevant commands and their representatives at PJHQ.[32] Given the location of the majority of the entitled personnel in Freetown there was no direct land route to a neighbouring state that did not pass through RUF controlled land and it was therefore not an option. There were therefore only two ways out – by air or by sea.

The air option required an assembly area where evacuees could be processed and a relatively secure airport to serve as the evacuation point. There were two potential airfields that were not in areas controlled by the RUF and therefore offered possible evacuation options. The first was at Hastings which was south-east of the capital Freetown. This was soon rejected because it was not known whether it was still usable. There was no information available on the state of the runway or its supporting infrastructure and it was therefore sensible to rule it out. Secondly, there was the international airport at Lungi which was known to be serviceable with a small ECOMOG garrison present. However, the international airport was physically separated from Freetown, where most evacuees were located, by five miles of water (where the Sierra Leone River flows into the Atlantic). There was no functioning ferry and the overland route to the airport involved a horseshoe shaped road leading clockwise from the airport via Lungi Lol, Port Loko, Rogberi Junction, over the Rokel Bridge, Masiaka, Waterloo and then to Freetown. The safety of this route could not be guaranteed so helicopters would be needed to ferry evacuees from Freetown to the airport if this option was selected.

The sea option again posed similar problems requiring an assembly point and either a secure route to the sea where boats could pick up the evacuees or somewhere to land helicopters if they were to be flown out to ships offshore. It also necessitated the appropriate ships to be located within range of Sierra Leone. With these two options in mind the PJHQ briefing team offered three possible evacuation plans:

1. Rapid deployment of air transport with Special Force support into Lungi airfield. This was viewed as fastest option with a notice-to-move (NTM) time of 24 hours, i.e. the forces could deploy within a 24-hour period.

2. Deployment of regular troops – the Airborne Task Force to Lungi Airport in a slower form of the first option taking several days – 1 PARA was then being held at a NTM time of five days.[33]

---

32 A Non-combatant Evacuation Operation (NEO) is defined in British parlance as 'an operation to relocate designated non-combatants threatened in a foreign country to a country of safety'. 'Non-combatant Evacuation Operations', *Joint Warfare Publication 3–51*, Joint Doctrine and Concepts Centre, August 2000, p. Glossary-6.
33 'Sierra Leone', MOD webpage, http://www2.army.mod.uk/para/history/sierra_leone.htm, accessed 17 January 2009.

3. Deployment of the Amphibious Ready Group (ARG) to conduct a sea evacuation. The ARG was then at Marseilles where 42 Commando were ashore undertaking firing exercises with the French. It would take approximately 10 days to reach Sierra Leone and conduct the evacuation and the ship movements could not be done covertly.

At the COBR meeting the MOD was encouraged to work up all three options in more detail for subsequent presentation to ministers later in the day. The COBR meeting also agreed that the various requests for further assistance that had been sent by the United Nations headquarters were clearly uncoordinated and consideration needed to be given concerning what should and what should not be given. The meeting did agree to recommend to ministers that any British deployment should not be placed under the rapidly dissolving UN command in Sierra Leone and should remain under national control.

What was clearly lacking was an appreciation of exactly what was happening on the ground. The meeting therefore recommended the dispatch of an Operational Reconnaissance and Liaison Team (ORLT) from the Permanent Joint Headquarters (PJHQ) to assess the situation in Sierra Leone. The ORLT was a new concept and the Sierra Leone operation was effectively its first trial. The ORLT consisted of a team of experienced staff officers who were capable of rapidly assessing how the military might assist the situation and then form the basis of a joint headquarters should a deployment be made. In this case the officials argued that the job of the ORLT should be to make a rapid assessment of the situation in conjunction with the British High Commission which would then inform the decisions taken in London; secondly, to assist the UNAMSIL commander Major-General Jetley where possible; and thirdly, to prepare for a possible NEO.

Ministerial approval proved a little complicated. The Defence Secretary, Geoff Hoon, was in his parliamentary constituency and there was a debate within his outer office whether to bring him back to London to expedite ministerial approval. The crisis management communications and facilities were best in the MOD and to leave him in his constituency which would impose some delay in obtaining the appropriate approvals. However, after discussion he decided to remain in his constituency for the simple reason that a return to London might have been picked up by the media and the potential British response revealed to the RUF. Verbal approval was therefore sought from him and the Prime Minister to send the ORLT.[34] After this was given the ORLT team, led by Brigadier David Richards,[35] accompanied by a small security detail and intelligence support departed the same

---

34 Interview with author.
35 David Richards is now a full 4-star General and Chief of the General Staff, the head of the British Army.

evening by RAF transport and arrived the following morning in Sierra Leone (6 May).

That afternoon (5 May) the Ministry of Defence's Crisis Management Organisation (DCMO) met to examine the military options in more detail and began to formerly alert the military units that might be required pending the report of the ORLT. Here the DCMO was aided by the institutional rivalry of a number of the potential units which sought to be involved. Uncontroversially, the Director of Special Forces (DSF) alerted the Special Forces standby squadron, which was on exercise in Scotland, that they might be required to conduct Option 1, and they were redeployed back to their base and their transport aircraft were put on alert to deploy them.

It was the rivalry between Options 2 and 3 that led to a variety of short cuts being taken. As mentioned earlier, a parachute battalion was covering both the Spearhead Battalion and Airborne Task Force (ABTF) standing roles.[36] As soon as they were notified early on the Friday morning there was a possibility of an operation they dispatched one of their command team to PJHQ with the brief to get them involved or not return.[37] He saw himself in direct competition with his Royal Marine counterpart who had received a similar brief from the Royal Marines headquarters that the new Amphibious Ready Group (ARG) must deploy. The rivalry between the Parachute Regiment and Royal Marines dates back to before the Falklands War. The Royal Marines felt that they needed an operation to emphasise their role since they had missed out on the 1991 Gulf War and more recently the Kosovo War. Ironically, the Parachute Regiment had similar feelings having missed out on the Gulf War and the deployment to Kosovo being in support of a peace agreement rather than a ground war. Both units were therefore keen to justify the retention of their specialist capabilities. Both knew that they could not directly compete with the Special Forces option, especially as both the Royal Marines and Parachute Regiment had close links to the United Kingdom's Special Forces (SBS and SAS respectively), being the major providers of its personnel. Instead, they both emphasised the potential scale of the task implying it was far too large for the Special Forces Standby Squadron to undertake on their own. Where they disagreed was in who was best placed to support the SF.

Unfortunately for the Royal Marines either airborne option (Special Forces or 1 PARA) was more appealing simply because of the time needed for the ARG to get to Sierra Leone and the problems of maintaining secrecy until the forces were on the ground. Ten days was too long to wait given the estimated time it would take the RUF to arrive in Freetown. Both airborne options required the securing

---

36 'Sierra Leone', MOD webpage, http://www2.army.mod.uk/para/history/sierra_leone.htm, accessed 17 January 2009.
37 Interview with author.

of Lungi Airport as the base for an evacuation and it was readily apparent that the airport would be vital ground not only for any evacuation but also as the route for UNAMSIL reinforcements to be brought into Sierra Leone from elsewhere. The loss of the airfield would have made the use of the ARG the only option available. Brigadier Richards' first task would, therefore, be to assess how much time the British had to respond, how secure the airport was and what options were available for evacuation and support to the UN mission in Sierra Leone. What was also clear was that the British would need to respond before the RUF arrived at Freetown or at the airport and that any disclosure about a British deployment might precipitate RUF action and further UNAMSIL collapse.

The DCMO organisation reviewed the options and having obtained Ministerial approval took a series of steps that would give the OLRT options depending on what type of mission the Prime Minister would decide upon. The operation was given the name *Operation Palliser* and approval was given to begin to divert assets and incur costs on the Friday night pending the advice from Brigadier Richards and the ORLT.[38]

A series of covert moves were approved. It was decided that the ARG should leave Marseilles on Sunday 7 May as planned and sail westwards past Gibraltar and thus have the option of deploying towards Sierra Leone.[39] 42 Commando started to re-embark its forces, reviewed the areas it had deficiencies in and began the process of obtaining additional personnel and equipment from the United Kingdom to meet the potential challenge. These were subsequently flown out to Gibraltar and then helicoptered on board the relevant ships as they sailed by. The aircraft carrier *HMS Illustrious* was on exercise in the Eastern Atlantic where she was testing out a combined RAF/RN Harrier/Sea Harrier air group and thus available to support any deployment.[40] *HMS Illustrious* and her battle group were therefore alerted to prepare to detach themselves from their exercise and deploy south towards Sierra Leone. The frigate *HMS Argyll*, a Type 23 frigate, was ordered to sail directly for Sierra Leone from the United Kingdom rather than to her deployment station in the South Atlantic.[41]

It was the next steps that could not be completely hidden but they were not picked up by the media.[42] A number of RAF transport aircraft were taken off other tasks in readiness to support a possible deployment of either the Special Forces

---

38 NTMs are defined times by which a unit will be ready for deployment.

39 Similar in size and composition to an army infantry battalion like 1 PARA, the battalion was then on exercise trialling a new company structure. Interview with author.

40 Nick Child, *The Age of Invincible: the ship that defined the modern Royal Navy* (Barnsley: Pen and Sword, 2009), p. 149.

41 Interview with author.

42 Interview with author.

squadron and/or 1 PARA. With estimates of some 1,000 personnel potentially needing evacuating a sizeable number of aircraft would be needed (ultimately eight Hercules, four Tristars and five chartered Antonovs would be used). These would not be enough if 1 PARA were to deploy so inquiries were made about contracting additional commercial airlift from the open market. The major problem for the British was that the most suitable helicopters were the RAF Chinooks, but it lacked any aircraft capable of transporting these helicopters to Sierra Leone because of their size (the RAF has since acquired six Boeing C-17s to fulfil this task). Instead, they would have to fly there themselves and it was estimated that this would take several days given their slow speed.[43] Authorisation was therefore given to deploy the two CH-47 Chinook helicopters from their base in the United Kingdom and divert a further 2 Chinooks en route to the Balkans initially to the Azores so that they would be nearer to the region.[44] In reality events led them to continue their deployment all the way to Sierra Leone in what became the longest self-deployment of helicopters in British history (approximately 3,000 miles).[45] Their role would be to provide the lift capacity from Freetown to the Lungi Airport and support the deployment of troops in country. The rapidity of the decision to deploy these helicopters meant that the permission required from the relevant governments to fly over their territory had to be obtained whilst the helicopters were in the air and their passage gave an indication to these states that a British military operation was in progress.[46] The governments of Senegal and France were approached with the view to using a French air base at Dakar in Senegal as a staging point if required and this they agreed to. Dakar was therefore designated the forward mounting base (FMB). The two flights of helicopters would use slightly different routes. As a result when two landed in Gibraltar to refuel the Spanish government refused to allow them to fly south via the Canary Islands and they had to fly via the Portuguese Azores instead.

The notice to move times (the expected response time) of the Special Forces Standby Squadron, 1 PARA and the ARG were reduced thereby maximising the options. For 1 PARA this caused some challenges. As mentioned above 1 PARA was covering both the Spearhead and Airborne Task Force Roles and it had different support units assigned to each task. For 1 PARA this meant recalling personnel from home and alerting its accompanying support assets. As A Company of 1 PARA was away on exercise in Jamaica a request was made to the other regiment which was supposed to provide an infantry company to fill in for the missing A

---

43 Patrick Allen, 'At the Drop of a Hat', *Defence Helicopter*, August–September 2000, pp. 8–12, p. 8.
44 Patrick Allen, 'The UK's Rapid Deployment to Sierra Leone', *RAF Yearbook 2001* (London: MOD, 2001), p. 21.
45 Interview with author; Patrick Allen, 'The UK's Rapid Deployment to Sierra Leone', *RAF Yearbook 2001* (London: MOD, 2001), pp. 8–12, p. 8.
46 Interview with author.

Company in the Spearhead order of battle and also to the on-call artillery battery.[47] However, neither of these units wanted to respond on a Friday night without greater direction from PJHQ and 1 PARA did not actually want them, preferring to use alternatives from within their airborne world.[48] Consequently, 1 PARA therefore looked within its own regiment and the wider 16 Air Assault Brigade community to make up for various deficiencies. Thus, D Company from 2 PARA recalled its personnel dispersed around the country and overseas and temporarily became part of 1 PARA. Other assets were drawn from 16 Air Assault Brigade including a battery of 7 Royal Horse Artillery, which was the artillery regiment permanently assigned to 16 Air Assault Brigade, and the brigade's Pathfinder Platoon to act as a reconnaissance element. For the personnel of 1 PARA these preparations had become fairly routine as they had been frequently stood up for an evacuation operation to Zimbabwe only for the mission to be cancelled.[49]

By way of contrast, the RAF was in the process of deploying a Jaguar squadron to the United States via the Azores to conduct to engage in exercises. There was a brief discussion whether the squadron should be held at the Azores for a possible deployment to Lungi but the RAF insisted that they continue with their deployment to the US and the ground forces would have to wait until *HMS Illustrious* arrived off the coast of Sierra Leone before they had the ability to provide fixed wing air support.[50]

The FCO also took a series of steps. It organised the diplomatic clearance for the Chinooks and later other aircraft to fly through various nations airspace and dispatched additional assets to support the British High Commission's efforts in information gathering thus providing it with the capacity to monitor the radio traffic of the RUF. The FCO also supported the United Nations efforts in bringing forward the additional contributions for UNAMSIL promised in February and persuaded the US to provide the requisite transport aircraft.

Operation Palliser Begins the Evacuation of EPs

During Saturday (6 May) news of further RUF attacks on Lunsar and Rogberi was received which meant that the land route from Freetown to the airport was no longer in government hands and therefore unsafe to use. This also indicated that the time available to the British was diminishing rapidly. Within the UNAMSIL headquarters Major-General Jetley admitted that he was out of options and ordered

---

47 'Sierra Leone', MOD webpage, http://www2.army.mod.uk/para/history/sierra_leone.htm, accessed 17 January 2009.
48 Interview with author.
49 Interview with author.
50 Interview with author.

the evacuation of the UN headquarters to the Mamy Yoko hotel on the Aberdeen peninsula near the coast in preparation for a last ditch stand if his appeals to Sankoh went unheeded. This was reported back to the United Kingdom and the Defence Secretary delegated authority to the relevant senior military officers to reduce the notice to move of 1 PARA further and for the Special Forces standby squadron to be deployed to the forward mounting base (FMB) at Dakar in Senegal.[51]

On arrival in Sierra Leone on the morning of Saturday 6 May Brigadier David Richards met the British High Commissioner to assess the situation and co-ordinate subsequent action. Fortunately Brigadier Richards had already made a number of visits to the area and he knew the main political players in Sierra Leone including President Kabbah. He also felt that he knew the view of minister's having had an important meeting with the then Foreign Secretary, Robin Cook, in Australia prior to the deployment of British forces in support of the United Nations mission to East Timor the previous year.[52]

Within Freetown there was considerable unease amongst the civilian population and a complete lack of confidence in the ability of UNAMSIL to protect them. The United Nations had begun the evacuation of its civilian agency staff and the transfer of its headquarters to the Mammy Yoko Hotel, near the beach on the Aberdeen Peninsula. It was trying to locate its missing personnel including the four British UNMOs. Richards was immediately concerned about the fragility of the UNAMSIL force. He discussed the situation with the UNAMSIL commander Major-General Jetley and the United Nations Special Representative who clearly did not agree with one another. He reported the situation back to London using his satellite communications capability giving an adverse assessment and expressed his concerns about the situation further deteriorating rapidly. With the agreement of the British High Commissioner, Richards requested the dispatch of the lead elements of the Joint Rapid Reaction Force to the Forward Mounting Base at Dakar, in order to reduce their response time. To further shorten the timeframe for deployment Richards also spoke directly with the 1 PARA command group directly and advised them of the situation. In response they began to move the whole battalion with its supporting units to South Cerney the Air Movements Centre (AMC) to ready themselves for deployment from the United Kingdom.[53]

---

51 'Forward Mounting Base – A base (also deployed operating base) established within the operational area, to support operations at forward operating bases. It will be resourced to a greater level than a forward operating base, including C2, logistics and administration support elements.' JWP 0-01.1.

52 See http://www.un.org/peace/etimor/etimor.htm, accessed 17 January 2009.

53 'Sierra Leone, MOD webpage, http://www2.army.mod.uk/para/history/sierra_leone.htm, accessed 17 January 2009.

This move was subsequently approved by PJHQ whilst the battalion was in transit and the battalion and its accompanying supporting assets spent the evening preparing for the deployment drawing on the Spearhead pack stores and issued ammunition.[54] Within the MOD a frantic search began for the appropriate malaria and other medications needed to support personnel deploying to Sierra Leone. Given the speed of deployment the majority of personnel deployed before taking the required pre-deployment course of medicine and some did not receive the appropriate medicines until after they had reached Sierra Leone.[55] RAF Tristar transport aircraft then flew them to Dakar where the first elements of 1 PARA arrived early on Sunday afternoon.[56] At the same time the Special Forces Standby Squadron had also begun to deploy to Dakar and elements of a race ensued. To facilitate a rapid response 1 PARA was told to deploy on light scales which meant that the lead companies left their main rucksacks behind for later dispatch. The speed of deployment led to a breakdown in the transport system which caused confusion and hardship as those responsible for transporting men and material lost track of who and what had been sent to Sierra Leone.[57] It would be a few days later when 1 PARA finally received its rucksacks containing amongst other things a change of clothes and bedding.

Whilst all this was occurring there were some divisions within the British government about the appropriate the relative priority for the British forces.[58] The Foreign Secretary identified the government's two key strategic objectives as: firstly, to sustain and support the United Nations which included implementing the Lomé Peace Agreement and enable UNAMSIL to fulfil its mandate and, secondly, to conduct contingency planning for an evacuation. In contrast the Defence Secretary had the evacuation of the EPs as his first priority and locating the missing British UNMOs as his second priority. He was well aware that the British deployment could undermine UNAMSIL but he felt this had to have a lower priority.

Following discussions with the United States, Nigeria, the United Nations and others in New York, the British government agreed that the situation should be stabilised and that UNAMSIL needed time to be brought up to its mandated strength and reorganised to make it more robust. The paralysis within UNAMSIL's military command and concerns about the capabilities of its commanders discouraged any idea of placing British forces under United Nations command. Thus, although stabilising the situation was given high importance the safety of the EPs was to be given overall priority. Nevertheless, the MOD and FCO agreed that if British

---

54 Interview with author.
55 Interview with author.
56 Interview with author.
57 Interview with author.
58 Interview with author.

forces were deployed for an evacuation operation they should remain in place until UNAMSIL was reinforced, otherwise it would look as though the United Kingdom was abandoning UNAMSIL, could cause panic in Sierra Leone. Obtaining cross-governmental agreement was hampered by DFID which was unable to fully engage in the crisis management process. Partly this was down to an institutional mindset which was concerned to distance itself from and limit any military involvement. Added to this was a lack of capacity to engage in the process. The department lacked secure video conferencing facilities which meant its personnel had to decamp either en masse to the FCO or MOD buildings for every discussion.[59] Within their building they struggled to handle secure information that was flowing into the system from other government departments and agencies and, as a result, their level of engagement was limited.

On the morning of Sunday 7 May the ORLT was formally re-tasked to become the forward headquarters for the British deployment and began to expand utilising staff officers then on exercise in nearby Ghana and also reinforcements from the United Kingdom. Given the rapidly deteriorating situation Blair, Cook and Hoon all gave their approval for full political and military decision-making powers to be delegated by the British government to the British High Commissioner (political) and Commander of the Joint Task Force (military), as Brigadier Richards was now designated.[60] This meant that it was up to them to judge when or if it became appropriate to carry out an evacuation operation and to give what assistance they could to UNAMSIL and the Government of Sierra Leone.

All this increased the importance of Lungi Airport heightened as the only evacuation and reinforcement route into Sierra Leone by air. Richards took the decision, with the agreement of President Kabbah of Sierra Leone, that British forces should discretely secure the airport by deploying there. As soon as the Special Forces Standby Squadron and lead company of 1 PARA arrived at Dakar on Sunday they were both put on aboard Special Forces C-130 Hercules transport aircraft which landed them at Lungi Airport just before dusk on the Sunday evening.[61] For C Company 1 PARA it meant taking spare ammunition from their other 1 PARA colleagues and 102 of them loading onto a single C-130 Hercules for a tactical landing at Lungi just before it got dark.[62] They were not sure what they would meet or even whether they would be attacked as they landed. In fact they were were met by a Liaison Officer from Richards' JTFHQ and the resident Nigerian battalion which formed part of the ECOMOG forces. They secured the

---

59 Interview with author.
60 Interview with author.
61 Interview with author.
62 'Sierra Leone', MOD webpage, http://www2.army.mod.uk/para/history/sierra_leone.htm, accessed 17 January 2009.

terminal building and awaited reinforcements from 1 PARA the following morning hoping they would arrive before the RUF arrived.[63]

At sea the aircraft carrier, *HMS Illustrious*, was detached from Exercise Linked Seas and ordered to Sierra Leone at best speed.[64] She had a combined RAF/RN Harrier Force embarked to test out the new Joint Force Harrier Concept as well as the Joint Force Air Component Command (JFACC) and would offer the ability to conduct offensive air operations if required.[65] The ARG also left Marseilles sailing directly for Freetown which it expected to reach a little over a week later.

Fortunately for C Company 1 PARA and the SF squadron the remainder of 1 PARA began arriving early the next morning (8 May) along with the first two Chinook helicopters.[66] This proved to be apt. With fear rising in Freetown there was a violent demonstration on Monday 8 May against Foday Sankoh and the Revolutionary United Front with around 10,000 Sierra Leoneans marching on his house.[67] As tension grew several of Sankoh's bodyguards opened fire and in the ensuing fighting 21 people were killed and Sankoh fled.[68]

By early afternoon the British High Commissioner with responsibility for the political lead asked Brigadier Richards to undertake a non-combatant evacuation operation (NEO) of all Entitled Personnel.[69] This commenced straight away. Within a few days 499 people had been evacuated. Interestingly a number changed their minds and chose to stay once the British forces had arrived and the situation rapidly began to stabilise.[70] The evacuation centre was established near the beach at the Mamy Yoko Hotel. All evacuees were told to make their way there before being ferried across the bay by the recently arrived RAF Chinook helicopters to Lungi Airport for onward transport by RAF aircraft to Dakar.

---

63 Interview with author.
64 *HMS Illustrious Millennium Commission* (London: Stacey International, 2002).
65 *HMS Illustrious Millennium Commission* (London: Stacey International, 2002).
66 Patrick Allen, 'The UK's Rapid Deployment to Sierra Leone', *RAF Yearbook 2001* (London: MOD, 2001), p. 22.
67 Brigadier D.J. Richards, 'Operation Palliser', *Journal of the Royal Artillery*, vol. CXXVII, no. 2, Autumn 2000, p. 11.
68 Brigadier D.J. Richards, 'Operation Palliser', *Journal of the Royal Artillery*, vol. CXXVII, no. 2, Autumn 2000, pp. 10–15, p. 11.
69 A Non-combatant Evacuation Operation (NEO) is defined in British parlance as 'an operation to relocate designated non-combatants threatened in a foreign country to a country of safety'. 'Non-combatant Evacuation Operations', *Joint Warfare Publication 3-51*, Joint Doctrine and Concepts Centre, August 2000, p. Glossary-6.
70 Major-General David Richards, 'Expeditionary Operations: Sierra Leone – Lessons for the Future', *World Defence Systems*, vol. 3, no. 2, July 2001, p. 135.

1 PARA's deployment to Sierra Leone was therefore divided between the protection of Lungi Airport and securing the assembly area in Freetown. Initially D Company, 2 PARA secured Freetown, B Company remained at the airport as the reserve and C Company was used to push out the defences from the airfield. It was this latter move that initially caused some friction with DFID personnel in Whitehall who had assumed that the military deployment would remain in the immediate proximity of the airfield. They failed to appreciate the need to keep the RUF outside artillery range of the airport or the need to secure the evacuation points.[71]

Just over two hours after the NEO was authorised the Foreign Secretary, Robin Cook, announced the deployment to the House of Commons beginning with the acknowledgement that it was 'one of the gravest statements that I have had to make to the House'.[72] He highlighted the RUF's breaking of the Lomé Peace Agreement and the current position of the UNAMSIL force including the loss of four Kenyan soldiers and the detention of approximately 500 UN personnel including one British UNMO.[73] Cook then emphasised the governments responsibility to its citizens in Sierra Leone as well as to those for whom the UK had consular responsibility.[74] Cook then informed the House of Commons of the scale of the British response:

> In view of the limited commercial opportunities to leave Sierra Leone and the current insecurity, we have taken the precautionary measure of deployment of a number of British military assets to West Africa. The forward elements of the current spearhead battalion, the 1st Battalion The Parachute Regiment arrived in Dakar, Senegal over the weekend. They are currently moving from Dakar to Freetown. In addition, HMS Ocean, support vessels with 42 Commando and a number of helicopters are moving towards the region and will be at Sierra Leone early next week. HMS Illustrious has been withdrawn from a NATO exercise to be available as needed.[75]

---

71 Interview with author.
72 Robin Cook, *House of Commons Parliamentary Debates*, Statement to the House 8 May 2000, vol. 349, session 1999–2000, cols.518-9, www.publications.parliament.uk/pa/cm199900/cmhansrd/vo000508/debtext/00508-11.htm#00508-11_spmin0, accessed 10 October 2006.
73 Robin Cook, *House of Commons Parliamentary Debates*, Statement to the House 8 May 2000, vol. 349, session 1999-2000, cols.518-9, www.publications.parliament.uk/pa/cm199900/cmhansrd/vo000508/debtext/00508-11.htm#00508-11_spmin0, accessed 10 October 2006.
74 Robin Cook, *House of Commons Parliamentary Debates*, Statement to the House 8 May 2000, vol. 349, session 1999-2000, cols.518-9, www.publications.parliament.uk/pa/cm199900/cmhansrd/vo000508/debtext/00508-11.htm#00508-11_spmin0, accessed 10 October 2006.
75 Robin Cook, *House of Commons Parliamentary Debates*, Statement to the House 8 May 2000, vol. 349, session 1999-2000, cols.518-9, www.publications.parliament.uk/

Cook did not state what the government intended to do once the NEO had been completed. Within two days of the NEO commencing the majority of those who wished to leave had been evacuated, those outside Freetown were more problematic. Ironically the number was not as high as that which had been expected because a number chose to stay once British forces were deployed. With this phase effectively resolved once the deployment of 1 PARA to conduct the NEO began Brigadier Richards began to focus in the short term on how to stabilise the situation in and around Freetown, reinforce UNAMSIL and check the RUF advance.[76] In other words, focus moved from the MOD to the FCO agenda.

A week after the evacuation the Secretary of State for Defence, Geoff Hoon, was able to give parliament a further update:

> British forces were deployed to allow for the safe evacuation of British nationals and other entitled personnel. Essential to that has been the task of securing Lungi airport, which, as the Foreign Secretary said, will be extremely valuable in allowing United Nations forces to build up to their mandated strength over the next month ...
>
> I am confident that the House would agree that the deployment of UK forces to Sierra Leone has been an outstanding success. Faced with a rapidly deteriorating situation, UK forces have evacuated almost 450 people. The airport was secured quickly and effectively. Although we have consistently made it clear that UK forces will not be deployed in a combat role as part of UNAMSIL, the presence of UK troops on the ground has helped stabilise the situation in Sierra Leone and we are providing technical advice to the UN as to how matters might be further improved.[77]

The evacuation had proved to be highly successful, however the question remained – what would the British government do and what would happen to its detained UNMO.

Initial Response of the British UNMOs

As mentioned earlier, three other British UNMOs were besieged at Makeni with a force of 70 UN Kenyan peacekeepers opted for an alternative plan. They had accepted the original 10 RUF personnel who had entered the DDR process on

---

pa/cm199900/cmhansrd/vo000508/debtext/00508-11.htm#00508-11_spmin0, accessed 10 October 2006.
  76 Interview with author.
  77 Geoff Hoon, House of Commons Parliament Debates, 'Sierra Leone', 15 May 2000, vol. 515, col. 23, accessed 10 October 2006.

30 April.[78] They had managed to avoid being taken hostage unlike some of their fellow UNMOs and sought refuge with the Kenyan peacekeepers. These were immediately besieged by an RUF force who urged the Kenyans to surrender the UNMOs in return for being guaranteed their own safety. The initial attack by the RUF was repulsed but the Kenyan force had relatively little ammunition, food or water supplies and the captured Zambian battalion that had been sent to relieve it was paraded past the besieged UN compound to emphasise their plight.[79] The British personnel, along with a another New Zealand UNMO who felt that the RUF would struggle to tell the difference between British and New Zealand personnel, therefore decided, with the agreement of the Kenyan commander and the senior British officer in the UNAMSIL headquarters in Freetown, to try and escape by walking through the RUF lines and then trekking westwards towards Freetown.[80] This they successfully did arriving at the UN base at Mile 91 on Monday 8 May some 24 hours after they were officially declared missing. When news reached the JTFHQ that the three British UNMOs from Makeni had reached the UN garrison at Mile 91 a Chinook helicopter was dispatched to pick them up and they were brought back to Freetown.[81] Subsequently, the Kenyan forces at both Mekeni and Magburaka fought their way out of their positions and rejoined the rest of the UNAMSIL forces in the west of the country.[82]

Discrete efforts were also begun to locate Major Harrison, the remaining British UNMO held captive by the RUF. Strictly speaking this was a United Nations responsibility and the British government did not want to increase the vulnerability of the other UN prisoners held by the RUF. However, it also wanted the option of freeing its UNMO if the situation deteriorated further. Major Andy Harrison from the 2nd Battalion the Parachute Regiment (2 PARA) had deployed along with 10 other UNMOs from various nations to Kailahun to help facilitate the Lomé Peace Agreement which required the RUF to decommission their weapons.[83] Also in the town was an Indian garrison of UNAMSIL peacekeepers to provide protection for the UNMOs. Harrison had been there several weeks when the 11 UNMOs were called to meet the local RUF commander. This was presumed to be

---

78 Major Phil Ashby, *Unscathed: Escape from Sierra Leone* (Basingstoke: Pan Macmillan Books, 2002), p. 191.

79 Major Phil Ashby, *Unscathed: Escape from Sierra Leone* (London: Pan Macmillan Books, 2002), p. 171.

80 Major Phil Ashby, *Unscathed: Escape from Sierra Leone* (London: Pan Macmillan Books, 2002), p. 225.

81 Interview with author.

82 'Fourth Report of the Secretary-General on the United Nations Mission in Sierra Leone', *S/2000/455*, 19 May 2000, p. 10, http://daccessdds.un.org/doc/UNDOC/GEN/N00/407/22/IMG/N0040722.pdf?OpenElement, accessed 15 March 2008.

83 'Return to the War Zone', interview by Ray Routledge, *Soldier*, September 2000, pp. 4–5.

in response to the 10 RUF fighters entering the DDR process in nearby Makeni. According to Harrison:

> We were told there was to be a peaceful protest and that we would be held by the RUF for a while because the UN had allegedly held some people in the town of Mekeni the previous night.[84]

He and his fellow UNMOs were paraded through Kailahun before being taken to a small rebel base in a neighbouring village. After a few days the local UN garrison began to deliver supplies to them, however, by day three of their captivity news arrived that two RUF soldiers had been killed at Makeni when they had attacked the UNAMSIL garrison. Harrison and a Russian UNMO were threatened but after heated negotiation between the RUF and Harrison the threat was not implemented. Nevertheless, it was made clear that should any of the UNMOs escape a similar number of those left behind would be killed. This was presumably in response to the successful breakout of four UNMOs from Makeni (see above). With his team leader ill Harrison took the initiative and several days later through bravado convinced his captives to let the UNMO contingent join the Indian UNAMSIL force at Kailahun. This meant that the UNMOs now had the protection of the 100-strong UNAMSIL force of Indian Gurkha troops.[85] His timing proved to be excellent, soon after RUF forces ran into the British Pathfinder Platoon at Lungi Lol (17 May) and sustained heavy casualties. As a Parachute officer Harrison would have no doubt felt the wrath of his RUF captors for this defeat and his escape to the Kailahun garrison could not have been more timely.

Conclusions

At the political level there was a lack of clear direction apart from the recognition of the need to do something. Cook's role as Foreign Secretary was important and reduced the level of Prime Ministerial engagement, something that would later alter in Afghanistan and Iraq. There was also a clear failure to coordinate across government in what many now refer to as a 'Comprehensive Approach'[86] and a woeful ignorance, particular by DFID of the implications and requirements of using the military. Their thinking that securing the airfield simply meant sitting on the runway is laughable and also dangerously concerning. There was also a good deal of divergence in the views of the FCO and MOD but these were offset

---

84 'Return to the War Zone', interview by Ray Routledge, *Soldier*, September 2000, pp. 4–5, p. 4.
85 'Return to the War Zone', interview by Ray Routledge, *Soldier*, September 2000, pp. 4–5, p. 4.
86 See www.stabilisationunit.gov.uk/resources/Comprehensive%20Approach%20Core%20Script.doc, accessed 29 January 2009.

within Sierra Leone by the close working of the BHC and CJTF. Here, Richards experience and knowledge of the players helped offset the inexperience and unfamiliarity of the new British High Commissioner.

Whilst the decision of the British government to deploy British forces to Sierra Leone came as a complete surprise to many, its professionalism was self-evident and it is worth remembering that there was a significant degree of good fortune in terms of where forces were deployed. The relative close proximity of the ARG and *HMS Illustrious* was fortuitous and meant that Brigadier Richards could take a number of calculated risks. The intelligence picture was not clear and the deployment of the Special Forces Standby Squadron and C Company of 1 PARA assumed that either the RUF would not reach the airport before the remainder of 1 PARA arrived or that these forces would be sufficient to hold the RUF pending the arrival of reinforcements at first light.

More significantly, 1 PARA was able to deploy on very light scales because it was known that the ARG was on its way and carried in full all the equipment and ammunition that would be needed to sustain the evacuation. In other words, if the RUF had been more assertive the ARG with 42 Cdo embarked would have been able to evacuate 1 PARA if need be. Thus the vulnerability of the airfield at Lungi was offset by other capabilities. The one major area lacking was that of fixed wing strike aircraft. Here the RAF's decision to continue the deployment of the Jaguar squadron to the United States, rather than hold them at the Azores with the potential to deploy them to either Dakar or Lungi, was odd.[87] This was subsequently negated once *HMS Illustrious* arrived with her air group. However, unknown to the RUF, the RAF air component commander insisted that none of the Harriers on board could overfly Sierra Leone until an appropriate level of combat search and rescue was provided in case an aircraft should be lost. This caused much consternation amongst other units who were taking risks with their deployments and the naval element of the air group subsequently ignored this edict with the result that Sea Harriers began flying over Freetown and elsewhere. RAF Harriers subsequently followed once it was finally accepted that the RAF Special Forces Chinooks could act in the combat search and rescue role.[88]

There was also a clear lack of familiarity of Sierra Leone and the resort was even made to guidance issued by the West African Frontier Force from the 1920s.[89] There were weaknesses in areas such as tropical medicine and the speed of deployment that none of those deployed at the start had received there requisite

---

87 Interview with author.
88 Interview with author.
89 Interview with author.

course of pre-deployment malaria tablets. Moreover, the potential side effects prevented aircrew from using the medications then in held by the MOD.[90]

---

90 Interview with author.

Chapter 5
Saving UNAMSIL and Confronting the RUF

Introduction

The day after the evacuation began Vice-Admiral Ian Garnett, the overall commander (Joint Force Commander – JFC) of the operation based at PJHQ, briefed the press and commented 'The troops are equipped to stay there for several weeks, because it might take quite a few days to evacuate all the UK people for whom we are responsible'.[1] In part this statement reflected the realities of those Entitled Personnel that were unable to reach Freetown and the continuing obligation to be able to evacuate the British High Commission should the need arise. However, the continuing flow of reinforcements, especially of the ARG and the aircraft carrier *HMS Illustrious*, gave the first public signs that the policy was likely to change.

The previous chapter highlighted the initial response of the British government and its decision to deploy military forces to Sierra Leone with the acquiescence of the Sierra Leonean government. This chapter examines how the mission evolved from the initial NEO to the first confrontations with the RUF and the development of a longer-term strategy. It ends with the diversion of *Operation Barras*, the rescue of a number of Royal Irish Rangers held captive by a group known as the West Side Boys (WSB), which is covered in the next chapter. To undertake this task the chapter has been divided into six parts. The first examines the initial debate within government about how to effect the situation. The second part analyses the initial deployment to secure Freetown and the Aberdeen peninsula. The third part then reviews the process of obtaining the release of the UN forces being held by the RUF. The fourth part considers the initial approach taken to confront the RUF. The fifth section examines the creation and deployment of a Short-Term Training Team (STTT) whilst the last section draws some conclusions.

The Initial Debate

As the first forces began to prepare deploy into Sierra Leone it was already being acknowledged that the British government would also need to consider the wider implications for UNAMSIL and the government of Sierra Leone. Tim Butcher

---

1 Michael Evans, 'UN seek new role for the Paras', *The Times*, 10 May 2000.

writing in the *Daily Telegraph* on the fifth day of the official deployment summed up the dilemma:

> The 9,000-strong United Nations operation in Sierra Leone has effectively been sidelined by a British operation less than one tenth its size.
>
> In five days the British force has established more stability than the UN. But this makes its eventual withdrawal more difficult because unless the UN force is made more effective, serious violence is likely to follow the departure of the British troops.[2]

Robin Cook's initial note to Geoff Hoon had highlighted this issue but it was not resolved before the deployment began. There continued to be calls for the British forces to join UNAMSIL from the United Nations and other governments, particularly those who who had already committed forces to UNAMSIL and were either being held hostage or besieged by the RUF.[3]

These appeals were, however, rejected by the British government for three reasons. Firstly, the British government and its armed forces in Sierra Leone distrusted the competence of the UN military command.[4] They felt that the UNAMSIL headquarters was out of its depth and it would only place more British forces in danger if they were placed under UN command. There were only two ways for Britain to retain full control of its forces: either it took full command of UNAMSIL, and this option was only possible if the British provided the largest troop contribution which it was not prepared to do, or it kept the British forces outside UNAMSIL and thus subject to the UK chain of command.

Secondly, there was the issue of domestic public opinion. Without a chance to mobilise domestic support or fully engage with the opposition parties it was not surprising that from the start there were calls from members of all the major political parties to debate the deployment and consider pulling out.[5] Neither the Conservatives nor Liberal Democrat opposition bought into the government's policy towards Sierra Leone and remained deeply sceptical about the commitment

---

2 Tim Butcher, 'UN force is upstaged by British expertise', *Daily Telegraph*, 12 May 2000.

3 Interview with author.

4 Richard Norton-Taylor and Chris McGreal, 'Britain rejects call to join UN peacekeepers in Sierra Leone', *The Guardian*, 11 May 2000; Simon Jenkins, 'Stuck in the mire of the white man's burden', *The Times*, 10 May 2000; Abiodun Alao and Comfort Ero, 'Cut short for taking short cuts: The Lomé Peace Agreement on Sierra Leone', *Civil Wars*, vol. 4, no. 3, Autumn 2001, pp. 117–34, p. 131.

5 George Jones, 'MPs seek debate on decision to send in the Paras', *Daily Telegraph*, 12 May 2000.

of the armed forces. The government rejected their calls for the House of Commons to be recalled and for a debate to be held on the deployment. The government was also very careful to avoid letting the House of Commons vote on the deployment. Constitutionally such a move would have been significant and potentially shifted power away from the government and monarch. Post-Iraq there have been calls for greater control over operations by the House of Commons and a demand that there should always be a vote.

Thirdly, the British government was still trying to establish what level of response it was prepared to make at the international level. There was pressure coming from a range of states and international organisations including the United States, the remaining members of the United Nations Security Council, the African Union, the contributing nations to UNAMSIL and the Sierra Leone Government. The US administration took a similar view to the British on the competence of UNAMSIL and both wished to avoid pushing for a new peace deal which they believed would be equally meaningless. However, they differed over their view of the way ahead. The US argued in favour of a Nigerian backed solution and focused its efforts on the training of Nigerian, Ghanaian and Senegalese troops for future peacekeeping operations whilst arguing for ECOMOG to lead.[6] The British government felt that ECOMOG would only complicate the situation further, especially given memories of their recent engagement, and this option was rejected by the British which left them in a position having to provide an alternative.

The first hints of a change in official policy came in a defence debate in the House of Lords. Baroness Symons, Minister of State at the MOD opened the debate:

> The primary purpose behind our decision to intervene in this crisis is to protect and evacuate British citizens and others for whom we have consular responsibility from a dangerous, uncertain and unpredictable situation. The Government's advice remains that all British citizens and others for whom we have consular responsibility should leave Sierra Leone as soon as possible.[7]

She then acknowledged that:

---

6 Abiodun Alao and Comfort Ero, 'Cut Short for Taking Short Cuts: The Lomé Peace Agreement on Sierra Leone', *Civil Wars*, vol. 4, no. 3, Autumn 2001, pp. 117–34, p. 131.
7 Baroness Symons, *House of Lords Parliamentary Debates*, Defence Debate, 12 May 2000, cols 1829–30, http://www.publications.parliament.uk/pa/ld199900/ldhansrd/vo000512/text/00512-01.htm#00512-01_head0, accessed 20 January 2009.

> we also believe that an effective UNAMSIL, organised and equipped to meet its mandate, coupled with renewed commitment by all parties to the Lome accord, offers the best hope for a lasting peace in Sierra Leone.[8]

As a result, she confirmed that British forces would retain control of Lungi airport in the short term to allow the ongoing evacuation and also enable the promised reinforcements for UNAMSIL to arrive safely. But Baroness Symons also recognised that:

> it cannot, and will not, be an open-ended commitment. British troops will continue to evacuate entitled persons and to secure Lungi airport while the UN forces build. We do not intend that British troops will become involved in combat other than if they are attacked. Nevertheless, this is a limited but significant military contribution and should permit UNAMSIL to reach its full strength and effectively discharge its mandate. That is the best hope for Sierra Leone and for its long-suffering people.[9]

This shift in policy was the probably the minimum the British could do without undermining UNAMSIL by pulling out. It offered the element that UNAMSIL lacked most of all and that was time to reorganise its forces, deploy its February mandated reinforcements and gain a picture of what exactly was happening. The hope was that in providing this window the British forces would be able to withdraw without the government of Sierra Leone and the UNAMSIL mission collapsing as Geoff Hoon, the Secretary of State of Defence, confirmed three days later in a statement to the Commons:

> I recognise that there have been questions about the length of our commitment. The UN plans to build up its forces to their authorised level of about 11,000 over the next month. We are in contact with those countries that are contributing troops to the UN force – in particular, with India, Jordan, Bangladesh and Nigeria – and are urging them to bring in troops as soon as possible to reinforce UNAMSIL. We expect that once the UN mission has been reinforced by those troops, our role at the airport will no longer be required. I assure the House that UK forces will stay no longer than is necessary.
>
> However, even when our forces withdraw, we will not end our political or diplomatic support for the UN and for Sierra Leone. When it is safe to do so, we

---

8 Baroness Symons, *House of Lords Parliamentary Debates*, Defence Debate, 12 May 2000, cols 1829–30, http://www.publications.parliament.uk/pa/ld199900/ldhansrd/vo000512/text/00512-01.htm#00512-01_head0, accessed 20 January 2009.

9 Baroness Symons, *House of Lords Parliamentary Debates*, Defence Debate, 12 May 2000, cols 1829–30, http://www.publications.parliament.uk/pa/ld199900/ldhansrd/vo000512/text/00512-01.htm#00512-01_head0, accessed 20 January 2009.

will continue with our programme of assistance to help train and build effective, democratically accountable Sierra Leonean armed forces that we announced in April. We will also continue to contribute military observers to the UN mission, and if required, technical advice to UNAMSIL.[10]

However, there was no alternative plan should this prove unsuccessful. For the UNAMSIL force to have the opportunity of being successful it needed three things in the short term. Firstly, it needed to secure its forces on the ground in and around the Aberdeen Peninsula. Secondly, it was essential that reinforcements were rapidly dispatched and arrived combat ready and with the approval of their respective governments to implement a Chapter VII mandate if necessary. Thirdly, it also needed to obtain the release of the elements of its forces held captive or trapped by the RUF. Time was therefore the critical dynamic at work and this the British government felt it could help provide by maintaining the deployment of the forces that had already reached Sierra Leone and continuing the build up in the form of *HMS Illustrious* and the Amphibious Ready Group. This the United Nations Security Council readily accepted although there continued to be pressure on the United Kingdom to place some or all of its forces under the command of the United Nations. Reflecting on the situation on 19 May 2000 the UN Secretary-General's report to the UN Security Council noted:

> At the time of preparation of this report, the situation in and around Freetown appeared to have stabilized, with no significant RUF movements reported towards the capital. The Government has mobilized forces which support it, including the Sierra Leone Army and Civil Defence Forces, to defence Freetown. A pivotal factor in restoring stability was the arrival of United Kingdom troops on 7 May and of a substantial British naval presence offshore a week later. The deployment of British troops at Lungi airport and in the western part of Freetown had as its objective the safe evacuation of nationals of the United Kingdom and others for whom it was responsible. Nevertheless, this presence boosted the confidence of the Sierra Leoneans, and enabled UNAMSIL to redeploy much-needed troops to areas east of Freetown. It is hoped that the United Kingdom will be able to maintain a military presence in the country until UNAMSIL has received the necessary reinforcements.[11]

---

10 Geoff Hoon, *House of Commons Parliamentary Debates*, 'Statement on Sierra Leone', 15 May 2000, session 1999–2000, col. 24, http://www.publications.parliament.uk/pa/cm199900/cmhansrd/vo000515/debtext/00515-05.htm#00515-05_spmin2, accessed 29 January 2009.
11 'Fourth Report of the Secretary-General on the United Nations Mission in Sierra Leone', *S/2000/455*, 19 May 2000, p. 10, http://daccessdds.un.org/doc/UNDOC/GEN/N00/407/22/IMG/N0040722.pdf?OpenElement, accessed 15 March 2008.

Securing Freetown and the Surrounding Area

In order to provide the time needed for UNAMSIL the British forces on the ground adopted five interconnected and reinforcing mechanisms. It was hoped that these would allow the British forces to withdraw within a few weeks with a maximum deployment period of a month and this formed the basis for subsequent military planning given the absence of political direction.

The first key requirement was to secure the key ground around Freetown and the airport. From the start the airport was viewed as the potential critical vulnerability for the Government of Sierra Leone, UNAMSIL and British forces.[12] It was the key route in and out of the country and if the RUF were able to take control of this the operation would befinished. C Company of 1 PARA was therefore retained at the airport thoughout the deployment of 1 PARA to ensure that this supply line remained open.[13]

Initially it had been planned that a 105mm Light Gun battery from 7 RHA Regiment would be flown into Lungi airport to provide heavy support if required. However, whilst the personnel were deployed the pressure that would have been placed on the already overstretched air transport fleet from the weight ammunition of ammunition and guns led to the decision not to deploy the guns and instead await the arrival of the battery of guns deployed with the ARG which could be helicoptered ashore if required. In Freetown D Company of 2 PARA were used to secure the evacuation points also also began to conduct patrols on Freetown's streets as a means of reassuring the civilian population.[14] For the British the situation became far more secure on Sunday 14 May 2000 when *HMS Illustrious* with her air group and the Amphibious Ready Group arrived.[15] The ARG not only had a full Royal Marine Commando but also all its accompanying units and stores. This virtually doubled the British land forces, more than doubled their firepower and gave them a much greater capacity to sustain themselves.[16]

Secondly, whilst this was occurring there were a number of steps taken to support UNAMSIL and assist in its reinforcement. The UNAMSIL forces that stood in the RUF's immediate way consisted of Nigerian and Jordanian battalions

---

12   Interview with author.
13   Tim Butcher, 'Paras dig in as rebels head for airport', *Daily Telegraph*, 12 May 2000.
14   Interview with author.
15   Alex Duval Smith and Jo Dillon, 'RN carrier off Freetown', *Independent on Sunday*, 14 May 2000.
16   Interview with author.

located Waterloo.[17] Further north a RUF began a fresh advance from Mange headed towards Port Loko and there were fears that the Nigerian battalion and accompanying Government forces would be unable to hold their positions.[18] RAF Chinook helicopters were immediately used to ferry UNAMSIL reinforcements and equipment from Lungi Airport as they arrived.[19] The British also appointed Liaison Officers to all the UNAMSIL units to advise them on the construction of defensive positions and likely lines of RUF advance.[20] These were assisted by the Royal Engineers that had accompanied the 1 PARA deployment and subsequently those deployed aboard the ARG.

Thirdly, the British forces backed the decision of the President Kabbah to form an 'Unholy Alliance' drawn from the various militias including the AFRC and the Civil Defence Force (CDF)/Kamajors and the remnants of the Sierra Leone Army. They armed themselves with the stocks of arms collected by the DDR process and amounted to some 6,000 fighters in total.[21] They were directed by a Joint Military Committee made up of the faction leaders and British personnel were again assigned as Liaison Officers to each group to give them guidance. Brigadier Richards went to great lengths to meet the various faction leaders and gain their support for the government led alliance. Amongst those mobilised were a group known as the West Side Boys who would later seize 11 British hostages (see Chapter 6).[22]

Fourthly, the British command put a great deal of effort into forming a picture of where the RUF were and establishing their capabilities and intentions. These ranged from the deployment of a Nimrod R1 reconnaissance aircraft to Ascension Island with tanker support to the use of the land forces own signals intelligence capability and that provided by the British High Commission.[23] All were helped by the RUF's lack of a secure communications capability and poor communications discipline which allowed the British to listen into their discussions.[24] In addition, helicopters and later Sea Harrier aircraft undertook reconnaissance flights whilst on

---

17 Brigadier D.J. Richards, 'Operation Palliser', *Journal of the Royal Artillery*, vol. CXXVII, no. 2, Autumn 2000, pp. 10–15, p. 11.
18 Brigadier D.J. Richards, 'Operation Palliser', *Journal of the Royal Artillery*, vol. CXXVII, no. 2, Autumn 2000, pp. 10–15, p. 11.
19 Interview with author.
20 Interview with author.
21 Brigadier D.J. Richards, 'Operation Palliser', *Journal of the Royal Artillery*, vol. CXXVII, no. 2, Autumn 2000, pp. 10–15, p. 11.
22 Alex Duval Smith, 'Paras backed by witchcraft warriors', *Independent on Sunday*, 14 May 2000.
23 See http://www.raf.mod.uk/equipment/nimrodr1.cfm, accessed 26 January 2009; http://www.spyflight.co.uk/nim.htm, accessed 26 January 2009.
24 Interview with author.

the ground British Special Forces were also used in the long-range reconnaissance role establishing the extent of the RUF advance and the size of units deployed.[25]

Fifthly, Brigadier Richards engaged in an extensive information campaign. In particular, he used local radio, which was the main means of mass communication, to emphasise the British commitment. In this he was assisted by the visibility of British troops on the streets of Freetown, the deployment of ships off the coast and on the Sierra Leone River and the use of aircraft and helicopters to overfly government controlled and RUF controlled territory. The ships were intentionally stationed within view of the coast as a visible deterrent whilst a couple of the accompanying frigates sailed up the Sierra Leone River and engaged in a live-fire demonstration. This did lead to some questions in parliament as Geoff Hoon played down the scale of the British deployment whilst Brigadier Richards for obvious reasons exaggerated the scale of the British deployment as a means of deterring the RUF.

Although all five mechanisms were successfully implemented the RUF continued to advance from the east and sporadically engaged with SLA/UNAMSIL forces. However, on 17 May 2000 they confronted British forces for the first time at a village called Lungi Lol some 12 miles north of Freetown near the airport. The village had been occupied by the Pathfinder Platoon of the Parachute Regiment the day before as a forward point to keep the RUF away from the airfield.[26] Refugees fleeing ahead of the RUF alerted the British to the approach of the RUF and when RUF rebels attacked the Pathfinder Platoon they were soundly repulsed. In a series of brief firefights that took place over several hours over 30 rebels were killed with no casualties to the British.[27] According to Brigadier Richards 'the psychological effect of this brief engagement was immense in deterring the RUF and further enhancing our status in the eyes of the UN and Sierra Leonians'.[28]

There was a further boost a few hours later when Foday Sankoh was found and taken to the Guardroom at Cockerill Barracks. Once news spread of his capture a hostile crowd gathered and the Sierra Leone Police Inspector General became concerned for Sankoh's safety. This posed a problem for British ministers, who had so far sought to avoid becoming too obviously involved.[29] Nevertheless, an RAF Chinook was dispatched, collecting Sankoh and his police escort and taking him to a place of safety in Sierra Leone. Legal advice led commanders to insist that he remained in Sierra Leone in the custody of the Sierra Leone police led by

---

25   Interview with author.
26   Interview with author.
27   'Swift, strong, flexible', *Soldier*, June 2000, pp. 4–5, p. 4.
28   Brigadier D.J. Richards, 'Operation Palliser', *Journal of the Royal Artillery*, vol. CXXVII, no. 2, Autumn 2000, pp. 10–15, p. 13.
29   Interview with author.

a retired British police officer Keith Biddle but in reality he remained a guest of the British military.[30]

The capture of Sankoh and the defeat of the RUF at Lungi Lol led to heightened concerns about RUF attacks on British forces seeking revenge. The decision was therefore taken to deploy the 105mm battery of light guns ashore from the recently arrived ARG and these were placed around the airport and manned by 7 Regiment Royal Horse Artillery, who had accompanied 1 PARA in the initial deployment, much to the consternation of the Royal Marine's own artillery battery whose guns they were. However, the immediate threat posed by the RUF soon diminished over the next few days following internal feuding within the RUF allowed the MOD to authorise the first roulement of British forces. After three or so weeks in the field 1 PARA was quietly replaced by 42 Cdo in late May and returned to the ABJTF role in the United Kingdom retaining the capacity to be rapidly flown back to Sierra Leone should they be needed. Their return to the United Kingdom was important because with them covering both the Airborne Task Force and Spearhead roles and the ARG deployed the United Kingdom lacked an immediate response force should another emergency deployment be required.

On taking over from 1 PARA the Royal Marines of 42 Cdo began to change the mission. They began to mobilise what was left of the local government infrastructure, for example, they encouraged the remnants of the police force to begin going out on patrol and arresting those engaged in banditry by accompanying the patrols and providing a deterrent.[31] They also gave significant help to the UNAMSIL force and again tried to encourage its forces to begin coming out from its bases.

The Return of the UN Captives

Whilst the British forces in Sierra Leone government sought to stabilise the situation before handing responsibilty back to UNAMSIL completely two other issues confronted ministers and Brigadier Richards. In the short term, the RUF held a considerable number of UN personnel captive, although none were British. In addition, they were besieging a number of UN compounds including the one at Kailahun where Major Andy Harrison was trapped with other UNMOs and a company of Indian Gurkha troops. Secondly, and linked to the first challenge, there remained the question of how to resolve the situation in Sierra Leone in the longer term. From a British perspective, the RUF could never be trusted and they would have to either voluntarily or be made to enter the DDR process. This meant that they would need to be confronted in some form.

---

30   Interview with author.
31   Interview with author.

After much internal discussion finally, the United Kingdom's longer term objectives for Sierra Leone were formally agreed at a ministerial meeting on 23 May. These were:

1. to establish a sustainable peace and security, stable democratic government, the reduction of poverty, respect for human rights and the establishment of accountable armed forces;

2. the UN's engagement to enhance its reputation in Africa and more widely;

3. in the shorter term to prevent another humanitarian disaster in Freetown;

4. see the UN detainees freed unharmed;

5. to avoid UK casualties and devise an exit strategy for UK forces which does not undermine either the Government of Sierra Leone (GOSL) or the UN but demonstrates the ability to avoid mission creep. [32]

These issues began to be confronted in parallel whilst the British forces on the ground stabilised the situation as outlined above. Strictly speaking the United Nations had responsibility for its personnel including Major Harrison. However, the British government was not at all confident that the UN would be able to safely extricate all these personnel and therefore began planning to retrieve Major Harrison if the situation deteriorated. From the start of the crisis Major-General Jetley had been negotiating the release of his personnel with representatives of the RUF and these were slowly released in dribs and drabs including 85 via Liberia which reflected the close links between the RUF and Liberia's President Charles Taylor.[33] This left the two garrisons at Kuiva and Kailahun.

Although the British developed plans to retrieve Major Harrison and kept the relevant Special Forces in Sierra Leone to carry them out their concern was for the remainder of the UN forces and prior to 30 May the UN prisoners the RUF still held.[34] Harrison and his family were kept fully in the picture about this and agreed to the delay. When the apparent inaction brought criticism within the UK media the family even resorted to writing to *The Times*.[35]

---

32 Interview with author.
33 'Last UN hostages released; more', *UN Wire*, 30 May 2000, http://www.unwire.org/unwire/20000530/9091_story.asp, accessed 26 January 2009.
34 Interview with author.
35 'Letter from Major and Mrs Harrison, 19 June 2000', *The Times*, 20 June 2000; Michael Evans, 'Major "home soon" wife hopes', *The Times*, 20 June 2000.

Finally the Kuiva garrison was evacuated leaving the Kailahun garrison as the only one still besieged by the RUF. The British and Indian commanders in the field came up with a joint plan to end the siege of the Kailahun garrison. On the morning of 10 July two British Chinook helicopters, which had remained in theatre in case they were needed for a rescue operation, landed Indian Special Forces at the approaches to Kailahun where they secured the exit points to the town.[36] The Chinooks then lifted out the injured from the Kailahun contingent plus the UNMOs including Major Harrison.[37] The Indian Gurkha soldiers then fought their way back to government controlled territory some 60 miles to the south supported by artillery fire. In all 600 men escaped suffering one dead and several wounded on the way.[38]

Confronting the RUF

There were only three options available to the British government if it chose to confront the RUF with military force. Firstly, for the British to deploy a force on their own. Their commander in the field estimated that this would need to be substantially more than a brigade in strength, i.e. over 5,000 personnel. Secondly, that UNAMSIL could chose to exercise its Chapter VII mandate and defeat the RUF. Thirdly, that a combination of the Sierra Leone Army and various loyal local militias could be organised and equipped to defeat the RUF.[39] For the British government the existing commitment of forces to the Balkans matched to a lack of domestic political and public support disinclined them from the first option. This left them a choice between UNAMSIL and the Sierra Leone Army. The United Nations Security Council passed a further resolution, 1299, which increased UNAMSIL's authorised strength to 13,000.[40] However, the focus remained on peacekeeping, despite calls from ECOWAS and others for a shift towards a policy of peace enforcement.[41] Moreover, the UNAMSIL force was initially unwilling to move outside its existing defensive positions. It remained concerned for its forces held hostage by the RUF.

---

36 Patrick Allen, 'The UK's Rapid Deployment to Sierra Leone', *RAF Yearbook 2001* (London: MOD, 2001), p. 24.

37 Interview with author.

38 Tim Collins, *Rules of Engagement: A Life in Conflict* (London: Headline Book Publishing, 2005), p. 10.

39 Interview with author.

40 'United Nation's Security Council Resolution 1299 (2000)', 19 May 2000, *S/RES/1299(2000)*, http://daccessdds.un.org/doc/UNDOC/GEN/N00/439/60/PDF/N0043960.pdf?OpenElement, accessed 30 January 2009.

41 Philip R. Wilkinson, 'Peace Support under Fire: Lessons from Sierra Leone', *ISIS Briefing Series on Humanitarian Intervention*, No. 2, June 2000, p. 2.

From a military viewpoint Brigadier Richards argued that UNAMSIL would never have the capability or willingness to take the RUF on but it could secure any ground that the RUF had been forced to relinquish. He therefore suggested that the third option was the only solution. For this to occur the SLA needed to be rebuilt into a manoeuvre force that could confront the RUF directly whilst the UNAMSIL force occupied and secured the territory that the reformed and reorganised Sierra Leone Army had liberated from the RUF.[42] In many respects this was similar to the earlier use by Executive Outcomes of the Kamajors matched to their technological capabilities and leadership.

Such a policy required the rearming of the SLA, a significant training effort being put into the partially demobilised SLA and the creation of an operational headquarters so that future operations could be properly planned and conducted. The rearming of the SLA required the United Nations to lift its arms embargo which it did and the British began to work on the SLA and its associated militias.[43] According to Brigadier Richards:

> We provided a team to pull the factions together and sort out their appalling logistic and communications problems. We built them an operations room and much more. Through this support and the influence we had with UNAMSIL, we found ourselves de facto directing the SLA campaign and heavily influencing the UN's.[44]

The first attempt at this proved successful and raised the morale of both the SLA and UNAMSIL, further undermining the RUF. However, the second attempt on 1 June proved less successful. A probing attack by RUF forces at Lunsar, 50 miles north-east of Freetown, led the Sierra Leone Army and the Jordanians to abandon their positions and retreat. It revealed major weaknesses in the capabilities of both, particularly in terms of leadership and poor coordination which would have to be addressed if the RUF were to be defeated.[45]

Formation of the Short Term Training Team (STTT)

This setback further encouraged the idea of deploying a short term British training team to assist the Sierra Leone Army in developing its basic infantry skills whilst

---

42 Interview with author.
43 'United Nation's Security Council Resolution 1299 (2000)', 19 May 2000, S/RES/1299(2000), http://daccessdds.un.org/doc/UNDOC/GEN/N00/439/60/PDF/N0043960.pdf?OpenElement, accessed 30 January 2009.
44 Major General David Richards, 'Expeditionary Operations: Sierra Leone – Lessons for the Future', *World Defence Systems*, vol. 3, no. 2, July 2001, p. 135.
45 Interview with author.

an international team would deploy, as previously planned before the deployment, and work on the development of democratic accountability of the SLA in the longer term. To achieve this 42 Cdo was tasked to begin to refurbish the Benguema Training Centre, a former British barracks, as the base for a Short Term Training Team (STTT), initially based around 2nd Battalion, The Royal Anglian Regiment, and 40 Sierra Leone officers were identified for staff training at a British run course in Ghana.[46] The STTT mission was given the title *Operation Basilica* and given the task of training two battalions worth of recruits for the SLA at anyone time. The course was planned to last six weeks and covered basic soldiering, hygiene and infantry skills so that the battalions that emerged would be in a position to confront the RUF.

The initial deployment came as a complete surprise to the Royal Anglians who had just finished a tour of duty in Cyprus and were returning to the United Kingdom in readiness to begin their training package prior to their deployment to Northern Ireland in November 2000.[47] Ministers decided to limit the size of the deployment to 250 personnel which included 45 instructors, an infantry company to provide a force protection element and supporting units to run the base.

The Royal Anglians arrived at the Benguema Training Centre at Waterloo, approximately 30 miles south-east of Freetown on 15 June just as the ARG withdrew. The STTT began training the first 1,000 recruits for the first two battalions. They had to be very strict on the recruitment criteria rejecting a significant number of former militia veterans who had lost limbs etc. and also those they thought were under 18 and therefore classed as children. This latter condition proved particularly problematic as few of the population had birth certificates or any other mechanism of proving their age and the STTT programme offered food and pay and was therefore of great appeal to many.[48]

The training programme was designed to improve unit cohesion and individual skills over a six week period. It included teaching on the Geneva Convention and was made conditional on the ending of the Sierra Leone Army's use of child soldiers. On 22 July the first two battalions passed out and a second STTT rotation of two battalions was started. The training had the full backing of the United Nations Security Council. In a report to the Security Council the Secretary-General outlined the programme:

> While the United Kingdom of Great Britain and Northern Ireland is providing extremely valuable training to the new SLA, it is clear that it will take time and resources before the Government can rely on a security force capable of

---

46 Dennis Barnes, 'Anglians in Africa', *Soldier*, September 2000, pp. 14–15.
47 Dennis Barnes, 'Anglians in Africa', *Soldier*, September 2000, pp. 14–15, p. 15.
48 Interview with author.

providing an effective presence throughout the country. The first batch of SLA soldiers trained by the United Kingdom completed a six-week programme on 22 July, and a second group is now undergoing training. According to current plans, the army will ultimately have a strength of about 8,500 troops organized to form 3 operational brigades. For the time being, however, the main burden of establishing and maintaining a credible security presence in Sierra Leone rests with the international community.[49]

Meanwhile, the build up of UNAMSIL continued and a battalion from Kenya was used to relieve 42 Cdo at Lungi Airport which was withdrawn to Royal Navy ships off shore in mid-June and when there was no RUF response they were withdrawn to the United Kingdom.

In the aftermath of the breakout of the UNAMSIL force from Kailahun in mid-July both sides took stock. Neither side wanted to initiate further combat during the Summer rainy season. For the government of Sierra Leone this window of relative calm allowed them to put a further two battalions through the second STTT. Meanwhile the Royal Anglians were replaced by the Royal Irish Regiment so that they could begin their pre-deployment training for Northern Ireland. For UNAMSIL it meant confirming the deployment of the existing force whilst discussions continued within the United Nations Security Council about further expanding its force size and mandate.

Conclusions

It is interesting to note that whilst the initial British deployment was fairly decisive in terms of the rapidity of decision-making. The weeks that followed witnessed a return to a more incremental approach as the British government sought a way out from its initial deployment without having undue consequences for the situation in Sierra Leone. Mounting an evacuation of entitled personnel was relatively straight-forward compared to the requirements of stability and searching for an answer to the effects of the decade long civil war. This can be seen by the gradual acceptance that the forces deployed initially for a few days would have to have their stay extended to a few weeks and the reinforcement plan continued whilst they stabilised the situation, helped UNAMSIL dig itself into defensible positions and began to organise the various militias and other groupings that had remained loyal to the Sierra Leone government into an organised army of sorts.

---

49 'Sixth Report of the Secretary-General on the United Nations Mission in Sierra Leone', *S/2000/832*, 24 August 2000, pp. 2–3, http://daccessdds.un.org/doc/UNDOC/GEN/N00/620/62/PDF/N0062062.pdf?OpenElement, accessed 15 March 2008.

However, it was soon apparent that the UNAMSIL force would never be able to take on the RUF directly, despite a succession of UN Security Council resolutions that steadily increased its authorised strength and its modus operandi. In truth UNAMSIL numbers were never really the issue, the problem was that the majority of the contributing countries were simply unwilling to undertake a Chapter VII mission even if they had the backing of the UN Security Council. This was not surprising given the decision of the British government to refuse to place its forces under UNAMSIL control. Moreover, it was relatively easy to criticise those that did deploy forces and ignore the far greater number of states who simply ignored the call of the United Nations Security Council for troop contributions.

Once the RUF were repulsed at Lungi Lol the British government was again able to consider an alternative – a reorganised Sierra Leone Army backed up by UNAMSIL as a solution. This also allowed the first transition of British personnel using the reinforcements with 42 Cdo replaced 1 PARA. However, the rout of the SLA and UNAMSIL force on 1 June showed that there was considerable work to be undertaken on the SLA and the British government finally acknowledged what their commander on the ground had said – that there needed to be a step change capability if the Sierra Leone Army was to defeat the RUF. The STTT operation was therefore developed using a small team of British trainers backed by a security company of some 250 in total. Thus, the British government could see that the British commitment to Sierra Leone could be contained and there was great relief when 42 Cdo was replaced by a new Kenyan battalion from UNAMSIL and *HMS Illustrious* and the ARG were able to depart. However, the STTT programme had its limitations and it would take more than a few weeks of basic infantry training to convert the Sierra Leone Army into a capable force. The result of all this was that by August the situation on the ground had been temporarily stabilised but the basic issues remained unresolved. The question that still lay before the Blair government was what was it prepared to do?

Chapter 6
Operation Barras – the Hostage Rescue

Introduction

The seizure of 11 members of the Royal Irish Regiment and their accompanying Sierra Leonean Army Liaison Officer could have turned the whole situation on its head.[1] Instead after a period of negotiation in which half the hostages were released by the West Side Boys the remainder were released in a dramatic assault by British Special Forces accompanied by elements of the 1 PARA. The operation was fraught with danger and required the Prime Minister to accept the potential loss of a significant number of personnel if one or more of the Chinook helicopters were shot down with upwards of 60 SAS personnel on board.[2] Instead, it proved to be a turning point in the whole campaign even though the RUF, which had been the main focus for the British forces, was not involved, as well as sending a wider signal about Britain's commitment both to its forces and to Africa in general.[3]

This chapter has been divided into four parts. The first considers the background to the seizure of the Royal Irish patrol by the WSB. The second section examines the hostage negotiation and the planning that was put into the deliberate assault. The third section then analyses the assault and its immediate aftermath before some conclusions are drawn.

The West Side Boys and the Seizure of the Royal Irish Patrol

The Royal Irish Regiment replaced the 2nd Battalion, Royal Anglians in the STTT role and within a few weeks found themselves with 11 of their personnel taken hostage. Their roulement with the Royal Anglians had occurred without any major problems; the Royal Anglians were needed back in the United Kingdom to prepare for their forthcoming deployment to Northern Ireland and the Royal Irish were the next duty general light infantry battalion. Like the Royal Anglians their deployment of some 200 personnel consisted of a training team plus a defence force based

---
   1   Interviews with author.
   2   Tim Collins, *Rules of Engagement: A Life in Conflict* (London: Headline Book Publishing, 2005), p. 18.
   3   Interview with author.

around their C Company.[4] At the same time, other assets in country were steadily reduced. The Chinook force had departed after the rescue at Kailahun in July and the Special Forces contingent also largely withdrew, which meant that they had less back-up than their predecessors but this was not perceived to be a problem. It was generally assumed that the RUF would not return to offensive operations until November when the rains would have stopped and there was a window of time to bring as much of the SLA through the STTT process as possible.

The WSB were one of a number of armed militias which would have been called brigands in an earlier error.[5] Their name derived from the New York Street gangs. Writing in *The Times* Michael Dynes characterised the West Side Boys as:

> Drugged, drunk and dangerous, the West Side Boys have created an extra layer of chaos in war-torn Sierra Leone since their renegade militia broke with President Kabbah's besieged government three months ago.
>
> The 30-strong force believed to be responsible for the capture of 11 British soldiers is renowned for youthful brutality and swaggering confidence. They are fortified by a seemingly infinite supply of so-called 'morale boosters', sachets of gin or vodka that are gulped down on an empty stomach to help them keep fighting, and are clad in a ragtag uniform of boots, T-shirts, baggy jeans and wraparound sunglasses.[6]

They had been led by Johnny Paul Koroma, the head of the 1997 coup, who by September 2000 was a colleague of President Kabbah. Koroma had decided to back Kabbah in May and the WSB had been one of the militias that had initially supported the government against the RUF. The WSB therefore had links to the government but as Koroma had decided to base himself in Freetown he was replaced as leader of the WSB by the self-style Brigadier-General Kallay. Kallay was a defector from the RUF but retained some loose links to the RUF that were never entirely clear and would provide a source of concern for the hostage negotiators.[7] Under Kallay, the WSB had drifted away from Koroma and the Sierra Leone government and they had ignored a subsequent Sierra Leone Government ultimatum to enter the DDR process and disarm. Instead, they chose to set up a

---

4 Tim Collins, *Rules of Engagement: A Life in Conflict* (London: Headline Book Publishing, 2005), p. 4.

5 'Who are the West Side Boys?', http://news.bbc.co.uk/1/hi/world/africa/901209.stm, accessed 10 November 2007.

6 Michael Dynes, 'Drink fuels aggression of brutal renegades', *The Times*, 28 August 2000.

7 Tim Collins, *Rules of Engagement: A Life in Conflict* (London: Headline Book Publishing, 2005), p. 12; Anton La Guardia, 'Army keeps its head as talks begin on captives', *Daily Telegraph*, 30 August 2000.

base in a collection of huts at a village called Gberi Bana on Rokel Creek, a fast-flowing river near the Occra Hills. From here they terrorised the local community extorting from them for their various needs.[8]

The relative calm was disturbed however by unforeseen events. On Friday 25 August 11 members of the Royal Irish Regiment and an accompanying Sierra Leone Army liaison officer were sent out on a routine patrol to visit the Jordanian UNAMSIL battalion based some 60 miles east of Freetown. The patrol was based on three Landrovers, one equipped with a heavy machine gun, and led by the company commander,[9] They were told by the Jordanians that the local villages were no longer in the hands of the West Side Boys who had apparently vacated the area. The company commander therefore decided that this was an opportunity that should be exploited and that it would be a good move to talk to the locals to start to get a feel for the area in preparation for UNAMSIL taking control. On arriving at the village of Magbeni the patrol was overwhelmed by at least 25 heavily armed West Side Boys whose armament included a Bedford lorry equipped with an anti-aircraft gun.[10] Instead of starting a firefight the company commander sensibly decided to avoid confrontation and the patrol was seized and taken prisoner. The manner of their capture was to cause considerable embarrassment in Whitehall, because of the earlier British criticism of the capture of UNAMSIL personnel in May, and the Company Commander was subjected to a Board of Inquiry.[11] The Royal Irish were rapidly moved by boat across the creek to the nearby village of Gberi Bana, the main WSB base where they would remain until freed 15 days later.

Negotiation and Planning

As soon as it was realised that the patrol was missing back at their base at the Benguema Training Centre an intensive air and surface search began in the remaining hours of daylight. As daylight faded PJHQ was alerted and the search for the missing patrol was resumed the following morning. However, the patrol

---

8 'Fifth Report of the Secretary-General on the United Nations Mission in Sierra Leone', *S/2000/751*, 31 July 2000, pp. 12–14, http://daccessdds.un.org/doc/UNDOC/GEN/N00/554/71/PDF/N0055471.pdf?OpenElement, accessed 15 March 2008; Tim Collins, *Rules of Engagement: A Life in Conflict* (London: Headline Book Publishing, 2005), p. 12.

9 Ewen MacAskill, 'Sierra Leone gang holding 11 soldiers want boss freed', *The Guardian*, 28 August 2000.

10 Tim Collins, *Rules of Engagement: A Life in Conflict* (London: Headline Book Publishing, 2005), p. 13.

11 Ewen MacAskill, 'Sierra Leone gang holding 11 soldiers want boss freed', *The Guardian*, 28 August 2000.

was not found and it soon became discovered that the patrol had been taken hostage by the WSB.[12]

The treatment of the hostages varied between atrocious behaviour, including beatings, mock executions and witnessing various members of the WSB abuse their other captives, to acts of friendliness.[13] Much depended on the individuals concerned and their relative state of mind. This largely depended on the level of alcohol and drug consumed by their captors on any given day. However, in general, the British Army personnel were comparatively well treated in comparison to their Sierra Leone Army Liaison Officer and the leadership of the West Side Boys viewed them as useful bargaining counters.

Whilst the British forces in Sierra Leone were operating under the jurisdiction of the Sierra Leone government it was readily apparent that the government of Sierra Leone lacked the necessary expertise to undertake negotiations for the release of the Royal Irish. Instead, President Kabbah allowed the British to undertake these negotiations themselves. A specialist team was rapidly put together which drew on experienced negotiators from the Metropolitan Police and also various military representatives.[14] The negotiations were led by the Commanding Officer of 1 Royal Irish, Lieutenant-Colonel Simon Fordham, who in the words of Tim Collins, then working directly got the Director of Special Forces in London and subsequent Commanding Officer of 1 Royal Irish, was:

> an able and clever man, who with the help of Metropolitan Police negotiators was able to effect a rapport with the terrorists. We in London knew that the hostage takers were impressed by his seniority and enjoyed talking to him as 'equals', and I'm in no doubt that he kept them as calm as possible and so bought time for a potential rescue operation.[15]

The British government also encouraged the former WSB leader, Johnny Paul Koroma, to use what influence he had with the group to obtain their release but this ultimately proved far less than was hoped.[16]

---

12 Ewen MacAskill, 'Sierra Leone gang holding 11 soldiers want boss freed', *The Guardian*, 28 August 2000.

13 Tim Collins, *Rules of Engagement: A Life in Conflict* (London: Headline Book Publishing, 2005), p. 13.

14 Michael Smith, 'SAS team ready to rescue hostages', *The Times*, 28 August 2000.

15 Tim Collins, *Rules of Engagement: A Life in Conflict* (London: Headline Book Publishing, 2005), p. 14.

16 Michela Wong, 'Former coup leader in Sierra Leone asked to help', *The Financial Times*, 28 August 2000.

The negotiating team were soon able to make contact with the West Side Boys and talks began initially with their leader, Foday Kallay, present. The West Side Boys made a specific demand for a satellite phone and the number for the BBC World Service in return for the release of all the hostages and equipment. The telephone was provided, together with a number for the BBC World Service.[17] A further agreement was made to provide fuel to drive the British vehicles out. Later that evening (30 August) after the agreed time had passed the Jordanian UNAMSIL battalion reported that five British hostages had been freed. They reported that all the hostages had been subjected to mental abuse, including mock executions.[18] This partial release encouraged the view in Whitehall that progress had been made and that negotiations should continue to try and obtain the release of the remaining captives.[19] This was viewed as the most likely avenue for success. Moreover, continuing to negotiate gave additional time to prepare military alternatives. The negotiations with the West Side Boys continued over the next few days but, significantly, their leader, Kallay, was no longer present. The local United Nations leadership learned that there was dissent within the ranks of the West Side Boys and there were doubts whether Kallay remained in command or was even still alive.[20] The release of the five Royal Irish captives and the response of the British to this appears to have encouraged the WSB to expand their demands. These swung between safe passes to the UK to start university degrees to posts in the government of Sierra Leone and almost certainly depended upon the individual actually negotiating at a particular point in time.[21]

Whilst all this was taking place the Conservative and Liberal Democrat opposition called for British forces to be withdrawn from Sierra Leone and queried what they were trying to achieve. They were also very critical of the vulnerability of the small numbers deployed and argued that this hostage seizure reflected a confused government policy.[22] A *Times* leader highlighted the predicament of the government:

> The 11 were too few; they were off guard; they were unprotected. They had better be rescued fast, by negotiation or by force, if the Government is not to be held culpably reckless of the safety of Britain's Armed Forces. The character and conduct of this mission must then be re-examined.[23]

---

17   Interview with author.
18   Interview with author.
19   Interview with author.
20   Interview with author.
21   Tim Collins, *Rules of Engagement: A Life in Conflict* (London: Headline Book Publishing, 2005), p. 15.
22   Severin Carrell, 'Blair rejects calls for British forces to be pulled out of Sierra Leone', *The Independent*, 30 August 2000.
23   'Caught Unawares', *The Times*, 28 August 2000, p. 19.

The Shadow Defence Secretary Iain Duncan-Smith noted:

> This is a matter of deep concern and our thoughts go out to the families of those who have been captured ... Whatever else happens, the Government must not lack the resolve to take whatever measures are necessary to secure their release.[24]

In other words Duncan-Smith, a former Guards officer, backed the use of force to release the hostages if it proved necessary.

Whilst a negotiated settlement was the preferred solution, preparations for military options were begun almost as soon as news of the Royal Irish seizure was received. Such an operation was traditionally the preserve of Britain's Special Forces but the scale of it forced them to seek additional help from the regular army. From the beginning it was emphasised to ministers that such an operation would be an assault and not a classic rescue operation such as the 1980 Iranian Embassy siege. The size of the West Side Boys contingent estimated at 200–300 and their location spread over a number of villages with a river dividing them in half precluded such an option.[25] Two military options were developed. The first, an emergency assault, would have been used if the lives of the hostages were thought to be at imminent risk and thus it would not have been at a time of the military's choosing. The second option, a deliberate assault, was a planned attack aimed at freeing the hostages at a time chosen by the commander in the field.[26]

The notice to move of various units was reduced and SAS personnel were recalled from Kenya where they had been on exercise. Tragically this led to a couple of SAS personnel being killed in a car accident on their journey back to the Kenyan capital. As for the regular army, ironically, it was the A Company of 1 PARA, which had missed out on *Operation Palliser*, which was the Airborne Lead Company on call and they formed a major component of the hostage rescue mission – *Operation Barras*. Rumours about the deployment and use of the SAS began to surface quite early. A *Times* report of 30 August stated that the SAS had been sent into the jungle to track down the rebel hideout.[27] This was a little premature and soon afterwards Geoff Hoon considered proposals for a rescue operation. They were approved and the initial deployment of units commenced over the weekend

---

24 Michael Smith, 'SAS team ready to rescue hostages', *The Times*, 28 August 2000.
25 Interview with author.
26 Tim Collins, *Rules of Engagement: A Life in Conflict* (London: Headline Book Publishing, 2005), p. 15.
27 Sam Kiley, 'Militia "could sell kidnap Britons to rebels"', *The Times*, 30 August 2000.

of 3–4 September 2000 with reconnaissance elements deployed into the jungle a couple of days later.[28]

Given the likelihood of significant casualties the government did not want to choose the military option unless they really had no alternative both Hoon and the Prime Minister, Tony Blair, had to weigh up various risks. The deployment of forces deep into Sierra Leone might be detected, and thus lead to precipitous action by the West Side Boys against the hostages. Yet, their exact location and well-being needed to be established. If an emergency assault was necessary, time was critical especially as an emergency assault would take at least 15 hours to mount from the United Kingdom. It was therefore agreed to the deployment of the requisite forces to Senegal to shorten the response time to around six hours. At the same time the authority to launch an emergency assault was delegated to the British High Commissioner and the Commander of British Forces in Sierra Leone to further shorten the time required.[29]

The elements of 1 PARA officially became part of the rescue plan on Wednesday 30 August and they began working out their requirements to deal with the village of Magbeni which was south of the creek whilst the Special Forces would release the hostages held in Gberi Bana.[30] The role of 1 PARA was threefold. Firstly, it would act as a diversion for the WSB who would be confronted by attacks on both sides of the river simultaneously, Secondly, it would prevent the WSB forces south of the river interfering with the rescue of the prisioners north of the river. Thirdly, by engaging directly with the West Side Boys 1 PARA was to severely reduce their capabilities and thus limit their actions in the future.[31] The 1 PARA elements were based on a reinforced company group (A Company) with extra battalion assets including sniper teams, the Patrols Platoon, heavy machine gun sections and a mortar section.[32] The inclusion of these assets was made to maximise the options of its commander and the firepower that could be deployed to help offset the numerical advantage of the WSB as it was acknowledged that there could be no back-up forces should the company become pinned down.

Some of the members of the company had only joined it a few weeks before from basic training and there was some discussion about replacing these inexperienced soldiers. However, it was decided that as they had passed training replacing them would have a negative effect on the individuals concerned and the company. A Company moved on Saturday 2 September to the OMC and then to

---

28   Interview with author.
29   Interview with author.
30   Interview with author.
31   Interview with author; see also Tim Collins, *Rules of Engagement: A Life in Conflict* (London: Headline Book Publishing, 2005), p. 18.
32   Interview with author.

Dakar where their training began from Sunday onwards.[33] The forces were held at Dakar to avoid detection and thus not encourage the WSB to take any precipitous action against the hostages. It did mean that they were still a few hours away from the WSB camp should an immediate response be required and this would involved spending a number of hours in a cramped Chinook before the mission began if an emergency assault was suddenly required.

Other preparations for a deliberate assault were taken in parallel. This included getting three Chinook to self-deploy initially to Dakar and also to bring forward the deployment of *RFA Argus* from the United Kingdom so that she could be diverted to Sierra Leone if needed.[34] It was hoped that she could be just off the Sierra Leone coast by the following weekend and thus available as an alternative base for the Chinooks closer to the WSB base but out of view from the land. She also embarked the equipment for a field medical unit to provide increased medical facilities to support an assault should it be needed.

Further meetings and discussions by radio with the West Side Boys occurred and in one radio discussion a demand for supplies was made and some were given. However, little substantive progress was made over the weekend and on Monday 4 September approval was given by the Defence Secretary for the forward deployment of the leading elements of the Task Force to Sierra Leone, although it was decided that the Chinook helicopters should remain at Dakar.[35] This meant that the rescue force could be picked up by the Chinooks on the way rather than for the troops to be sat in the helicopters for a number of hours prior to an assault. The Chinooks were held back because it was felt that the deployment of the soldiers could be hidden but if the helicopters were seen, which was likely, the West Side Boys would take this to be a sign of imminent British action and act against the hostages. At this stage it was believed that the balance of risk favoured accepting a longer reaction time rather than cause a precipitous West Side Boys response.

Negotiations continued on 6 September. However, Kallay was still missing and those West Side Boys involved seemed increasingly unpredictable. In discussion with the negotiating team on 6 September the officer in charge of the patrol sounded tired and demoralised indicating that the mood in the village where they were being held was bad. However, the negotiations were continued and a portable generator was handed over. The West Side Boys even indicated that the negotiating team could expect good news on Thursday 7 September and the next 24 hours were identified by the negotiating team as important in determining whether the West Side Boys were serious about further releases.

---

33   Interview with author.
34   Interview with author.
35   Interview with author.

However, no good news was received and the mood at the daily COBR meeting in London was sombre. British Special Forces had managed to get close enough to the WSB base by the Tuesday but had not seen any sign of the hostage for some 24 hours. At the most recent meeting with the WSB it was clear that the group were making preparations to move and there was a real concern that the hostages might either be killed or handed over to the RUF as a bargaining chip.[36] It was therefore decided on 7 September to recommend that the following day's ministerial meeting make the decision whether to launch a deliberate assault in light of developments on the ground. To facilitate this it was agreed that the Chinooks should also be deployed to Sierra Leone and, as *RFA Argus* had not yet reached the area, the risk of the Chinooks being detected accepted as less than the dangers of the WSB taking flight with the hostages.[37] At the subsequent ministerial meeting it was decided that the time had come to take military action. The meeting was briefed by the Director of Special Forces' Chief of Staff. According to Tim Collins who was there:

> It fell into two parts: Operation Barras, the rescue, and Operation Amble, which aimed to involve the local SLA on the periphery, in order to give them some credit for the apparent outcome and to demonstrate the effectiveness of the British training to any other not-so-innocent bystanders.
>
> We would strike at dawn. The Chinooks would suppress known enemy billets on their approach, and their door gunners would take down the 12.7mm heavy machine guns as they landed on the football pitch. SAS teams already in place would provide covering fire. Simultaneously, Lynx helicopters from the Special Forces detachment would strafe the area to the south of the river, preventing use of the captured vehicles and more importantly the captured machine gun, keeping reinforcements at bay and creating an opportunity for the Para distraction force to land and assault the rebel village of Gberi Bana to the south.
>
> The main assault troops, guided from the football pitch by the observation teams already in place, would close in on the hostages and take them to safety. A four-man team would go after Kallay. We wanted him alive. A sixteen-strong troop would cover the rescue force and dispatch any West Side Boys who tried to interfere.[38]

---

36 Interview with author; Sam Kiley, 'Militia "could sell kidnap Britons to rebels"', *The Times*, 30 August 2000.
37 Interview with author.
38 Tim Collins, *Rules of Engagement: A Life in Conflict* (London: Headline Book Publishing, 2005), p. 18.

Despite the protestations of the representative from the Prime Minister's office it was decided that British forces would not conduct any follow-on operation (*Operation Amble*) but that the Sierra Leone Army should be encouraged to clear the West Side Boys from the Occra Hills as soon as possible thereafter.[39]

Kallay then returned to the negotiations with new political demands as well as for some equipment and provisions. The political demands were impossible for the British government to meet and the West Side Boys seemed keen to secure still more hostages. The view in Sierra Leone and at that day's Whitehall meeting was that the negotiated release of the remaining hostages was most unlikely and that their lives were now in extreme danger.[40]

The Deliberate Assault and its Aftermath

The commander on the ground indicated that his preferred intention was to proceed with the deliberate assault at first light on the following day – Saturday – and Ministers approved this. However, it took longer than planned to get the ground forces into position and the assault was put back by 24 hours.[41] At first light on Sunday 10 September a deliberate assault was launched. Overwhelming force was used to achieve tactical surprise and to try and maintain a level of engagement that would paralyse any West Side Boys response, thus minimising the risk to the assault force and to the hostages. Chinook and Lynx helicopters flew in at very low altitude to achieve surprise as daylight broke. The Lynx helicopters laid down suppressive fire aided by the reconnaissance party on the ground and a government of Sierra Leone Hind attack helicopter which was added into the package at the last minute when one of the Lynx helicopters had technical problems and would not work.[42] Two Chinooks flew directly over the location of the captives on the northern side of the river and Special Force troops disembarked by rope. The rescue team safely snatched the hostages but one of the rescue team, Bombardier Tinnion, was critically wounded.[43] In a brilliant and highly dangerous piece of flying an RAF Chinook returned to picked him up despite a heavy fire-fight and flew him to *RFA Lancelot*, a naval landing ship in the port of Freetown, that was set up to act as the main casualty receiving point. However, Tinnion died before he reached the ship despite the best efforts of the medical team accompanying the assault.

---

39 Tim Collins, *Rules of Engagement: A Life in Conflict* (London: Headline Book Publishing, 2005), p. 19.
40 Interview with author.
41 Interview with author.
42 Interview with author.
43 Tim Collins, *Rules of Engagement: A Life in Conflict* (London: Headline Book Publishing, 2005), p. 20.

Meanwhile, in the operation on the south side of the river A Company of 1 PARA landed in two waves from the third Chinook south of the river to clear the village of Magbeni of West Side Boys. The aim was to neutralise the heavy weapons of the West Side Boys, recover the vehicles lost when the patrol was seized and destroy the military facilities available to the West Side Boys. Unfortunately the landing site used by the paratroopers turned out to be a swamp. As the ground was open and close to the villages the reconnaissance team had not been able to physically test the ground and had assessed it as the firmest ground available.[44] The PARAs therefore had to wade 150 yards through chest high swamp to approach the village of Magbeni from the west. In almost a repeat of the attack on Goose Green during the Falklands Conflict one of the early casualties was the commander of the assaulting force along with most of his command team.[45] His deputy quickly took over and completed the operation and the village was cleared of WSB, their other captives freed and the vehicles of the Royal Irish were retrieved and flown out.

Conclusions

In summing up the operation at a press conference Geoff Hoon stated:

> The operation sends a number of powerful messages. Firstly, it is a yet further demonstration of the refusal of successive British Governments to do deals with terrorists and hostage takers. Secondly, we hope the West Side Group and other rebel units in Sierra Leone will now realise the futility of continuing unlawful operations and instead accept the rule of law and the authority of the democratically elected Government of Sierra Leone. Thirdly, we hope all those who may in future consider taking similar action against UK Armed Forces will think carefully about the possible consequences and realise there is nothing to be gained by such action.[46]

Hoon neatly summed up the various constituents that the rescue was aimed at. For the government the hostage crisis was about managing risk. Issues about casualties, proportionality and the decision to use force were inextricably linked with concerns about potential winners and losers from the deliberate assault. A great deal was at risk for the British government. Its' attitude towards ensuring that its hostages were released and the manner in which they were released sent signals to the RUF and to other groups within Sierra Leone, the African continent and globally. If the assault had indeed failed and there had been a significant loss of life then the policy of the British government towards Sierra Leone would have

---

44 Interview with author.
45 Interview with author.
46 'Final Press Conference Statements by Secretary of State and Chief of the Defence Staff', 10 September 2000.

been forced to change and almost certainly involved the complete withdrawal of British forces. The resultant impact on the RUF, UNAMSIL and the Sierra Leone government would have been considerable. Moreover, it would have raised questions about government intervention policy three years before the invasion of Iraq in 2003. As it was the operation was a great success and had a major impact on the situation in Sierra Leone.

Chapter 7
The Defeat of the RUF

Introduction

Even before the seizure of the Royal Irish soldiers by the West Side Boys there was recognition within the British government that their existing policy on Sierra Leone was not working to the extent they had hoped for.[1] Moreover, the Conservative and Liberal Democrat front benches continued to question what the British forces in Sierra Leone were trying to achieve and it was recognised within the MOD and wider government that the situation in Sierra Leone needed to be brought to an end.[2]

This chapter examines how the British government successfully achieved a final end to Sierra Leone civil war by forcing the RUF into the disarmament, demobilisation and rehabilitation process. To undertake this task the chapter has been divided into four parts. The first examines events that led to the ceasefire in November 2000. The second section then analyses how this was built upon and led to the ending of hostilities. The third section examines the aftermath of the conflict before a final section makes some conclusions.

Achieving a Ceasefire

The United Nations Security Council adopted resolution 1313 (2000) on 4 August 2000. This provided the basis for subsequent action. The resolution firstly emphasised that the RUF had engaged in 'widespread and serious violations of the Lomé Peace Agreement' and thus firmly placed all the blame on the RUF.[3] It then concluded that:

> until security conditions have been established allowing progress towards the peaceful resolution of the conflict in Sierra Leone there will continue to be a threat to UNAMSIL and the security of the state of Sierra Leone, and that in

---

1 Richard Beeston, 'Cook needs an exit from West African foray', *The Times*, 28 August 2000.
2 Interview with author.
3 UN Security Council Resolution 1313 (2000), 4 August 2000, http://daccessdds.un.org/doc/UNDOC/GEN/N00/591/96/PDF/N0059196.pdf?OpenElement, accessed 18 March 2008.

order to counter that threat, the structure, capability, resources and mandate of UNAMSIL require appropriate strengthening; ...[4]

The resolution then emphasised the importance of maintaining control of the Lungi and Freetown peninsulas, and their major approach routes. In the short term it authorised UN forces to act 'robustly to any hostile actions or threat of imminent and direct use of force'.[5] In the longer term it agreed to significantly enhance UNAMSIL's capabilities and pledged to:

> To deploy progressively in a coherent operational structure and in sufficient numbers and density at key strategic locations and main population centres and, in coordination with the Government of Sierra Leone to assist, through its presence and within the framework of its mandate, the efforts of the Government of Sierra Leone to extend state authority, restore law and order and further stabilize the situation progressively throughout the entire country, and, within its capabilities and areas of deployment, to afford protection to civilians under threat of imminent physical violence ...

The United Nations Security Council agreement that UNAMSIL should be further reinforced and tasked to consolidate territory captured from the RUF by the Sierra Leone Army had a number of implications. Firstly, it was entirely dependent on retaining and attracting credible peacekeepers whose governments were prepared for them to use force and incur casualties if necessary. Secondly, that the Sierra Leone Army and its allies should be built up sufficiently in order that they would be in a position to militarily defeat the RUF.

There was, therefore, considerable pressure within the United Nations for a British contribution to UNAMSIL, even of only a token number, because this would emphasise the British commitment to Sierra Leone and the United Nations. This pressure from the United Nations headquarters was understandable. They had approached a number of other countries to make military contributions but these had expressed their concern about the lack of western contingents and the obvious first western candidate for them was the United Kingdom.[6] There was therefore a clear case for a British contribution to assist the United Nations in bringing UNAMSIL up to its' authorised strength with appropriately committed and equipped forces.

---

4 UN Security Council Resolution 1313 (2000), 4 August 2000, http://daccessdds.un.org/doc/UNDOC/GEN/N00/591/96/PDF/N0059196.pdf?OpenElement, accessed 18 March 2008.

5 UN Security Council Resolution 1313 (2000), 4 August 2000, http://daccessdds.un.org/doc/UNDOC/GEN/N00/591/96/PDF/N0059196.pdf?OpenElement, accessed 18 March 2008.

6 Interview with author.

However, the MOD remained concerned about UNAMSIL's leadership.[7] It continued to argue that only by deploying a full brigade would it become the largest troop contributor and therefore able to guarantee command of UNAMSIL. Anything less than that would mean the British contribution would fall under the command of the existing UNAMSIL command structure which the MOD felt to be unacceptable.[8] Moreover, this would mean the armed forces going well beyond the overseas deployment levels agreed in the 'Strategic Defence Review' and place significant pressure on them.[9] More generally, the Blair government believed that it was better for the United Nations if the British continued to provide an on-call brigade capable of rapid response rather than a long term commitment of a brigade of peacekeepers to a particular mission which others were capable of undertaking.[10] The events of May 2000 showed that the United Kingdom was one of the few countries in the world with such a rapid deployment capability and they felt it should not be wasted on a static mission.

At a ministerial meeting in early September 2000 the British government set out its requirements for the future of Sierra Leone.[11] A number of non-negotiable points were agreed. These included an end to all RUF abductions and attacks, the immediate freedom of access throughout Sierra Leone for UNAMSIL and government forces and for the Government of Sierra Leone to have control of the diamond areas and its income.[12]

To achieve these objectives, a number of further steps were approved. It was agreed that the Sierra Leone Army should have additional British advisors seconded to its headquarters to help conduct future operations. In reality this meant that the British would take over the control of the operational headquarters and elements from the PJHQ were initially deployed and then replaced by the headquarters of 1 Mechanised Brigade.[13] To placate the United Nations it was decided to provide additional planning support at its headquarters in New York via a few additional staff officers.[14] More significantly, UNAMSIL would also receive additional British staff officers to help it to prepare and undertake operations including

---

7   Interview with author.
8   Interview with author.
9   'The Strategic Defence Review', *Cm. 3,999* (London: HMSO, 1998), http://www.mod.uk/NR/rdonlyres/65F3D7AC-4340-4119-93A2-20825848E50E/0/sdr1998_complete.pdf, accessed 13 July 2009.
10 Interview with author.
11 Interview with author.
12 Interview with author.
13 Baroness Symons of Vernham Dean, 'Statement on Sierra Leone', *House of Lords Parliamentary Debates*, 10 October 2000, cols 169.71; Paul Williams, 'Fighting for Freetown: British Military Intervention in Sierra Leone', *Contemporary Security Policy*, vol. 22, no. 3, December 2001, p. 140.
14 Interview with author.

the key post of Chief of Staff. As Chief of Staff, Brigadier Duncan formulated a campaign plan for UNAMSIL to confront the RUF in conjunction with the help of the Sierra Leone Army. As events transpired this was not enacted but it did represent the beginning of a change in mindset within UNAMSIL's headquarters.[15]

It was judged that the effect of the Short Term Training Team (STTT) had been considerable in terms of individual training, but the ability to undertake more complex operations remained limited without a significant British contribution to battle procedure and execution. The problem was twofold: the poor command and control capability of the SLA and the weakness of combat support elements.[16] As a result, the British government decided to continue the STTT process after STTT3 but with a change in emphasis. Instead in the subsequent three training courses a mixture of infantry and more specialised training was undertaken. Thus, whilst STTTs 1–3 trained six SLA infantry battalions in total, STTTs 4–6 trained only three more with the spare capacity used to focus on specialist units. Suitable equipment was also required and the United States was asked to help together with a sizeable provision of British equipment drawn from stocks in the United Kingdom.[17]

In the aftermath of the hostage rescue the Sierra Leone Army conducted a sweep of the Occra Hills to eliminate the last pockets of West Side Boys using the two battalions trained by the Short Term Training Team's first course. Many of the West Side Boys now chose to disarm and by the end of September over 350 West Side Boys, including a number of child soldiers, had entered the DDR process.[18] It was also significant that during the hostage negotiations the RUF decided to return the United Nations vehicles seized in May. This gave a further boost to the UNAMSIL whilst the surrender of the WSB helped to revitalise the DDR process.

However, the decision by the United Nations to alter UNAMSIL's remit created political difficulties for the Jordanian and Indian governments.[19] The shift away from impartiality towards support for the Government of Sierra Leone against the opposition led them to decide to withdraw their forces.[20] The problem was they were two of the highest troop contributors amounting to almost 5,000 personnel.

---

15 Interview with author.
16 Interview with author.
17 Interview with author.
18 'Seventh Report of the Secretary-General on the United Nations Mission in Sierra Leone', *S/2000/1055*, 31 October 2000, p. 3, http://daccessdds.un.org/doc/UNDOC/GEN/N00/717/71/IMG/N0071771.pdf?OpenElement, accessed 18 March 2008.
19 Interview with author.
20 'Seventh Report of the Secretary-General on the United Nations Mission in Sierra Leone', *S/2000/1055*, 31 October 2000, p. 8, http://daccessdds.un.org/doc/UNDOC/GEN/N00/717/71/IMG/N0071771.pdf?OpenElement, accessed 18 March 2008.

Moreover, they had provided some of the most robust forces as well as a good deal of support forces. The composition of UNAMSIL at 30 October 2000 is shown in Table 7.1.[21]

Table 7.1   Composition of UNAMSIL, 30 October 2000

Bangladesh	792
Ghana	785
Guinea	789
India	3,151
Jordan	1,817
Kenya	889
Nigeria	3,205
Zambia	788
Others	294
Total	12,510

This caused considerable concern within the United Nations and for the British government. New troops would replace the experienced UNAMSIL forces from November onwards with the rainy season at an end. It was felt in the United Kingdom and in the UN that this potential vulnerability might be exploited by the RUF. To help deter the RUF, and indicate the continuing commitment of the United Kingdom to Sierra Leone, the Defence Secretary therefore ordered the diversion of the ARG to spend a week off the Sierra Leone coast in November in order that it conduct an Amphibious Demonstration as a show of force whilst the Indian and Jordanian forces were replaced.[22]

Whilst all this was going on in secret it was also clear from information being intercepted by the British that the RUF was split over the way ahead.[23] This reflected the earlier division of its leadership between those who wanted a political

---

21   'Seventh Report of the Secretary-General on the United Nations Mission in Sierra Leone', *S/2000/1055*, 31 October 2000, p. 10, http://daccessdds.un.org/doc/UNDOC/GEN/N00/717/71/IMG/N0071771.pdf?OpenElement, accessed 18 March 2008.

22   'Amphibious Demonstration. This is an operation conducted to deceive an enemy or illustrate a capability. They must pose a credible threat to a land commander which then requires him to allocate sufficient forces to counter that contingent risk. Demonstrations can be used as components of shaping operations and exploiting operations, prior to or during an amphibious assault. The demonstration is perhaps the most elegant expression of amphibious capability. The limited liability offered by poising at sea, both in a military and political context, provides a unique form of leverage which can easily and rapidly be converted into combat action ashore.' 'The British Maritime Doctrine', *BR.1806* (London: The Stationery Office, second edition 1999), p. 136.

23   Interview with author.

and those who wanted a military resolution. The political element wanted to re-enter the Lomé peace process whilst other elements wanted to maintain the status quo. To help buy time for UNAMSIL to reconfigure itself, the British government supported the government of Sierra Leone in its decision to attend a meeting at Abuja between representatives of the Government of Sierra Leone, UNAMSIL, ECOWAS and the RUF. Out of these discussions a temporary ceasefire agreement was negotiated between the Government of Sierra Leone and the RUF. The agreement signed on 10 November provided for:

> A monitoring role for UNAMSIL; full liberty for the United Nations to deploy throughout the country; unimpeded movement of humanitarian workers, goods and people throughout the country; the return of UNAMSIL weapons and other equipment seized by the RUF; the immediate resumption of the programme of disarmament, demobilisation and reintegration; and a review of the implementation of the agreement after 30 days.[24]

The RUF clearly saw this as the first step towards a return to the Lomé Peace Agreement. In contrast, the Sierra Leone and British governments and UNAMSIL all viewed it as a potentially helpful mechanism during a process of changeover of UNAMSIL personnel.[25] They felt that time in terms of UNAMSIL reorganisation and the training of the Sierra Leone Army was against the RUF and thus the longer it lasted the more it suited them. However, where they varied was over the fear of staxis.

Achieving Peace

The transition of UNAMSIL personnel was successfully achieved with the deployment of two more Bangladesh battalions, a Ukrainian Maintenance and Training Battalion and some additional Kenyan forces.[26] The United Nations Secretary-General continued to argue for a further increase in UNAMSIL to 20,500 personnel including 260 UNMOs but this was ignored by the UN Security Council.[27]

---

24 'Eighth Report of the Secretary-General on the United Nations Mission in Sierra Leone', *S/2000/1199*, 15 December 2000, p. 1, http://daccessdds.un.org/doc/UNDOC/GEN/N00/797/01/IMG/N0079701.pdf?OpenElement, accessed 18 March 2008.

25 Interview with author.

26 'Eighth Report of the Secretary-General on the United Nations Mission in Sierra Leone', *S/2000/1199*, 15 December 2000, p. 4, http://daccessdds.un.org/doc/UNDOC/GEN/N00/797/01/IMG/N0079701.pdf?OpenElement, accessed 18 March 2008.

27 'Eighth Report of the Secretary-General on the United Nations Mission in Sierra Leone', *S/2000/1199*, 15 December 2000, p. 10, http://daccessdds.un.org/doc/UNDOC/GEN/N00/797/01/IMG/N0079701.pdf?OpenElement, accessed 18 March 2008.

Subsequently, the RUF announced that despite the ceasefire UNAMSIL was barred from entering RUF-controlled territory until certain addition conditions were met which included the release of their leader Foday Sankoh.[28] Much to the frustration of the British government, which feared staxis, the UNAMSIL forces did not seek to challenge this bar on its movement arguing that time was on their side.[29] For many in Sierra Leone it resulted in the most peaceful Christmas/ Ramadan for a decade.[30] The initial 30-day ceasefire was subsequently extended by a further 90 days.

The British government continued to press for a challenge to the RUF and on 15 March 2001 a 220-strong Nigerian UNAMSIL contingent firstly moved into the RUF controlled town of Lunsar. Officials and police from the Sierra Leone Government were supposed to have followed shortly afterwards but they did not do so and the RUF continued to man roadblocks despite the presence of UNAMSIL.[31] Further forward moves by UNAMSIL were strongly encouraged by the British government who felt little progress was being made but the UNAMSIL command did not seem keen to enforce the disarmament and further advances were delayed until April and then only limited moves were made.[32]

Behind the scenes the RUF was struggling as the British government, with support from the US administration, began to focus on reducing the illegal trade in Sierra Leone diamonds which had helped fund the RUF and their links to President Charles Taylor in Liberia. Some of the RUF leadership could see that the end was in sight and on 2 May 2001 representatives of the Sierra Leone Government, ECOWAS and UNAMSIL again meeting with the RUF at Abjua. It was agreed that the Civil Defence Force and RUF should simultaneously disarm and that a timetable and process for implementing the DDR process should be agreed.[33] Importantly, the Sierra Leone Army was to be left intact but open to recruit from those who had passed through the DDR process. Five days later the international community decided to impose a diamond embargo on Liberia as a means of putting pressure on President Taylor and ending the supply of illicit funding to the RUF. Just over a week later the Sierra Leone Government, UNAMSIL and the RUF again met to discuss the DDR process. It was agreed that the disarmament of the

---

28 'Eighth Report of the Secretary-General on the United Nations Mission in Sierra Leone', *S/2000/1199*, 15 December 2000, p. 2, http://daccessdds.un.org/doc/UNDOC/GEN/N00/797/01/IMG/N0079701.pdf?OpenElement, accessed 18 March 2008.
29 Interview with author.
30 'Interview of Brigadier Riley', Radio 4 Today Programme, 1 January 2001.
31 Interview with author.
32 Interview with author.
33 'Tenth Report of the Secretary-General on the United Nations Mission in Sierra Leone', *S/2001/627*, 25 June 2001, p. 1, http://daccessdds.un.org/doc/UNDOC/GEN/N01/423/17/IMG/N0142317.pdf?OpenElement, accessed 18 March 2008.

RUF and some government militias should be restarted and this time the process was entered into immediately with significant RUF disarmament. By September 2001 the UN Secretary-General was able to report to the Security Council that the peace process continued to make progress with the 'disarmament of combatants of the Revolutionary United Front (RUF) and the Civil Defence Forces (CDF) has so far been completed in four districts, including the diamond-producing Kono district.[34] Apart from a brief skirmish early on between Civil Defence Forces and the RUF in the Kono district the ceasefire has generally continued to hold. Moreover, UNAMSIL had been able to deploy across most of the country which meant that 'more areas have become accessible to humanitarian workers and the civilian population, and the Government has taken steps, albeit modest, to restore civil authority in some areas formerly controlled by RUF'.[35] Most importantly, the UN Secretary-General was able to report that:

> the disarmament, demobilization and reintegration process has made remarkable progress. Since the programme resumed on 18 May, a total of 16,097 (6,523 RUF, 9,399 CDF and 175 AFRC/ex-Sierra Leone Army) combatants had been disarmed as at 3 September, out of an estimated 25,000. A total of 6,502 weapons and 728,058 assorted pieces of ammunition have so far been collected.
>
> 22. After the disarmament exercise in Kambia and Port Loko districts, the programme was launched simultaneously in Kono and Bonthe districts on 1 July and concluded on 17 August. A total of 5,451 combatants (3,478 RUF and 1,973 CDF) disarmed in the volatile Kono district. The programme was subsequently launched in Moyamba and Koinadugu districts, on 15 and 20 August respectively. If the current pace is sustained, the disarmament process in the remaining six districts could be completed by November/December 2001.[36]

The six months from May 2001 saw a remarkable transformation in Sierra Leone. By September 2001 over 16,000 fighters had been disarmed and the RUF was allowed to re-enter the political process. By the following March the DDR process had dealt with over 50,000 people and the RUF had ceased to exist as a military force.

---

34 'Eleventh Report of the Secretary-General on the United Nations Mission in Sierra Leone', *S/2001/857*, 7 September 2000, pp. 1, 4, http://daccessdds.un.org/doc/UNDOC/GEN/N01/529/63/PDF/N0152963.pdf?OpenElement, accessed 30 Januaru 2009.

35 'Eleventh Report of the Secretary-General on the United Nations Mission in Sierra Leone', *S/2001/857*, 7 September 2000, pp. 1, 4, http://daccessdds.un.org/doc/UNDOC/GEN/N01/529/63/PDF/N0152963.pdf?OpenElement, accessed 30 Januaru 2009.

36 'Eleventh Report of the Secretary-General on the United Nations Mission in Sierra Leone', *S/2001/857*, 7 September 2000, pp. 1, 4, http://daccessdds.un.org/doc/UNDOC/GEN/N01/529/63/PDF/N0152963.pdf?OpenElement, accessed 30 Januaru 2009.

Aftermath

In May 2002 elections were held and Ahmad Kabbah was re-elected President as his SLPP party won 83 out of 112 seats. The RUF won no seats at all. Johnny-Paul Koroma, the leader of the 1997 coup, won one of the AFRC's two seats but significantly received over 90 per cent of the Sierra Leone Army vote. In the aftermath of these elections there was, perhaps surprisingly, no attempted coup or withdrawal from the electoral process by any of the defeated groups. The process towards reconstruction and rehabilitation continued.

The end of the fighting brought further consequences. In December 2002 the British High Commissioner was briefed by the Chief Prosecutor of the Sierra Leone Special Court in strict confidence.[37] The Special Court, like the International Criminal Tribunal for the former Yugoslavia (ICTY) in Yugoslavia, had been set up under United Nations auspices and modelled on ICTY to bring those responsible for atrocities and crimes against humanity to justice. The Chief Prosecutor indicated that the court planned to issue its first indictments and make as many as 15 arrests sometime between mid-January and March. The indictees were likely to include former RUF leaders Foday Sankoh, Issa Seesay and Sam Bockarie, former coup leader Johnny Paul Koroma, the Minister for Internal Affairs Sam Hinga and President Charles Taylor of Liberia. The importance and potential danger of this was recognised within the British government and the MOD was asked to provide support. For the MOD the problem was one of other commitments. It still needed to maintain its existing commitments such as the Balkans, Cyprus and Northern Ireland, undertake a major deployment of forces to Iraq and provide sufficient forces available to cover any further industrial action by British firefighters (*Operation Fresco*). It was agreed to stand down some of those earmarked for *Operation Fresco* for a two-week period and deploy a Gurkha company from the then Spearhead battalion together with a navy frigate under the name *Operation Keeling*. These were sent to Sierra Leone in March 2003 to coincide with the likely date of the arrests and act as a deterrent alongside an information campaign stressing Britain's support for the court process. The operation was a total success with the majority of those indicted successfully arrested and peace was preserved.

Recovering from the effects of such a long civil war and endemic corruption that has been present far longer is taking time. By the end of December 2005 the UN Secretary-General was able to report to the Security Council that the principal issue was that of governance. This did not mean that the threat of a return to violence had gone away and the report highlighted that 'there are still a number of factors which pose potential threats to the security and political stability the country currently enjoys. These include the widespread destitution

---

37 Interview with author.

and disaffection, especially among the unemployed youth; corruption, which is still prevalent in the public sector; weaknesses in the judicial system; and resource constraints and other capacity shortfalls inhibiting the Government's ability to deliver services to the population'.[38] Nevertheless, the expectations of the ordinary Sierra Leonean remained high which meant that 'the Government is still facing considerable challenges in putting together an effective strategy for communicating its vision and programmes to the public and in creating an environment conducive to effective participation of and closer collaboration with civil society and the private sector in enhancing democratic governance'.[39]

Since then Sierra Leone has had a period of relative peace and stability. By the end of 2005 the UNAMSIL force was able to be wound up and its forces completely withdrawn.[40] It has been replaced by the United Nations Integrated Office in Sierra Leone (UNIOSIL) which was set up under United Nations Security Council resolution 1620.[41]

In subsequent elections there was a peaceful transfer of power with President Kabbah handing over office to the successful opposition party. This bodes well for Sierra Leone and although the issue of corruption remains. Sierra Leone society is slowly beginning to rebuild itself and work slowly continues on improving the economic and social well-being of the civilian population.

Tensions remain and the trial of Charles Taylor accused of masterminding the RUF and the decade long civil war initially began in Freetown but was soon moved to The Hague because of fears of uprest.[42] These began in 2007 and the trial was expected to be a long one with Taylor pleading not guilty.

---

38 'Twenty-seventh report of the Secretary-General on the United Nations Mission in Sierra Leone', *S/2005/777*, 12 December 2005, http://daccessdds.un.org/doc/UNDOC/GEN/N05/630/47/PDF/N0563047.pdf?OpenElement, accessed 21 January 2009.

39 'Twenty-seventh report of the Secretary-General on the United Nations Mission in Sierra Leone', *S/2005/777*, 12 December 2005, http://daccessdds.un.org/doc/UNDOC/GEN/N05/630/47/PDF/N0563047.pdf?OpenElement, accessed 21 January 2009.

40 Funmi Olonisakin, *Peacekeeping in Sierra Leone: The Story of UNAMSIL* (Boulder, CO: Lynne Rienner, 2008), p. 129.

41 United Nations Security Council Resolution 1620 (2005), 31 August 2005, http://daccessdds.un.org/doc/UNDOC/GEN/N05/477/15/PDF/N0547715.pdf?OpenElement, accessed 2 February 2009.

42 David Charter, 'Africa's warlords look on in alarm as "revolutionary" faces UN court', *The Times*, 4 June 2007, p. 27.

Conclusions

In many respects the speed of peace almost matched the speed of the collapse of UNAMSIL and the British deployment the previous May. It was noteworthy that the British government only really came to a final decision about its approach to the situation in Sierra Leone in September 2000 and then began to implement a coherent plan. Until this point the response had largely been reactive in nature and it had never been what government now refers to as a 'Comprehensive Approach'.[43] Even after the September 2000 decision the response was largely focused around the military response with the FCO working in conjunction with the MOD. DFID and the other departments of state were far less engaged and there was no major direction from the Prime Minister's office. Indeed, it was noticeable that the Prime Minister's representative was overruled and *Operation Amble* did not take place. The STTT process, the clear military commitment, exhaustion, the lessoning of Charles Taylor's grip on Liberia and the hope that the Lomé Peace Agreement could be returned to all played a role in encouraging those within the RUF who wanted a political settlement that the November ceasefire was the best option available. The subsequent closing of the illegal trade in Sierra Leone diamonds took the major resource line from the RUF and the RUF entered the DDR process relatively benignly. This was certainly difficult to have imagined back in May 2000 and shows how elements came together to tip the balance towards peace and reconciliation.

---

43 'JointDiscussionNote(JDN)4/05:TheComprehensiveApproach',version20080125 (London: MOD, 2008), http://www.mod.uk/NR/rdonlyres/25A7F4A2-31C2-49D8-A857-4D31750CBD6F/0/20071218_jdn4_05_U_DCDCIMAPPS.pdf, accessed 30 January 2009.

Chapter 8
Impact of the Operation

As the title of this book implies, the British deployment of its armed forces to Sierra Leone in May 2000 was one of the few successful uses of the military by the Blair administration. The Sierra Leone experience had a number of consequences for government policy. This chapter seeks to critically examine the impact of this military intervention within government policies at home and overseas. To undertake this task the chapter has been subdivided into four sections. Firstly, what was the impact of the war on the Blair government and, in particular, its views on the use of force? Secondly, how were the lessons drawn by the British used to influence the defence transformation agenda within NATO and the European Union? Thirdly, to what extent did this conflict influence the subsequent evolution of British defence policy? The fourth section reflects on the lessons which were drawn from the Sierra Leone operation by the British military.

The Impact on the Blair Government

Writing shortly after the initial deployment to Sierra Leone in May 2000 *The Economist* suggested that:

> At any time in the past two years, you could have asked the authors of Britain's Strategic Defence Review what sort of crisis they were preparing to face more often, and the answer would have been the same: a slide into anarchy in some developing-world state, probably African and quite possibly on the coast, in which British lives were at risk and a broader humanitarian disaster loomed. In other words, Sierra Leone. Which is where the Labour government's aspiration to use the military as a 'force for good' all over the world – even in areas which lack the strategic stakes of the Balkans or the Middle East – could face its make-or-break test.[1]

The Sierra Leone example appeared to prove that military force could be used as a 'force for good' and could have a lasting impact positive impact.[2] It tapped into the internationalist agenda that had been part of the Labour Party from its very early days. The apparent success of the Sierra Leone experience encouraged

---

1   'The Logic of Sierra Leone', *The Economist*, 20 May 2000, p. 38.
2   Nyta Mann, 'Blair says Britain is "force for good"', *BBC Online*, 5 January 2002, http://news.bbc.co.uk/1/hi/uk_politics/1743985.stm, accessed 2 March 2009.

the Prime Minister and his government to take this a stage further and adopt the ideas of cosmopolitan militaries in which armed forces could be used to support humanitarian intervention.[3] In the following year, after the attacks on America on 11 September 2001, a US-led coalition began military operations against the Taliban government of Afghanistan and al Qaeda, the group held responsible for the attacks on America.[4] From the first day of the war the United Kingdom was intimately involved in the operation launching cruise missile from its submarines and deploying Special Forces and other assets to help topple the Taliban regime.[5] As the US sponsored Northern Alliance started to successfully push the Taliban out of Afghanistan it was the Blair government that argued that the international community needed to support the changing situation in Afghanistan, prevent the humanitarian disaster many feared and begin the process of rebuilding Afghanistan. In other words the war expanded from one focused on destroying al Qaeda and toppling the Taliban to one of completely changing Afghanistan permanently. Blair successfully pushed for Britain to initially lead the international force (ISAF) that deployed initially to Kabul to support the Interim Authority and it would be Britain that led the subsequent NATO takeover and expansion of this mission in 2006 with the deployment of forces to the south and east of Kabul.[6]

Similarly in Iraq 2003 Blair used British forces to support the US-led invasion partly to search for Saddam Hussain's alleged hoard of weapons of mass destruction but also to overthrow a ruthless dictator.[7] In other words, the Sierra Leone experience built on that of Kosovo in 1999 and made the use of Britain's armed forces a more appealing and less daunting prospect because there was an expectation of success. Sierra Leone provided added impetus to the ideas of humanitarian intervention ideas espoused in Blair's Chicago speech which would

---

3 See Lorraine Elliott and Graeme Cheeseman (eds), *Forces for good? Cosmopolitan militaries in the 21st century* (Manchester: Manchester University Press, 2005).

4 United National Security Council, Resolution 1373 (2001), *S/RES/1373 (2001)*, 28 September 2001, http://ods-dds-ny.un.org/doc/UNDOC/GEN/N01/557/43/PDF/N0155 743.pdf?Open Element, accessed 17 October 2007.

5 Tony Blair, 'House of Commons Parliamentary Debates', 8 October 2001, vol. 372, session 2001–2002, cols 811, 813, www.publications.parliament.uk/pa/cm200102/cmhan srd/vo011008/debindx/11008-x.htm, accessed 10 November 2007.

6 'Minister Cetin Speaking Notes Change of Command Press Conference,' 4 May 2006, http://www.nato.int/isaf/docu/speech/2006/speech_04may06.htm, accessed 3 February 2009.

7 Tony Blair, *House of Commons Parliamentary Debates*, 'Iraq', 18 March 2003, session 2002–2003, col. 760, http://www.publications.parliament.uk/cgi-bin/newhtml_hl ?DB=semukparl&STEMMER=en&WORDS=toni%20blair%20iraq&ALL=tony%20 blair%20iraq&ANY=&PHRASE=&CATEGORIES=&SIMPLE=&SPEAKER=&COL OUR=red&STYLE=s&ANCHOR=30318-06_spmin2&URL=/pa/cm200203/cmhansrd/ vo030318/debtext/30318-06.htm#30318-06_spmin2, accessed 3 February 2009.

only begin to be question in the lead up to the invasion of Iraq in 2003. According to Anthony Seldon, a biographer of Blair:

> After successful actions in Kosovo in 1999, Sierra Leone, Indonesia and East Timor in 2000, and Afghanistan in 2001, his focus shifted from the risks to the soldiers and pilots to the effectiveness of their actions ... Over the space of four years, from late 1998 to 2002/3, he changed to a leader who was actually confident about the use of military action.[8]

The Sierra Leone experience also implied that the use of the military was a relatively precise tool for politicians to use. Although the British had used overwhelming force at both Lungi Lol and during *Operation Barras* these were perceived to be both legitimate and perhaps more significantly they were out of sight of the media. Instead, what was seen was a deployment of forces that looked both potent and restrained as British troops patrolled the streets of Freetown whilst Royal Naval ships could be seen off the coast of Sierra Leone and in Freetown harbour. Added to this impression was the RUF's history of barbarity which allowed the government and media to portray the situation as a simple case of good versus evil. The experience of Iraq from 2003 and Afghanistan from 2006 has helped re-address the perceptions of precision and reminded politicians and public opinion that the use of the armed forces can never be surgically precise whatever their intentions. The inadvertent killing of civilians and ones own military personnel, so-called blue-on-blue incidents, has placed a dampener on the use of the military.

The apparent success of Sierra Leone also encouraged the Blair government to continue its African emphasis and work continued to promote good governance, alleviate debt and bring an end to the continent's various wars.[9] However, the lack of domestic support for the Sierra Leone operation and the commitment of Britain's armed forces to other conflicts proved to decisive in preventing any further British interventions in the continent. Darfur and Zimbabwe continued to remain issues for the British government throughout Blair's time in office but no British forces were committed apart from a few logistics personnel to support the African Union mission to Darfur.

The Lessons Drawn in Terms of Defence Transformation for the EU and Beyond

In an early article in the *Berliner Zeitung* Maritta Tkalec indicated the impact that the British operation May 2000 in Sierra Leone might have. Entitled 'Neo-colonialism with a Human Face' she argued:

---

8   Anthony Seldon, *Blair Unbound* (London: Simon and Schuster, 2007), pp. 167–8.
9   Anthony Seldon, *Blair Unbound* (London: Simon and Schuster, 2007), p. 324.

> Good news is no news in the media world. Consequently, one of the best stories of the year has attracted little attention. Sierra Leone, a small country in West Africa, did *not* experience a terrible new massacre, hundreds of women and children were *not* raped, thousands of people did *not* have their limbs chopped off. However, all these brutal atrocities were committed in 1999 when rebel forces captured to Sierra Leonean capital Freetown. At the beginning of May this year, the rebels reached the outskirts of the city again. The local population were in a state of panic – they knew what could happen. No one trusted the 10,000 UN soldiers from India, Nigeria or Zambia to defend them; 500 of them had been taken hostage by the rebels ...
>
> The first major British military intervention in Africa *since the Suez crisis* in 1956 is a success. The five-week 'blitzkrieg of the Brits', as one British tabloid wrote, not only saved Freetown from a repeated massacre it also rescued the Blue Helmet mission in Sierra Leone. This intervention interrupts the long series of disastrous international attempts to provide assistance in African crisis regions – Somalia, Rwanda and Angola to mention just a few ...
>
> But it was the speed and determination of the intervention which brought success. Other courses of action, which might have been more usual in a democracy, were not taken because they were regarded as unacceptable detours in this case. A week later – perhaps after a parliamentary debate or extensive coordination with NATO partners to obtain a UN mandate – the only action would have been to bemoan the suffering after the atrocities.[10]

The Kosovo experience had highlighted to the MOD that Europe's military capabilities (including Britain's) lagged significantly behind those of the United States and needed to be substantially transformed.[11] Blair had already encouraged a more European focus within defence and the British and French governments agreed at their meeting in St Malo in December, 1998, that the EU 'must have the capacity for autonomous action, backed up by credible military forces, the means to decide to use them, and a readiness to do so, in order to respond to international

---

10 Emphasis in original. Maritta Tkalec, 'Neocolonialism with a human face', *Berliner Zeitung*, 21 June 2000.

11 See Lord Robertson (1999), speech to the RIIA Conference 'European Defence: The Way Ahead', 7 October 1999; William S. Cohen and General Henry H. Shelton (1999), Senate Armed Services Committee, 14 October 1999, http://armed-services.senate.gov/statemnt/1999/991014wc.pdf, accessed 3 February 2009; 'Defence Capabilities Initiative (1999), *NATO Press Release NAC-S(99)69*, 25 April 1999, www.nato.int; General Wesley Clark, Admiral James Ellis Jr and Lieutenant-General Michael Short (1999), Senate Armed Services Committee, 21 October 1999, http://armed-services.senate.gov/statemnt/1999/991021wc.pdf, accessed 3 February 2009.

crises'.[12] This followed on from an earlier speech by Prime Minister Tony Blair some two months before at Portschach.[13] The subsequent Helsinki Headline Goals produced by the European Union in December 1999 after the Anglo-French London Summit of November 1999 developed proposals for reform that focused on the development of a Corps level capability in which some 50,000–60,000 personnel would be deployed within 60 days and sustained in the field for a year. In other words a force based on that deployed by KFOR to Kosovo in June 1999. However, progress continued to be slow and British frustrations were reinforced during the initial deployment of ISAF forces to Afghanistan in December 2001.

Instead, the Sierra Leone experience again influenced policy as it set the scene for increasing cooperation with Britain's European partners particularly the French, in Africa. At the November 2003 Franco-British summit a declaration on co-operation in Africa was agreed:

> Our two countries are convinced that their common vision and action can, at the heart of the European Union, contribute to peace and security, the reinforcement of democracy and good governance, poverty reduction and the development of the continent.[14]

Operation Artemis was a French-led European Union response to the request from the United Nations Secretary-General to launch an operation within two weeks of United Nations Security Council Resolution 1484.[15] This called for a multinational interim emergency force to be deployed in Bunia in the Democratic Republic of Congo.[16] Following on from this the French and British governments have proposed that:

---

12 *Joint Declaration Issued at the British-French Summit*, Saint Malo, France, 3–4 December 1998; see Robert Dover, *Europeanisation of British Defence Policy* (Aldershot: Ashgate, 2007); Andrew Dorman, 'Reconciling Britain to Europe in the Next Millennium: The Evolution of British Defense Policy in the Post-Cold War Era', *Defense Analysis*, vol. 17, no. 2, Summer 2001, pp. 187–202.

13 Richard Hatfield, 'The Consequences of St Malo', Paris, Institut Français des Relations Internationales, 28 April 2000, news.mod.uk/news/press/news_press_notice.asp?newsItem_id=468, accessed 10 November 2007.

14 'Declaration on Franco-British Co-operation in Africa', Franco-British Summit, London, 24 November 2003, http://www.elysee.fr/magazine/deplacement_etranger/sommaire.php?doc=/magazine/deplacement_etranger/2003/11/24/80640_page_13.htm, accessed 10 November 2007.

15 See http://ec.europa.eu/world/peace/geographical_themes/africa/artemis/index_en.htm, accessed 2 March 2008.

16 United Nations Security Council Resolution 1,484 (2003), 30 May 2003, http://daccessdds.un.org/doc/UNDOC/GEN/N03/377/68/PDF/N0337768.pdf?OpenElement, accessed 10 November 2007.

> The EU should aim to build on this precedent so that it is able to respond through ESDP to future similar requests from the United Nations, whether in Africa or elsewhere. The EU should be able and willing to deploy in an autonomous operation within 15 days to respond to a crisis. The aim should be coherent and credible battle-group sized forces, each around 1500 troops, offered by a single nation or through a multinational or framework nation force package, with appropriate transport and sustainability. These forces should have the capacity to operate under a Chapter VII mandate. They would be deployed in response to a UN request to stabilise a situation or otherwise meet a short-term need until peace-keepers from the United Nations, or regional organisations acting under a UN mandate, could arrive or be reinforced.[17]

Thus the new working assumption for the European Union use of military force shifted from large-scale operations in the Balkans to much smaller scale operations in Africa. The mechanism to support this, a 1,500 strong battlegroup, simply took the Spearhead Battalion/Airborne Task Force concept that had formed the basis of the *Operation Palliser* deployment and used it as a template for the rest of the European Union.[18] In other words the British government at no cost to itself used the Sierra Leone experience as the new template for European defence adaptation.[19] As a consequence the members of the European Union have now agreed to create 13 rapidly deployable battle groups.[20]

The Impact on British Defence Policy

The impact of the Sierra Leone operation has taken some time to filter through into defence policy. The then official defence policy was based on the 1998 'Strategic Defence Review' which George Robertson had undertaken during Labour's first 14 months in office.[21] Robertson had been replaced by Geoff Hoon at defence after the Kosovo War and Sierra Leone was Hoon's first war. It therefore had a considerable impact on him and gave him a particular set of insights into the future

---

17 'Declaration on Strengthening European Co-operation in Security and Defence', Franco-British Summit, London, 24 November 2003, http://www.fco.gov.uk/Files/kfile/UKFrance_DefenceDeclaration,0.pdf.

18 'EU Battlegroups', EU Council Secretariat Factsheet, E BG01, 2005, http://consilium.europa.eu/uedocs/cmsUpload/BattlegroupsNov05factsheet.pdf.

19 Andrew Dorman, *Transforming to Effects Based Operations: Lessons from the United Kingdom Experience* (Carlisle, PA: Strategic Studies Institute, 2008), http://www.strategicstudiesinstitute.army.mil/pubs/display.cfm?pubID=831, accessed 2 March 2009.

20 Gustav Lindstrom, 'Enter the EU Battlegroups', *Chaillot Paper no. 97* (Paris: ISS, 2007), http://www.iss.europa.eu/uploads/media/cp097.pdf, accessed 13 July 2009.

21 Ministry of Defence, 'The Strategic Defence Review' (London: The Stationery Office, Cm 3999, July 1998), http://www.mod.uk/NR/rdonlyres/65F3D7AC-4340-4119-93A2-20825848E50E/0/sdr1998_complete.pdf, accessed 18 November 2008.

requirements for defence policy. Whilst these were being absorbed a year and a day after the *Operation Barras* rescue the United States was attacked by hijacked airliners which were deliberately crashed into the World Trade Center in New York and the Pentagon in Washington DC. In the aftermath of the attacks Hoon published an initial response 'The Strategic Defence Review: A New Chapter' in 2002.[22] The goal was to:

> Move away from always assessing defence capability in terms of platforms or unit numbers. It is now more useful to think in terms of the effects that can be delivered – we must consider what effect we want to have on an opponent and at what time.[23]

In terms of substantive policy there was not much change over the earlier SDR. A little bit more emphasis was given to home defence. Where it differed significantly was in its buy into the ideas of 'Defence Transformation'.[24] For Blair and Hoon Sierra Leone had shown the benefit of small numbers of highly capable forces. The 'New Chapter' took a number of steps forward towards embracing these concepts, notably embracing network enabled capability (NEC) and the threat posed by asymmetric warfare.[25] However, it was the subsequent two part defence white papers 'Delivering Security in a Changing World', that followed in 2003 and 2004, that fully reflected the impact of Sierra Leone.[26] They argued that only by adopting a comprehensive

---

22 'The Strategic Defence Review: A New Chapter', *Cm.5,566* (London: TSO, 2002), http://www.mod.uk/DefenceInternet/AboutDefence/CorporatePublications/PolicyStrategy/StrategicDefenceReviewANewChaptercm5566.htm, accessed 7 November 2007.

23 Geoff Hoon, House of Commons Defence Committee, 'A New Chapter to the Strategic Defence Review', *HC.93-I*, Report of Session 2002–2003, 2003, para. 66, http://www.parliament.the-stationery-office.co.uk/pa/cm200203/cmselect/cmdfence/93/93.pdf, accessed 10 November 2007.

24 Alvin and Heidi Toffler, *War and Anti-War: Making Sense of Today's Global Chaos* (New York: Mass Market Paperback, 1995); Thomas J. Czerwinski, 'The Third Wave: What the Tofflers Never Told You', *Strategic Forum*, no. 72 (Washington, DC: National Defense University, 1996); there is a vast library of material on changing the nature of security and warfare. See, for example, Ken Booth and Tim Dunne (eds), *Worlds in Collision: Terror and the Future of Global Order* (Basingstoke: Palgrave Macmillan, 2002); Samuel P. Huntington, *The Clash of Civilizations: Remaking of World Order* (New York: Touchstone, 1996); George and Meredith Friedman, *The Future of War: Power, Technology and American World Dominance in the Twenty-First Century* (New York: St Martin's Griffin, 1996); Colonel John B. Alexander, *Future War: Non-Lethal Weapons in Twenty-First Century Warfare* (New York: Thomas Dunne Books, 1999); John Leech, *Asymmetries of Conflict: War without Death* (London: Frank Cass, 2002); Colin McInnes, *Spectator War: The West and Contemporary Conflict* (London: Lynne Rienner, 2002); Robert J Bunker (ed.), *Non-State Threats and Future Wars* (London: Frank Cass, 2003).

25 See http://www.iwar.org.uk/rma/resources/uk-mod/nec.htm.

26 'Delivering security in a Changing World: The Defence White Paper', *Cm. 6,041-I* (London: TSO, 2003), http://www.mod.uk/DefenceInternet/AboutDefence/Corpor

security approach in which defence was a part would British interests be best served. They shifted the defence focus away from traditional inter-state war towards other challenges and in particular what Rupert Smith coined as 'wars amongst the people'.[27] The belief was that traditional inter-state warfare was likely to occur far less often because of western advantages in traditional warfare. This thinking has subsequently begun to be challenged by the likes of Colin Gray and the armed forces are clearly split over the future direction of conflict.[28] The ongoing Afghanistan experience has led to a move towards the concept of 'hybrid wars'.

Secondly, despite the British government's level of political engagement in Sierra Leone, the size of its investment and the commitment of a sizeable UN mission, Sierra Leone had not been identified as a location for a potential deployment of British forces and no specific training had been undertaken for this operation. Rather the geographical focus was on Europe and an 'arc of concern' that ran from North Africa to the Middle East. This operation, reinforced by the subsequent requirement to deploy forces to Afghanistan after the attacks on America highlighted the geographical limitations of the 1998 'Strategic Defence Review' and encouraged its thinking towards shorter, high intensity operations using armed forces that had a significant technological advantage over their potential opponents. Thus, the geographical view of defence and the level of simultaneous operations were revisited in the 2003 defence review 'Delivering Security in a Changing World'.[29]

The third shift was the emphasis now placed in the speed of response and follows on from the line of thinking espoused by the likes of Donald Rumsfeld. As the Sierra Leone operation had literally occurred overnight it reinforced the argument that the United Kingdom needed to hold some units at very high readiness and this endorsed the Airborne Task Force, ARG and Spearhead battalion concepts and confirmed the need for Parachute and Marine units. However, this did not entirely protect them when it came to revisiting the army's infantry structure.[30] The

---

atePublications/PolicyStrategy/DeliveringSecurityInAChangingWorldDefence WhitePaper2003.htm; 'Delivering security in a Changing World: Future Capabilities', *Cm. 6,269* (London: TSO, 2004), http://www.mod.uk/DefenceInternet/AboutDefence/Corporate Publications/PolicyStrategy/DeliveringSecurityInAChangingWorldFutureCapabilities cm6269.htm, accessed 7 November 2007.

27   Rupert Smith, *The Utility of Force: the Art of War in the Modern World* (London: Penguin, 2006).

28   Colin Gray, *Another Bloody Century: Future Warfare* (London: Phoenix, 2006).

29   Andrew Dorman, *Transforming to Effects Based Operations: Lessons from the United Kingdom Experience* (Carlisle, PA: Strategic Studies Institute, 2008), http://www.strategicstudiesinstitute.army.mil/pubs/display.cfm?pubID=831, accessed 2 March 2009.

30   See 'Reorganising the Infantry: Drivers of Change and What This Tells Us about the State of the Defence Debate Today', *British Journal of Politics and International Relations*, vol. 8, no. 4, 2006.

problems with the Spearhead elements that were supposed to bring 1 PARA Battle Group up to strength in May 2000 were subsequently repeated in 2003–2004 as the army sought to sustain a significant level of military commitment to Iraq and found that it had few battalions that were fully up to strength.[31] The review of the the army's structures, and in particular its infantry regiments, proved highly controversial but the argument of the then Chief of the General Staff, General Sir Mike Jackson, was that it ws better to have fewer fully manned battalions and the number of battalions was reduced from 40 to 36. Interestingly, his deputy at the time in the role of Vice-Chief of the General Staff was a now Major-General David Richards!

Jackson came under significant pressure to cut one of the Parachute battalions as part of this reduction and he acknowledged that the country did not need three battalions in the parachute role as it was unlikely ever to use that method of entry except for very small forces. The reason why the three battalions were retained was their role in serving as a recruiting pool for Britain's Special Forces. Moreover, *Operation Palliser* began to show that the role of Britain's Special Forces would begin to bring them into ever closer contact with their conventional counterparts.[32] In Afghanistan in 2001 and Iraq in 2003 Royal Marine units were used to supplement the Special Forces and bring supportive conventional firepower as 1 PARA had offered to do in May 2000 and A Company of 1 PARA had done in the *Operation Barras* rescue. In the 2004 infantry reforms 1 PARA was transferred to the command of the Director of Special Forces along with a newly created Special Reconnaissance Regiment.[33]

The technological dominance of the British forces in Sierra Leone and also later in Afghanistan encouraged an emphasis on acquiring three key elements: sensors capable of identifying targets; a communications network able to transfer this information to commanders to decide on a response; and the strike assets capable of accurately hitting the target within the requisite timeframe.[34] This, in part, explains the drive towards developing a Network-Enabled Capability (NEC) which brings these elements together.[35]

---

31 Interviews with author.

32 Geoffrey Hoon, *House of Commons Parliamentary Debates*, Statement on 'Future Infantry Structure', 16 December 2004, session 2004–2005, col. 1796, http://www.publications.parliament.uk/pa/cm200405/cmhansrd/vo041216/debtext/41216-06.htm#41216-06_head0, accessed 3 February 2009.

33 Geoffrey Hoon, *House of Commons Parliamentary Debates*, Statement on 'Future Infantry Structure', 16 December 2004, session 2004–2005, col. 1796, http://www.publications.parliament.uk/pa/cm200405/cmhansrd/vo041216/debtext/41216-06.htm#41216-06_head0, accessed 3 February 2009.

34 House of Commons Defence Committee, 'Defence White Paper 2003', Third Report of Session 2003–2004, *HC.465-I* (London: The Stationery Office, 2004), p. 7.

35 *Operations in Iraq: First Reflections* (London: MOD, 2003), www.mod.uk, p. 24.

Reflections on the Lessons Learned by the Ministry of Defence

Soon after the initial deployment Geoff Hoon, the Defence Secretary, noted in the House of Commons that:

> The deployment of British troops for a limited period on these tasks is a model of the rapid deployment concept that was at the heart of the Strategic Defence Review.[36]

For those involved in the initial deployment the abiding memory was the speed of the response.[37] The Chairman of the Joint Chiefs indicated to the British that the Americans would not have been able to react so quickly.[38]

However, the picture was a little misleading. The initial operation in May 2000 was fortunate in having both the Amphibious Ready Group and a carrier group nearby, and thus able to rapidly redeploy far quicker than would normally have been expected and this allowed Brigadier Richards to take a number of risks with his deployment by air. Perhaps, more typically, the subsequent rescue in September was hampered by the lack of an off the coast base for the Chinook helicopters. The fact that *RFA Argus* arrived too late highlighted that there is a need to balance home-based quick response forces with forward deployed forces. Moreover, there were two lifts for 1 PARA as only three Chinooks were available. However, the steady reduction in defence spending as a proportion of gross domestic product has meant that the MOD has had to make a number of defence reductions through a lack of resources. Thus overall numbers of units, such as destroyers and frigates, continues to gradually decline and an emphasis is placed on the ability to respond quickly in the short term rather than sustain the deployment of military assets around the globe. The recent economic downturn has now caused fundamental questions to be asked about the sustainability of the current defence budget and Britain's future defence capabilities.[39]

---

36 Secretary of State for Defence's Statement on Sierra Leone, House of Commons, 15 May 00, http://news.mod.uk/news/press/news_press_notice.asp?newsItem_id=723, accessed 13 July 2009; see also Andrew Dorman 'Transforming to Effects-based warfare: Lessons from the United Kingdom Experience', Strategic Studies Institute, US Army War College, 2008.
37 Interviews with author.
38 Interview with author.
39 See Paul Cornish and Andrew Dorman, 'National Defence in the Age of Austerity', *International Affairs*, vol. 85, no. 4, July 2009, pp. 733-53; Paul Cornish and Andrew Dorman, 'Blair's Wars and Brown's Budgets: From Strategic Defence Review to Strategic Decay in Less than a Decade', *International Affairs*, vol. 85, no. 2, March 2009, pp. 247–61.

The Sierra Leone operation also appeared to show that the United Kingdom is one of a very few countries to have developed a joint headquarters, comprising all three Services, capable of rapid deployment at short notice over long distances and able to function at the operational level, planning and managing the use of military force in theatre to achieve the strategic goals set by the government.[40] In fact the realities of government integration and direction were gently forgotten. According to the commander on the ground, Brigadier David Richards, Sierra Leone showed the importance of being able to operate at this level of activity.

> The Joint Force Headquarters (JFHQ) has become fundamental to the way the UK conducts operations 'out of area'. In part it is the reason why the UK has been able to mount Op Palliser in an exceptionally short time. More significantly, the HQ was a major reason why the Joint Task Force was able to create order out of chaos, put the UN back on its feet, reconstitute the Sierra Leone Army, give the rebels a bloody nose and depart, all within six weeks.[41]

In contrast a *Times* Leader soon after the initial deployment commented:

> The dispatch of British paratroops to Sierra Leone was a textbook example of "rapid reaction", demonstrating the effectiveness of combined operations planning and the ability of Britain's Armed Forces, badly overstretched as they are, to swing swiftly into action in an emergency ...
>
> But sound military planning requires, as its indispensible counterpart, political clarity. Precise because there is none in Sierra Leone, it is all the more important that the Chiefs of Staff should have a clear understanding about what contingencies their political masters in Britain expect them to prepare against.[42]

The wider governmental apparatus for decision-making has remained a problem, especially at home in Whitehall. The *Operation Palliser* deployment showed a clear lack of an understanding of how a military operation is conducted across

---

40 Interview with author; 'The operational level is the level of war at which campaigns are planned. Operational art – the skilful employment of military forces to attain strategic goals through the design, organisation, integration and conduct of campaigns or major operations – links military strategy to tactics. It dies this by establishing operational objectives, initiating actions and applying resources to ensure the success of the campaign. These activities are the responsibility of the Joint Commander, and of the Joint Task Force Commander once deployed to the Joint Operations Area where the campaign takes place'. 'British Defence Doctrine', *Joint Warfare Publication 0-01*, second edition, MOD, 2001, p. 21.

41 Major-General David Richards, 'Expeditionary Operations: Sierra Leone – Lessons for the Future', *World Defence Systems*, vol. 3, no. 2, July 2001. p. 134.

42 'In Sierra Leone: British forces must be given a clear and limited mission', *The Times*, 10 May 2000.

government. Other departments of government, particularly DFID, had no appreciation of MOD's standard operating procedures or the requirements of the armed forces.[43] For example, DFID tried to insist that the British Army elements stayed on the runway to protect it and deeply concerned to find them over 20 miles in land. Moreover, at least in DFID's case, they had no provision for dealing with highly classified material and lacked the secure communications of other departments. This meant that they had to leave their building to attend secure meetings and also read secure information which was inefficient and caused some time delay.[44]

The British system for managing such operations via Cabinet Office, DCMO and PJHQ had been developed over the previous decade and drew on the experience gained from both the 1982 Falklands Conflict and 1991 Gulf War. On the ground the British High Commission (BHC) and the Joint Task Force Headquarters (JTFHQ) effectively acted as the political and military leads and worked hand-in-glove with one another. The availability of the BHC as a facility proved invaluable as did the facilities at Dakar.

The Blair and now the Brown governments continue to emphasise the idea of a 'Comprehensive Approach' in which all the different departments of state are brought together to achieve the political effects that government wants. Only later in the wars in Iraq and Afghanistan has the lack of a British 'Comprehensive Approach' become evident. Giving evidence to the House of Commons Foreign Affairs Committee Lord Ashdown argued:

> Look and see what business has done today. Modern commerce has stripped down the vertical hierarchies, has networked organisations and restructured them to serve their customer. That is what modern organisations have done and if you have not done that, you are not going to succeed. Meanwhile, all the British Departments of State remain in vertical stovepipes, replicating the systems of yesterday. So, what do we have to do? Are we going to reconstruct the whole of our politics and the whole of our state structures to mimic industry? I doubt it. But what we do have to do is to work cross-departmentally.[45]

He then went on to argue that:

---

43 Interview with author.
44 Interview with author.
45 Lord Ashdown, House of Commons Foreign Affairs Committee, 'First Report – Foreign and Commonwealth Office Annual Report 2006–7', *HC.50*, session 2006–7, Oral Evidence 17 July 2007 (London: TSO, 2007), answer 203, http://www.publications.parliament.uk/pa/cm200708/cmselect/cmfaff/50/7071704.htm, accessed 2 February 2009.

In the business of foreign affairs and the area of post-conflict reconstruction, which I have been involved in and is becoming a very large part of foreign affairs, it is not what Foreign Offices do that matters, but what they do together with other Departments, for example, with the Ministry of Defence and the Home Office on police reform. What you do with other countries matters as well; this is essentially a multilateral organisation. And it is what you do with the multilateral organisations, the UN organisations, that matters.

This is about joined-up government. How do we apply that? The Foreign and Commonwealth Office needs to become good at – and what it is very bad at, by the way – is project management. It is very good at reporting and sitting dizzily above the scene and providing elegant telegrams for home, but what it should be saying is, "Here are the improvements that are needed to resolve this problem: here is the Ministry of Defence contribution, here is the Treasury contribution and here is the Department for International Development's contribution of aid; here is what we can do by bringing some police reforms in". Then we can change the nature of a failing state. Our job in this process is not to pretend that we can do it all, but to project manage it. If someone asked me what the Foreign and Commonwealth Office has to do now, it would be to learn the art of project management. The Department for International Development, by the way, is rather a good project manager, but the Foreign and Commonwealth Office is extremely bad.[46]

Yet the problems of a disconnected government incapable of bringing the disparate elements of government together to a common end were clearly visible throughout the Sierra Leone conflict.

Sierra Leone also revealed a more general challenge for ministers. Defence Ministers are required to balance their constitutional responsibility to be open and accountable to Parliament whilst at the same time trying to avoid revealing anything that might run counter to the security needs of the operation and indeed of similar operations which become necessary in the future.[47] During May 2000 there was a tension between informing Parliament precisely what British forces were doing at the same time as maximising the deterrent effect on the RUF by being vague about what British forces were there to do and implying that their remit was far greater. This tension can never be completely reconciled in operations of this kind and with a media able to bring both worlds together any creative tensions will inevitably be exposed.

---

46 Lord Ashdown, House of Commons Foreign Affairs Committee, 'First Report – Foreign and Commonwealth Office Annual Report 2006–7', *HC.50*, session 2006–7, Oral Evidence 17 July 2007 (London: TSO, 2007), answer 203, http://www.publications.parliament.uk/pa/cm200708/cmselect/cmfaff/50/7071704.htm, accessed 2 February 2009.

47 Interview with author.

A number of problems arose because of the speed of the deployment. Some personnel were deployed without a full set of inoculations and the arrangements for ensuring that personnel remained protected revealed difficulties.[48] This was a consequence of the European focus during the Cold War and the post-Cold War focus on Europe and the Middle East. The British military's historical experience of operating in West Africa had faded and had to be restored. Yet, there were British UNMOs as part of UNAMSIL, there had been a succession of defence attaches that had covered the region, there was a British training team in nearby Ghana and the British Army regularly trained in Kenya. Similarly the procedures for monitoring personnel and vaccinations had to be revamped. Nevertheless, when operations require such a rapid deployment it is perhaps inevitable that some individuals may not have been fully prepared. The operation also highlighted the value of local knowledge. Brigadier Richards was able to make a rapid appraisal and then seize the initiative and stabilise the UN's position because of his familiarity with the area.

The timeframe of the initial deployment also showed that there could never be a guarantee that there would always be preparatory training to bring units up to full capability. This does not mean that there had been no training in this type of scenario. There had been a series of exercises conducted by elements of 5 Airborne and their successors 16 Air Assault Brigade in the NEO role and it was seen as a likely task for the brigade.[49] There was an interim NEO doctrine in operation at the time but few of the participants were fully conversant with it and it was noticeable that it was replaced virtually straight after *Operation Palliser* by *Joint Warfare Publication 3–51* which drew on the experiences taken from this operation.[50] In general, the forces deployed tended to fall back on their Northern Ireland experience and the 'rules of engagement' that applied there until they were advised to the contrary.[51] In this case it worked but it did reveal that the armed forces generally returned to their most recent experience as a default setting which is not necessarily the best approach.

In the case of *Operation Palliser* the situation was in large part offset by the slow response of the RUF and the fact that in terms of command group training a number of units were quite experienced. For example, the command team for 1 PARA had been largely together for over a year and apart from the various

---

[48] 'New computer system marks a revolution in military medical records', *MOD*. 26 April 2006, http://www.mod.uk/DefenceInternet/DefenceNews/DefencePolicyAndBusiness/NewComputerSystemMarksARevolutionInMilitaryMedicalRecords.htm, accessed 17 October 2007.

[49] Interview with author.

[50] 'Non-combatant Evacuation Operations', *Joint Warfare Publication* 3–51, Joint Doctrine and Concepts Centre, August 2000.

[51] Interview with author.

exercises they had conducted they had also been deployed to Kosovo as part of the initial ARRC deployment into that territory in June 1999.[52] The ARG had been on a series of exercises as part of testing the ARG concept of operations. As part of this they had conducted a series of operations culminating in a live-fire exercise in France. They were used to working with each other and in the ARG's case had the support of the command infrastructure aboard the accompanying ships.[53]

The cultural dynamic is important here and often underappreciated. Both the Royal Marine and Parachute Regiment communities are relatively small and have strong links into the United Kingdom's Special Forces community, mainly because the Special Forces community draws so heavily from them.[54] This meant that both 1 PARA and 42 Cdo RM were at ease at working with the Special Forces who they trusted and this was reciprocated. Moreover, the core land units – Special Forces, 1 PARA and 42 Cdo – were highly motivated and prided themselves on coping in difficult situations.[55] Many of those deployed were drawn from 16 Air Assault Brigade and thus they had all in general conducted this type of exercise. There was therefore a collective understanding within the land component. The construction of the deployment from within 16 Air Assault Brigade rather than from the Spearhead order of battle clearly helped the operation. During the initial deployment phase use was made of informal social networks to obtain reinforcements in the form of D Company 2 PARA as well as supporting units such as the Pathfinder Platoon and the artillery battery from 7 Royal Horse Artillery.[56] There was a clear reluctance within the Parachute Regiment to draw on other army units earmarked as part of the Spearhead function.[57] As a result, one of the principal lessons taken was that in future all Spearhead elements would engage in collective training before they were declared to the Spearhead role and thus help to encourage trust and understanding between different units.[58] Similarly the ARG had also exercised in the NEO role and was able to dovetail into the existing deployment.

Moreover, it is worth remembering that the level of sustained operations was far less at this point in time than in more recent years and there was a desire by many to be involved as a means of justifying their continued existence. This meant the official notice-to-move times were radically reduced and in a number of cases forces took the initiative to deploy/prepare before the system formally gave them

---

52 Interview with author.
53 Interview with author.
54 Interview with author.
55 Anthony C. King, 'The existence of cohesion in the armed forces', *Armed Forces and Society*, vol. 33, no. 4, 2007, pp. 638–45.
56 Interview with author.
57 Interview with author.
58 Interview with author.

notification.[59] For example, the whole of 1 PARA plus its accompanying assets went to the South Cerney Forward Mounting Base rather than just the Spearhead Lead Echelon.

Where there was inexperience the results were mixed. The Joint Force Air Component Command (JFACC) was being trialled aboard *HMS Illustrious* and was in the process of being stood up.[60] It had been developed following the Kosovo experience as an organisation that could command and control an independent air campaign by the British. Such capability had been lost many years earlier and instead run through NATO. It proved in this case less successful than hoped partly because there was less of a need to create a coordinated air picture within the context of this operation and this added an extra command level. In the first few days the air component merely consisted of the four RAF Chinooks and a succession of C-130 Hercules delivering men and equipment into Sierra Leone.[61] Moreover, although *HMS Illustrious* arrived off the coast of Sierra Leone on 11 May she did not begin to use her aircraft until 17 May because of concerns about a lack of combat search and rescue capability to retrieve any lost pilots.[62]

The other inexperienced force element was the ORLT deployed with Brigadier Richards in command. At the time this deployment was seen as a test of the concept and all those who participated in the operation agreed that it worked.[63] The ORLT formed the basis for the JFTHQ with additional staff deployed from London and also Ghana where there was a British training team at the peacekeeping centre. The ORLT had conducted a number of exercises prior to the deployment and thus drew upon a relatively experienced team. Any weaknesses were partially compensated by Brigadier Richards familiarity with the key participants in Sierra Leone as well as being very familiar with 16 Air Assault Brigade. This was further evidenced by the decision to place the Special Forces component under the JTFHQ rather than for this capability to be run independently.[64] The ORLT/JTFHQ concept worked well because the idea had been appropriately thought through, resourced and contained an experienced core team. It ensured that the operation could be conducted at the operational level from the beginning and also highlighted the benefit of local expertise – in this case Brigadier Richards. The key to the success was Richards' ability to utilise the network he had to maximum advantage because of his own knowledge. In other words the network acted as a force multiplier building on existing strengths.[65]

---

59 Interview with author.
60 Interview with author.
61 Interview with author.
62 *HMS Illustrious Millenium Commission* (London: Stacey International, 2002).
63 Interview with author.
64 Interview with author.
65 Interview with author.

Within the British forces there was a general expectation that the communications would not work and that was to be expected.[66] Too often this proved to be the case but in this deployment it probably did not matter given the capabilities of the RUF and there was a general expectation that the weaknesses would have to be got around. In terms of communications a number of 'get arounds' were used, in particular, the use of Liaison Officers was highlighted as important and to a certain degree the Special Forces and their communications provided the glue that held the system together.[67] Moreover, the proximity of many of the units at Lungi International Airport meant that recourse could be made to face-to-face communications. In the short term 1 PARA also 'borrowed' a number of satellite phones from UNAMSIL and the general provision of satcoms was increased at both this level and at JTFHQ after this operation.[68] The overall communications capacity provided by government satellites was insufficient and recourse had to be made both to US military and commercial operators to provide the necessary capacity. There have been a number of steps taken to improve this capacity with the most recent being the PFI contract for Skynet 5.[69]

Secure communications to the senior civilian defence leadership were problematic. At the time the Secretary of State for Defence lacked secure mobile communications and this caused some problems as he was in his constituency when the crisis began and the department did not think it was wise to make the public move of returning him to Main Building.[70] However, the worse communications were across government with DFID officials having to move to other departments to conduct secure meetings. This led to some delays in information exchange as people came to MOD or other secure facilities.

Despite its impact on overall policy the operation did not significantly influence subsequent defence procurement decisions. For example, there were obvious limitations posed by the airlift and the lack of a heavy lift capability at the time was evident.[71] This meant that reliance had to be placed on chartered Antonovs.[72] Fortunately a number of Ukrainian ones were available at the time but their use did place limitations on what equipment could be moved forward. Although it showed the importance of being able to transport personnel and equipment rapidly by air it did not lead to a significant increase in this capability. During the course of the operation the Ministry of Defence confirmed its existing

---

66 Interview with author.
67 Interview with author.
68 Interview with author.
69 http://www.mod.uk/DefenceInternet/DefenceNews/EquipmentAndLogistics/Third BritishBuiltCommunicationsSatelliteWillGoIntoOrbit.htm, accessed 17 November 2007.
70 Interview with author.
71 http://www.raf.mod.uk/equipment/c-17.html, accessed 17 November 2007.
72 Michael Evans, 'Cook sends Marines to Sierra Leone', *The Times*, 8 May 2000.

plans that four C-17 transport aircraft would be leased from Boeing to provide an outsized lift capability.[73] However, the size of the Royal Air Force's transport fleet still remains an issue and it has struggled to support subsequent operations in Iraq and Afghanistan.[74] The four C-17s were subsequently along with two additional aircraft but the Airbus A400M programme remains years late.[75]

Conclusions

There is little doubt that the apparent success of the British deployment of military forces to Sierra Leone had a significant impact on the evolution of the government, and more particularly, the Prime Minister's view on the role of force within the modern international system. Less well known is the impact this first war had for Blair's new Defence Secretary, Geoff Hoon. The impact on both would subsequently significantly influence the evolution off British policy towards a European defence capability and Britain's own defence policy.

Both bought into the defence transformation narrative in different ways but both clearly subscribed to the idea of using Britain's military in a short, swift way to achieve precise results. The government line became that significant advantages may well follow from the early and effective use of military capabilities. The most frequently cited example to support this thesis was the deployment of British forces to Sierra Leone in May 2000.[76] The official line became that British troops deployed over the course of a weekend, succeeded in evacuating all the entitled personnel who wanted to leave the country, restored order in the capital Freetown, restored the crumbling UN peacekeeping mission and prevented the Revolutionary United Front from occupying the capital carrying out further atrocities. The reality was a little less clear cut, the British were fortunate where assets happened to be and there are doubts still remaining about what the RUF actually intended. Moreover, the previous use of Executive Outcomes had shown how the RUF could be successfully countered.

---

73 'The Logic of Sierra Leone', *The Economist*, 20 May 2000, p. 38.
74 Interview with author.
75 'Ministry of Defence: Major Projects Report 2008', *HC.64ii* session 2008–2009 (London: National Audit Office, 2008), pp. 1–10, http://www.nao.org.uk/publications/0809/mod_major_projects_report_2008.aspx, accessed 3 February 2009.
76 Major General David Richards, 'Expeditionary Operations: Sierra Leone – Lessons for the Future', *World Defence Systems*, vol. 3, no. 2, July 2001, pp. 134–6; Brigadier David Richards, 'Operation Palliser', *Journal of the Royal Artillery*, vol. CXXVII, no. 2, Autumn 2000, pp. 10–15; 'Sierra Leone', www.army.mod.uk/para/history/sierr_leone.htm, accessed 7 September 2007.

This view was reinforced after the 11 September 2001 attacks on America and appeared to substantiate this view about pre-emptive action. Moreover, the early operations in Afghanistan reinforced the view first set out in the 1998 Strategic Defence Review that it is better to go to the crisis than wait for it to come to you. However, the subsequent experience of wars in Iraq from 2003 and Afghanistan from 2006 onwards has eroded this assumption somewhat and the problem develops that a military deployment becomes the default option without any thought behind what was to be achieved. This was the case in Sierra Leone where the mission for the armed forces was not at all clear as they deployed. This is not new, in 1969 the British Army was deployed onto the streets of Northern Ireland to take the pressure off the police force for 48 hours. Thirty-eight years later *Operation Banner* finally came to an end. In 1992 the British sent a battalion to support the UN peacekeeping force in Bosnia with the simple remit – do something.[77] Both Iraq and Afghanistan have shown that the military element alone cannot resolve a situation and at best can buy time.

The problem was that in many ways Sierra Leone was too easy for the British and thus provided an artificial example from which to draw lessons. The Revolutionary United Front and the West Side Boys were not the most dynamic or thoughtful of opponents whilst the British military command was in many ways at its best with a commander in the field who was familiar with the region, its politics and the relevant individuals. The campaign therefore represented an ideal rather than normal model from which to take lessons.

As is usually the case Britain's armed forces undertook a series of lessons learned projects covering the various different operations. But Sierra Leone highlighted some much bigger problems with British government which were not addressed and which continue to beset it in the conduct of military operations today. The British system of government remains loosely coordinated and whilst there has been a considerable amount of discussion about the ideal of a 'Comprehensive Approach' this still remains no more than a MOD discussion note that the rest of government have failed to either adopt or redefine. The Sierra Leone experience highlight how problematic it is for government departments to actually agree with one another. The result was that there were frequent impasses and a lack of decision-making. In the case of the *Operation Palliser* the commander on the ground had to take the initiative and await subsequent approval for his steps. In this case he appears to have got them right but there was no guarantee that then next general will have a similar level of political acumen. Moreover, although Britain has a long history of military involvement in Sierra Leone it still had managed to forget how to conduct operations in that environment and had to re-learn them.[78] The Director of Special Forces admitted that the *Operation Barras* rescue mission

---

77   Interview with author.
78   Interview with author.

might not have been possible had it not been for the experience gained during *Operation Palliser*.

It is therefore clear there are still problems with how the British government thinks about and uses military forces. Many of the subsequent failings in both Iraq and Afghanistan can be seen in Sierra Leone but these were not, in general, identified in the lessons learned process whilst was entirely internal to the Ministry of Defence. All this raises questions about how experience and history is used within and by government and the armed forces. What is clear is that none have a firm grasp of history or an adequate corporate memory which means that the one thing that can be guaranteed is that the mistakes of the past will be repeated with potentially more serious consequences.

Select Bibliography

Official

Tony Blair, 'Doctrine of the International Community', speech made 23 April 1999, Chicago, www.number-10.gov.uk/output/page917.asp.

Tony Blair, 'Our Nation's Future', speech made Plymouth 12 January 2007, http://www.number10.gov.uk/output/Page10735.asp.

Lakhdar Brahimi (chair), 'Report of the Panel on Peacekeeping Operations'. *S/2000/809*, The United Nations, August 2000, www.un.org/peace/reports/peace_operations.

'British Defence Doctrine', *Joint Warfare Publication 0-01*, second edition, MOD, 2001.

'The British Maritime Doctrine', BR1806 (London: The Stationery Office, second edition 1999).

Cabinet Office, 'National Security Strategy of the United Kingdom' (London: Cabinet Office, 2008).

CIA World Fact Book, https://www.cia.gov/library/publications/the-world-factbook/geos/sl.html.

General Wesley Clark, Admiral James Ellis Jr and Lieutenant-General Michael Short (1999), Senate Armed Services Committee, 21 October 1999, http://armed-services.senate.gov/statemnt/1999/991021wc.pdf.

William S. Cohen and General Henry H. Shelton (1999), Senate Armed Services Committee, 14 October 1999, http://armed-services.senate.gov/statemnt/1999/991014wc.pdf.

'Declaration on Franco-British Co-operation in Africa', Franco-British Summit, London, 24 November 2003, http://www.elysee.fr/magazine/deplacement_etranger/sommaire.php?doc=/magazine/deplacement_etranger/2003/11/24/80640_page_13.htm.

'Declaration on Strengthening European Co-operation in Security and Defence', Franco-British Summit, London, 24 November 2003, http://www.fco.gov.uk/Files/kfile/UKFrance_DefenceDeclaration,0.pdf.

'Defence Capabilities Initiative', *NATO Press Release NAC-S (99)69*, 25 April 1999, http://www.nato.int/docu/pr/1999/p99s069e.htm.

'Delivering Security in a Changing World: The Defence White Paper', *Cm. 6,041-I* (London: TSO, 2003).

'Delivering Security in a Changing World: Future Capabilities', *Cm. 6,269* (London: TSO, 2004).

Department for International Development, 'Eliminating World Poverty: A Challenge for the 21st Century', *Cm. 3,749* (London: TSO, 1997), http://www.dfid.gov.uk/pubs/files/whitepaper1997.pdf.

'EU Battlegroups', EU Council Secretariat Factsheet, EU BG01, 2005, http://consilium.europa.eu/uedocs/cmsUpload/BattlegroupsNov05factsheet.pdf.

Foreign and Commonwealth Office, 'Africa Conflict Prevention Pool: The UK Sub-Saharan Strategy for Conflict Prevention', www.fco.gov.uk/Files/kfile/UK%20Sub-Saharan%20Strategy%20for%20Conflict%20Prevention.pdf.

Foreign and Commonwealth Office, 'History of Conflict in Sierra Leone', www.fco.gov.uk/Files/kfile/SierraLeoneHistoryOfConflict,0.pdf.

Foreign and Commonwealth Office, FCO, 'Private Military Companies: Options for Regulation', *HC.577*, session 2001–2002 (London: The Stationery Office, 2002).

HMS Illustrious Millennium Commission (London: Stacey International, 2002).

House of Commons Defence Committee, 'The Strategic Defence Review: The View of the Defence Select Committee', *Defence Management Journal*, vol. 1, no. 2, December 1998, pp. 14–17.

House of Commons Defence Committee, 'A New Chapter to the Strategic Defence Review', *HC.93-I*, Report of Session 2002–2003, 2003, http://www.parliament.the-stationery-office.co.uk/pa/cm200203/cmselect/cmdfence/93/93.pdf.

House of Commons Defence Committee, 'Defence White Paper 2003', Third Report of Session 2003–04, *HC.465–I* (London: The Stationery Office, 2004).

House of Commons Defence Committee, 'Eighth Report: Operational Costs in Afghanistan and Iraq: Spring Supplementary Estimate 2007-8', *HC.400*, session 2007–2008 (London: TSO, 2008).

House of Commons Foreign Affairs Committee, 'Second Report: Sierra Leone', *HC.116*, session 1998–1999 (London: TSO, 1999), http://www.publications.parliament.uk/pa/cm199899/cmselect/cmfaff/116/11601.htm.

House of Commons Foreign Affairs Committee, 'Fourth Report – Kosovo', *HC.28*, session 1999–2000 (London: TSO, 2000).

House of Commons Foreign Affairs Committee, 'First Report – Foreign and Commonwealth Office Annual Report 2006–7', *HC.50*, session 2006–2007 (London: TSO, 2007), http://www.publications.parliament.uk/pa/cm200708/cmselect/cmfaff/50/7071704.htm.

House of Lords Select Committee on the Constitution, 'Waging War: Parliament's Role and Responsibility', session 2005–2006, *HL.236–I* (London: TSO, 2006).

JDCC, 'Non-combatant Evacuation Operations', *Joint Warfare Publication 3–51*, Joint Doctrine and Concepts Centre, August 2000.

Joint Declaration issued at the British-French Summit, Saint Malo, France, 3–4 December 1998.

Ministry of Defence, *Kosovo: Lessons from the Crisis* (London: TSO, 2000).

Ministry of Defence, *Operations in Iraq: First Reflections* (London: MOD, 2003).

Ministry of Defence, 'Joint Discussion Note (JDN) 4/05: The Comprehensive Approach', version 20080125 (London: MOD, 2008), http://www.mod.uk/NR/rdonlyres/25A7F4A2-31C2-49D8-A857-4D31750CBD6F/0/20071218_jdn4_05_U_DCDCIMAPPS.pdf.

'New Labour because Britain deserves better' (London: Labour Party, 1997), http://labour-party.org.uk/manifestos/1997/1997-labour-manifesto.shtml.

'Presidency Conclusions, Helsinki European Council, 10–11 December 1999', www.ue.eu.int/ueDocs/cms_Data/docs/pressData/en/ec/ACFA4C.htm.

'Private Military Companies: Options for Regulation', *HC.577*, session 2001–2002 (London: The Stationery Office, 2002), http://www.fco.gov.uk/Files/kfile/mercenaries,0.pdf.

'The Governance of Britain', *Cm. 7070* (London: TSO, 2007).

'The Governance of Britain Analysis of Consultations', *Cm. 7342–III* (London: TSO, 2008).

'The Strategic Defence Review', *Cm. 3,999* (London: HMSO, 1998), http://www.mod.uk/NR/rdonlyres/65F3D7AC-4340-4119-93A2-20825848E50E/0/sdr1998_complete.pdf.

'The Strategic Defence Review: A New Chapter', *Cm. 5,566* (London: TSO, 2002).

UN Secretary-General, 'Third Report of the Secretary-General on the United Nations Mission in Sierra Leone', *S/2000/186*, 7 March 2000, p. 2, http://daccess-ods.un.org/TMP/4843224.html.

UN Secretary-General, 'Fourth Report of the Secretary-General on the United Nations Mission in Sierra Leone', *S/2000/455*, 19 May 2000, http://daccessdds.un.org/doc/UNDOC/GEN/N00/407/22/IMG/N0040722.pdf?OpenElement.

UN Secretary-General, 'Fifth Report of the Secretary-General on the United Nations Mission in Sierra Leone', *S/2000/751*, 31 July 2000, http://daccessdds.un.org/doc/UNDOC/GEN/N00/554/71/PDF/N0055471.pdf?OpenElement.

UN Secretary-General, 'Seventh Report of the Secretary-General on the United Nations Mission in Sierra Leone', *S/2000/1055*, 31 October 2000, http://daccessdds.un.org/doc/UNDOC/GEN/N00/717/71/IMG/N0071771.pdf?OpenElement.

UN Secretary-General, 'Eighth Report of the Secretary-General on the United Nations Mission in Sierra Leone', *S/2000/1199*, 15 December 2000, http://daccessdds.un.org/doc/UNDOC/GEN/N00/797/01/IMG/N0079701.pdf?OpenElement.

UN Secretary-General, 'Tenth Report of the Secretary-General on the United Nations Mission in Sierra Leone', *S/2001/627*, 25 June 2001, http://daccessdds.un.org/doc/UNDOC/GEN/N01/423/17/IMG/N0142317.pdf?OpenElement.

UN Secretary-General, 'Eleventh Report of the Secretary-General on the United Nations Mission in Sierra Leone', *S/2001/857*, 7 September, http://daccessdds.un.org/doc/UNDOC/GEN/N01/529/63/PDF/N0152963.pdf?OpenElement.

UN Secretary-General, 'Twenty-seventh Report of the Secretary-General on the United Nations Mission in Sierra Leone', *S/2005/777*, 12 December 2005, http://daccessdds.un.org/doc/UNDOC/GEN/N05/630/47/PDF/N0563047.pdf?OpenElement.

World Health Statistics 2007 (Geneva, Switzerland: World Health Organization, 2007), http://www.who.int/whosis/whostat2007.pdf.

Others

Rita Abrahamsen and Paul Williams, 'Ethics and Foreign Policy: the Antinomies of New Labour's "Third Way" in Sub-Saharan Africa', *Political Studies*, vol. 49, no. 2, 2001, pp. 249–64.

Adekeye Adebajo, *Building Peace in West Africa: Liberia, Sierra Leone and Guinea-Bissau* (Boulder, CO: Lynne Rienner Publishers, 2002).

Abiodun Alao and Comfort Ero, 'Cut Short for Taking Short Cuts: The Lome Peace Agreement on Sierra Leone', *Civil Wars*, vol. 4, no. 3, Autumn 2001, pp. 117–34.

Ken Aldred et al., *The Strategic Defence Review: How Strategic? How Much a Review?* (London: Brasseys, 1998).

Colonel John B. Alexander, *Future War: Non-Lethal Weapons in Twenty-First Century Warfare* (New York: Thomas Dunne Books, 1999).

Patrick Allen, 'At the Drop of a Hat', *Defence Helicopter*, August-September 2000, pp. 8–12.

Patrick Allen, 'The UK's Rapid Deployment to Sierra Leone', *RAF Yearbook 2001* (London: MOD, 2001).

Anon., 'Swift, Strong, Flexible', *Soldier*, June 2000, pp. 4–5.

Major Phil Ashby, *Unscathed: Escape from Sierra Leone* (Basingstoke: Macmillan), 2002.

Paddy Ashdown, *The Ashdown Diaries*, Vol. 2, *1997–99* (London: The Penguin Press, 2001).

Dennis Barnes, 'Anglians in Africa', *Soldier*, September 2000, pp. 14–15.

Alex J. Bellamy, 'Motives, Outcomes, Intent and the Legitimacy of humanitarian intervention', *Journal of Military Ethics*, vol. 3, no. 3, 2004, pp. 216–32.

Mark Bennister, 'Tony Blair and John Howard: Comparative Predominance and 'Institution Stretch' in the UK and Australia', *British Journal of Politics and International Relations*, vol. 9, no. 3, August 2007, pp. 327–45.

General Henri Bentégeat, '1998–2008: 10 years of ESDP', *Impetus: Bulletin of the EU Military Staff*, Autumn/Winter 2008, pp. 6–7.

Patrick Bishop, *3 PARA: Afghanistan, Summer 2006, This is War* (London: HarperPress, 2007).

Ken Booth and Tim Dunne (eds), *Worlds in Collision: Terror and the Future of Global Order* (Basingstoke: Palgrave Macmillan, 2002).

Tom Bower, *Gordon Brown: Prime Minister* (London: HarperCollins, 2004).

Rachel Brett and Irma Sprecht, *Young Soldiers: Why They Choose to Fight* (Boulder, CO: Lynne Rienner Publishers, 2004).

Robert J. Bunker (ed.), *Non-State Threats and Future Wars* (London: Frank Cass, 2003).

John Callaghan, *The Labour Party and Foreign Policy: A History* (London: Routledge, 2007).

Alastair Campbell, *The Blair Years: Extracts from the Alastair Campbell Diaries* (London: Hutchinson, 2007).

Michael Chege, 'Sierra Leone: The State that Came Back from the Dead', *Washington Quarterly*, vol. 25, no. 3, Summer 1992, pp. 147–60.
Nick Child, *The Age of Invincible: The Ship that Defined the Modern Royal Navy* (Barnsley: Pen and Sword, 2009).
Warren Chin, 'Why Did it all Go Wrong? Reassessing British Counterinsurgency in Iraq', *Security Studies Quarterly*, vol. 12, no. 4, Winter 2008. pp. 119–35.
Dan D. Chipman, 'General Short and the Politics of Kosovo's Air War', *Air Power History*, Summer 2002, pp. 30–39.
General Wesley K. Clark, 'The United States in NATO: The Way Ahead', *Parameters*, vol. 29, no. 4, Winter 1999–2000, pp. 2–15.
General Wesley K. Clark, *Waging Modern War* (New York: Public Affairs, 2001).
Michael Codner, 'The Strategic Defence Review: How Much? How Far? How Joint is Enough?', *RUSI Journal*, vol. 143 no. 4. August 1998, pp. 5–11.
Tim Collins, *Rules of Engagement: A Life in Conflict* (London, Headline, 2005).
Richard Connaughton, *Military Intervention and Peacekeeping: The Reality* (Aldershot: Ashgate, 2001).
Richard Connaughton, 'The Mechanics and Nature of British Interventions into Sierra Leone (2000) and Afghanistan (2001–2)', *Civil Wars*, vol. 5, no. 2, Summer 2002, pp. 77–95.
Richard Connaughton, *A Brief History of Modern Warfare: The True Story of Conflict from the Falklands to Afghanistan* (London: Constable and Robinson, 2008).
Robin Cook, *The Point of Departure* (London: Simon and Schuster, 2003).
Paul Cornish and Andrew Dorman, 'Blair's Wars and Brown's Budgets: From Strategic Defence Review to Strategic Decay in Less than a Decade', *International Affairs*, vol. 85, no. 2, March 2009, pp. 247–61.
Paul Cornish and Andrew Dorman, 'National Defence in the Age of Austerity', *International Affairs*, vol. 85, no. 4, July 2009, pp. 733–53.
Humphry Crum Ewing, 'After the UK Strategic Defence Review: The Need for an Ongoing Reasoned Critique of Positions, Policies and Operations', *Defense and Security Analysis*, vol. 14, no. 3, 1998, pp. 323–30.
Thomas J. Czerwinski, 'The Third Wave: What the Tofflers Never Told You', *Strategic Forum*, no. 72 (Washington, DC, National Defense University, 1996).
Alex Danchev, 'Tony Blair's Vietnam: The Iraq War and the "Special Relationship" in Historical Perspective', *Review of International Studies*, vol. 33, no. 2, April 2007, pp. 189–203.
R.P.M Davis, *History of the Sierra Leone Battalion of the Royal West Africa Frontier Force* (Freetown: Government Printer, 1932).
Andrew Dorman, 'The Irrelevance of Air Power: The Potential Impact of Capability Divergence in NATO post-Kosovo', *Airman Scholar*, Spring 2000, pp. 53–8.
Andrew Dorman, *Defence under Thatcher* (Basingstoke: Palgrave Macmillan, 2002).

Andrew Dorman, 'Reconciling Britain to Europe in the Next Millennium: The Evolution of British Defense Policy in the Post-Cold War Era', *Defense Analysis*, vol. 17, no. 2, Summer 2001, pp. 187–202.

Andrew Dorman, 'Reorganising the Infantry: Drivers of Change and What This Tells Us about the State of the Defence Debate Today', *British Journal of Politics and International Relations*, vol. 8, no. 4, 2006.

Andrew Dorman, 'Britain and its Armed Forces Today', *Political Quarterly*, vol. 78, no. 2, April–June 2007, pp. 320–27.

Andrew Dorman, *Transforming to Effects Based Operations: Lessons from the United Kingdom Experience* (Carlisle, PA: Strategic Studies Institute, 2008), http://www.strategicstudiesinstitute.army.mil/pubs/display.cfm?pubID=831.

Andrew Dorman and Greg Kennedy (eds), *War and Diplomacy* (Washington, DC: Potomac Books, 2008).

Beth K. Dougherty, 'Right-Sizing International Criminal Justice: A Hybrid Experiment in the Special Court for Sierra Leone', *International Affairs*, vol. 80, no. 2, March 2004, pp. 311–28.

Robert Dover, *Europeanisation of British Defence Policy* (Aldershot: Ashgate, 2007).

Mark Doyle, BBC West Africa Correspondent, 'Letter to the Editor', *New Statesman*, 2 October 2000, pp. 37–8.

John Dumbrell, *A Special Relationship: Anglo-American Relations from the Cold War to Iraq.* (Basingstoke: Palgrave Macmillan, 2006).

David H. Dunn, 'Innovation and Precedent in the Kosovo War: The Impact of Operation Allied Force', *International Affairs*, vol. 85, no. 3, May 2009, pp. 531–46.

Lorraine Elliott and Graeme Cheeseman (eds), *Forces for Good? Cosmopolitan Militaries in the 21st Century* (Manchester: Manchester University Press, 2005).

C. Ero, 'Sierra Leone Security Complex', *The Conflict, Security and Development Group Working Paper no. 3* (London: Centre for Defence Studies, 2002).

James Fergusson, *A Million Bullets: The Real Story of the British Army in Afghanistan* (London: Bantam Press, 2008).

William Fowler, *Operation Barras: The SAS Rescue Mission: Sierra Leone 2000* (London: Weidenfeld and Nicolson, 2004).

George and Meredith Friedman, *The Future of War: Power, Technology and American World Dominance in the Twenty-First Century* (New York: St Martin's Griffin, 1996).

Christopher Fyfe, *A History of Sierra Leone* (Oxford: Oxford University Press, 1962).

Jeremy Ginnifer and Kaye Oliver, *Evaluation of the Conflict Prevention Pools: Sierra Leone; Country/Regional Case Study 3* (London: DFID, 2004).

Michael R. Gordon and Bernard E. Trainor, *Cobra II: The Inside Story of the Invasion and Occupation of Iraq* (London: Atlantic Books, 2007).

Colin Gray, *Another Bloody Century: Future Warfare* (London: Phoenix, 2006).

William Hague, *William Pitt the Younger* (London: HarperCollins, 2004).
William Hague, *Wilberforce* (London: HarperCollins, 2007).
Grant T. Hammond, 'Myths of the Air War over Serbia: Some "Lessons" not to Learn', *RAF Air Power Review*, vol. 4, no. 2, Summer 2001, pp. 68–81.
Michael Heseltine, *Life in the Jungle: My Biography* (London: Hodder and Stoughton, 2000).
John L. Hirsch, *Diamonds and the Struggle for Democracy* (Boulder, CO: Lynne Rienner Publishers, 2001).
John L. Hirsch, 'War in Sierra Leone', *Survival*, vol. 43, no. 3, Autumn 2001, pp. 145–62.
Samuel P. Huntington, *The Clash of Civilizations: Remaking of World Order* (New York: Touchstone, 1996).
IISS, 'Crisis in Sierra Leone. The Failure of UN Peacekeeping', *Strategic Comments* (Oxford: Oxford University Press for the IISS), vol. 6, no. 9, November 2000.
Lieutenant-General Sir Mike Jackson, 'KFOR: The Inside Story', *The RUSI Journal*, vol. 145, no. 1, February 2000, pp. 13–19.
General Sir Mike Jackson, *Soldier: The Autobiography* (London: Bantam Press, 2007).
Simon Jenkins, *Thatcher and Sons: A Revolution in Three Acts* (London: Penguin, 2006).
Tim Judah, *Kosovo: War and Revenge* (London: Yale University Press, 2nd edition 2002).
John Kampfner, *Blair's Wars* (London: The Free Press, 2003).
Robert Kaplin, 'The Coming Anarchy', *Atlantic Monthly*, February 1994.
David Keen, *Conflict and Collusion in Sierra Leone* (New York: Palgrave, 2005).
Anthony C. King, 'The Existence of Cohesion in the Armed Forces', *Armed Forces and Society*, vol. 33, no. 4, 2007, pp. 638–45.
John Leech, *Asymmetries of Conflict: War without Death* (London: Frank Cass, 2002).
Gustav Lindstrom, 'Enter the EU Battlegroups', *Chaillot Paper no. 97* (Paris: ISS, 2007), http://www.iss.europa.eu/uploads/media/cp097.pdf.
Ed Macy, *Apache: The Man, the Machine, the Mission* (London: HarperCollins, 2008).
Brigadier-General Michel Maisonneuve, 'The OSCE Kosovo Verification Mission', *Canadian Military Journal*, Spring 2000, pp. 49–52.
Colin McInnes, 'Labour's Strategic Defence Review', *International Affairs*, vol. 74, no. 4, October 1998, pp. 823–45.
Colin McInnes, *Spectator War: The West and Contemporary Conflict* (London: Lynne Rienner, 2002).
Craig McLean and Alan Patterson, 'A Precautionary Approach to Foreign Policy? A Preliminary Analysis of Tony Blair's Speeches on Iraq', *British Journal of Politics and International Relations*, vol. 8, no. 3, August 2006, pp. 351–67.

Funmi Olonisakin, *Peacekeeping in Sierra Leone: The Story of UNAMSIL* (Boulder, CO: Lynne Rienner, 2008).

Eoin O'Malley, 'Setting Choices, Controlling Outcomes: The Operation of Prime Ministerial Influence and the UK's Decision to Invade Iraq', *British Journal of Politics and International Relations*, vol. 9, no. 1, February 2007, pp. 1–19.

Gerrard Quille, '"Battle Groups" to Strengthen EU Military Crisis Management?', *European Security Review*, no. 22, 2003.

William Reno, *Corruption and State Politics in Sierra Leone* (New York: Cambridge University Press, 1995).

Brigadier D.J. Richards, 'Operation Palliser', *Journal of the Royal Artillery*, vol. CXXVII, no. 2, Autumn 2000, p. 11.

Major General David Richards, 'Expeditionary Operations: Sierra Leone – Lessons for the Future', *World Defence Systems*, vol. 3, no. 2, July 2001, pp. 134–6.

Brigadier David Richards, 'Operation Palliser', *Journal of the Royal Artillery*, vol. CXXVII, no. 2, Autumn 2000, pp. 10–15.

Thomas E. Ricks, *Fiasco: The American Military Adventure in Iraq* (London: Allen Lane, 2006).

Lord Robertson, speech to the RIIA Conference 'European Defence: The Way Ahead', 7 October 1999.

Simon Schama, *Rough Crossings: Britain, the Slaves and the American Revolution* (London: BBC Books, 2005).

Anthony Seldon, *Blair* (London: The Free Press, 2004).

Anthony Seldon (ed.), *Blair's Britain, 1997–2007* (Cambridge: Cambridge University Press, 2007).

Anthony Seldon, *Blair Unbound* (London: Simon and Schuster, 2007).

Clare Short, *An Honourable Deception? New Labour, Iraq, and the Misuse of Power* (London: The Free Press, 2005).

P.W. Singer, *Corporate Warriors: The Rise of the Privatized Military Industry* (New York: Cornell University Press, 2003).

Rupert Smith, *The Utility of Force: The Art of War in the Modern World* (London: Penguin, 2006).

Ewen Southby-Tailyour, *3 Commando Brigade: Helmand, Afghanistan – Sometimes the Best Form of Defence is Attack* (London: Random House, 2008).

Tim Spicer, *An Unorthodox Soldier: Peace and War and the Sandline Affair* (Edinburgh: Mainstream Publishing, 1999).

Patrick Stephens, *Tony Blair: The Price of Leadership* (London: Politico's Publishing, 2004).

Andrew Stewart, 'An Enduring Commitment: the British Military's Role in Sierra Leone', *Defence Studies*, vol. 8, no. 3, September 2008, pp. 351–68.

Sir Hilary Synott, *Bad Days in Iraq* (London: I.B. Tauris, 2008).

Margaret Thatcher, *The Downing Street Years* (London: HarperCollins, 2003).

Rod Thornton, 'Case Study 2 – Northern Ireland August 1969–March 1972', *The British Approach to Low-intensity Operations*, study for the MOD and US

Office of Force Transformation, http://www.oft.osd.mil/initiatives/ncw/docs/LIO%20Part%20II%20Final%20with%20UK%20MOD%20Release.pdf.

Alvin and Heidi Toffler, *War and Anti-War: Making Sense of Today's Global Chaos* (New York: Mass Market Paperback, 1995).

Edward Turay and Arthur Abraham, *The Sierra Leone Army: A Century of History* (Basingstoke: Macmillan, 1987).

Brian Urquhart, 'Some Thoughts on Sierra Leone', *New York Book Reviews*, 15 June 2000.

Al J.Ventnor, 'Taking Control in Sierra Leone: The Rules of the Limited Operation have been Imposed on the War', *Jane's International Defense Review*, September 2000, pp. 60–62.

Geoffrey Wheatcroft, *Yo, Blair!* (London: Politico's Publishing, 2007).

Philip R. Wilkinson, 'Peace Support under Fire: Lessons from Sierra Leone', *ISIS Briefing Series on Humanitarian Intervention*, no. 2, June 2000.

Paul Williams, 'Fighting for Freetown: British Military Intervention in Sierra Leone', *Contemporary Security Policy*, vol. 22, no. 3, December 2001, pp. 140–68.

Harold Wilson, *The Labour Government, 1964–70: A Personal Record* (London: Weidenfeld and Nicolson, 1971).

Douglas P. Yurovich, *Operation Allied Force: Air Power in Kosovo. A Study in Coercive Victory* (Carlisle, PA: US Army War College, 2001).

Index

1st Battalion of the Parachute Regiment (1 PARA) 5, 63, 71–81, 84–5, 92–3, 95, 101, 103, 108–9, 113, 135–6, 140–43
2nd Battalion of the Parachute Regiment (2 PARA) 75, 80, 83, 92, 141

Afghanistan 3–4, 9, 10–13, 26–8, 84, 128–9, 131, 134–5, 138, 144 6
African Union 40, 47, 89, 129
Airborne Task Force 63, 71, 73, 75, 95, 132, 134
Allied Rapid Reaction Corps (ARRC) 25, 48, 141
All People's Congress (APC) 35, 36
amnesty 39, 46
Amphibious Ready Group (ARG) 27, 71, 73–5, 79, 84–5, 87, 92–3, 95, 99, 101, 119, 134, 136, 141
Armed Forces Revolutionary Council (AFRC) 40, 42, 93, 122–3
arms and arms trafficking 15, 38, 40–42, 48, 55, 93, 98

Balkans, the 3, 10, 12, 19–20, 24, 42–3, 47, 63, 74, 97, 123, 127, 132
Bangladesh 50, 90, 119–20
Bosnia 12, 20, 25, 63, 68, 145
Britain 5, 9–10, 12–16, 18, 20, 21, 23, 28, 32–3, 43–4, 47, 58–9, 62, 65, 88, 99, 103, 107–8, 123, 127–31, 135–7, 144–5
    see also United Kingdom
British Army 23, 33, 48, 72, 106, 138, 140, 145
Brown, Gordon 1, 7–11, 14, 18, 138

Cameron, David 2, 7
Chege, Michael 31, 36, 37
Chief of the Defence Staff (CDS) 17, 21, 23, 6–8
child soldiers 51, 99, 118

Civil Defence Forces (CDF) 42, 45–6, 54, 91, 93, 122
civil war 4, 20, 26, 29–44, 58, 64–5, 100, 115, 123–24
colonial rule 32–4
'Comprehensive Approach' 84, 125, 138, 145
Conservative Party 7, 14, 15, 17, 88, 107, 115
Cook, Robin 15, 18, 19, 67, 77, 80, 81, 88
Cyprus 23, 63, 99, 123

Darfur 10, 129
defence cuts 66
defence spending 18, 39, 136
democracy 35, 40, 130, 131
Department for International Development (DFID) 15–16, 26, 55, 64–6, 69–70, 78, 80, 84, 125, 137–9, 143
diamond mining/diamonds 31, 34, 37–9, 46, 53, 55–6, 59, 121, 125
Director of Special Forces (DSF) 70, 72, 106, 111, 135, 145
disarmament, demobilisation and reintegration (DDR) 26, 48, 52–5, 58, 82–3, 93, 95, 104, 118, 120–2, 125

East Timor 9, 13, 77, 129
Economic Community of West African States (ECOWAS) 4, 42–3, 97, 120–21
Economic Community of West African States Monitoring Group (ECOMOG) 4, 40–42, 45–7, 49–53, 59, 71, 79, 89
elections 1, 8–11, 27, 32, 35–6, 39, 45, 49, 123–4
entitled personnel (EPs) 4–5, 43, 61, 65, 67–8, 70, 76, 78, 80, 82, 87, 100, 144
European Union (EU) 5, 10, 20, 24, 61–2, 70, 127, 129–32

evacuation 47, 61–85, 87, 90–92, 100
Executive Outcomes (EO) 38–41, 98, 144

Falklands Islands 9, 63, 73
  Conflict 5, 33, 113, 138
Foreign and Commonwealth Office (FCO) 15, 16, 26, 41, 43, 62, 64, 69, 70, 76, 78, 81, 84, 125, 139
forward mounting base (FMB) 75, 76, 142
France 19, 23, 43, 75, 141

Ghana 33, 50, 79, 99, 119, 140, 142
Guinea 29, 35, 38, 40, 43, 50, 55, 68, 119
Guthrie, Charles 17, 18, 23, 67

Harrison, Andy 83–4, 95–7
HMS Illustrious 74, 76, 79, 81, 84–5, 87, 91–2, 101, 142
Hoon, Geoff 26, 62–3, 67, 72, 79, 82, 88, 90, 94, 108–9, 113, 132–3, 136, 144
hostage taking/hostages 50, 51, 56, 63, 82, 88, 93, 97, 103–14, 118, 130
humanitarian intervention 3, 7, 9, 14, 16, 128
Hussein, Saddam 3, 12, 18, 128

international community 4, 9, 13, 16, 22, 26, 28, 40, 43, 45, 47–8, 50, 54, 58, 62, 64, 67, 100, 121, 128
Iraq 1–4, 7–13, 26, 27–8, 84, 89, 114, 123, 128–9, 135, 138, 144–6
  War 1–2, 4

Jackson, Mike 25, 47, 135
Jetley, Vijay Kumar 51, 53, 56, 59, 68, 72, 76–7, 96
Joint Force Air Component Command (JFACC) 79, 142
Joint Task Force 68, 79, 137
  Headquarters (JTFHQ) 79, 83, 138, 142, 143

Kabbah, Ahmad 39–43, 68, 77, 79, 93, 104, 106, 123–4
Brigadier-General Kallay 104
Kallay, Foday 104, 107, 110–12
Kamajors 40–41, 54, 93, 98

Kampfner, John 9, 14, 17–18
Kenya 11, 100, 108, 119, 140
Koroma, Johnny Paul 40, 104, 106, 123
Kosovo 9, 12–13, 18–21, 23, 25–6, 43, 47–8, 59, 63, 73, 128–2, 141–2

Labour Party 1–3, 7, 8, 14–18, 28, 47, 65, 127, 132
  Government 17, 65
  New 1, 2, 28
Liberal Democrat Party 21, 88, 107, 115
Liberia 5, 29, 37–38, 40, 46, 55, 96, 121, 123, 125
Lomé Peace Agreement 4, 26, 29, 43, 44, 45–59, 78, 81, 83, 89, 115, 120, 125

Milošević, Slobodan 19, 20–21, 23–4, 47
Ministry of Defence (MOD) 14, 16–17, 26, 47, 63–5, 67, 70–72, 77–8, 81, 84–5, 89, 95, 115, 117, 123, 125, 130, 136–9, 143, 145–6
  Crisis Management Organisation (DCMO) 72–3, 138
mission creep 5, 96
Momoh, Joseph Saidu 31, 36, 38

network enabled capability (NEC) 133, 135
Nigeria 42, 50, 78, 90, 119, 130
non-combatant evacuation operation (NEO) 70, 72, 80–81, 87, 140–41
North Atlantic Treaty Organisation (NATO) 10, 12–13, 17, 19–26, 47–8, 62, 81, 127–8, 130, 142
Northern Ireland 2, 23, 63, 67–8, 99, 100, 103, 123, 140, 145

Operational Reconnaissance and Liaison Team (ORLT) 61, 69, 72, 74, 79, 142
Operation Amble 111, 112, 125
Operation Barras 5, 87, 103–114, 129, 133, 135, 145
Operation Desert Fox 9, 12, 13, 18
Operation Palliser 4, 73, 76, 108, 132, 135, 137, 140, 145, 146

Penfold, Peter 40, 41, 62

Index

Permanent Joint Headquarters (PJHQ) 63, 70–73, 75, 77, 87, 105, 117, 138
Private Military Company (PMC) 38, 40
    Sandline 40–41, 47, 65

rape 37, 40, 69
Revolutionary United Front (RUF) 4, 5, 26, 27, 29, 36–40, 43, 45–7, 50–59, 61, 63, 65, 68–70, 72, 73, 76, 79–85, 87, 88, 91–101, 103–4, 111, 113–14, 115–25, 129, 139, 140, 143, 144, 145
RFA Argus 110, 111, 136
Richards, David 59, 72–4, 76–7, 79–81, 84, 93–5, 97–8, 135–7, 140, 142, 144
Robertson, George 17, 23, 26, 132
Royal Air Force (RAF) 25, 43, 64, 72, 74, 76–7, 85, 93–4, 97, 112, 142, 144
Royal Irish Regiment 5, 87, 100, 103, 105–8, 113, 115
Royal Marines 73, 95
Royal Navy 33, 100
Rules of Engagement (ROE) 67, 105

Sankoh, Foday 36–8, 43, 46, 55, 57, 68–9, 80, 94, 121, 123
Senegal 75–6, 81, 109
Short, Clare 13, 15, 25, 65
Short Term Training Team (STTT) 87, 98–101, 103–4, 118, 125
Sierra Leone Army (SLA) 5, 34–6, 38–40, 46–7, 51–2, 54, 57, 91, 93–4, 97–9, 101, 104–6, 112, 116–18, 120–23, 137
Sierra Leone People's Party (SLPP) 34–6, 39, 123
Special Forces 5, 27, 70, 72–7, 79, 84–5, 94, 96, 103–4, 106, 108–9, 111, 128, 135, 141–3, 145
Strategic Defence Review (SDR) 17–18, 25, 47, 117, 127, 132–4, 136, 145

Taylor, Charles 5, 36, 38, 96, 121, 123–5
Thatcher, Margaret 1, 2, 7

United Kingdom (UK) 5, 8, 10, 12, 17, 19, 23, 25, 27, 31, 33–4, 41, 44, 47–8, 61–3, 65–6, 68–70, 73–4, 76–9, 81–2, 87–8, 90–1, 95–6, 99, 100, 103, 107, 109–10, 113, 116–19, 128, 134, 137, 141
see also Britain
United Nations (UN) 4, 9, 12, 23, 26, 27, 29, 31, 39–42, 44, 45–59, 61–2, 64–5, 67–71, 73, 76–8, 81–3, 87–101, 107, 115–20, 123–4, 131–2, 134, 137, 139–40, 144–5
    Military Observers (UNMOs) 26, 42, 49, 51, 52–6, 61, 63, 70, 77–8, 81–4, 91, 95, 97, 120, 140
    Mission in Sierra Leone (UNAMSIL) 4, 5, 45–59, 62–4, 67–70, 72, 73, 76–9, 81–4, 87–95, 97–8, 100, 101, 105, 107, 114–22, 124–5, 140, 143
    Observer Mission to Sierra Leone (UNOMSIL) 4, 42, 43, 46, 48, 49, 68
    Security Council 40, 42, 48, 57–8, 62, 64–5, 67, 70, 89, 91, 97, 99, 100, 101, 115–16, 124, 131
    Peacekeeping Mission 45–69
United States of America (USA) 18–19, 22, 23, 24, 31, 32, 43, 58, 76, 78, 85, 89, 118, 130, 133

West Side Boys (WSB) 5, 87, 93, 103–13, 115, 118, 145
World Health Organisation (WHO) 4, 29

Yugoslavia 19, 20, 123

Zimbabwe 48, 63, 76, 129